SEGREGATED SOLDIERS

SEGREGATED SOLDIERS

MILITARY TRAINING

AT

HISTORICALLY BLACK COLLEGES

IN THE

JIM CROW SOUTH

MARCUS S. COX

WITH A FOREWORD BY
LIEUTENANT GENERAL RUSSEL L. HONORÉ

LOUISIANA STATE UNIVERSITY PRESS
BATON ROUGE

Published by Louisiana State University Press
lsupress.org

Copyright © 2013 by Louisiana State University Press
All rights reserved. Except in the case of brief quotations used in articles or reviews, no part of this publication may be reproduced or transmitted in any format or by any means without written permission of Louisiana State University Press.

Louisiana Paperback Edition, 2024

Designer: Barbara Neely Bourgoyne
Typefaces: Din Schrift and Gotham, display; Whitman, text

Cover image courtesy John B. Cade Library/Archives and Manuscripts Department/ Southern University and A&M College.

Library of Congress Cataloging-in-Publication Data
Cox, Marcus S., 1965–
 Segregated soldiers : military training at historically Black colleges in the Jim Crow South / Marcus S. Cox ; with a foreword by Lieutenant General Russel L. Honoré.
    pages cm
 Includes bibliographical references and index.
 ISBN 978-0-8071-5176-1 (cloth : alk. paper) — ISBN 978-0-8071-5177-8 (pdf) — ISBN 978-0-8071-5178-5 (epub) — ISBN 978-0-8071-8379-3 (paperback) 1. Military education—Southern States—History. 2. African American soldiers—Southern States—Training of. 3. African American soldiers—Southern States—History. 4. African American universities and colleges—Southern States—History. 5. African Americans—Education (Higher)—History. 6. Segregation in higher education—Southern States—History. 7. United States—Armed Forces—African Americans—History. 8. United States—Race relations—History. I. Title. II. Title: Military training at historically Black colleges in the Jim Crow South.
 U409.S9A53 2001
 355.0071'175—dc23

2012042804

For my Nana and Grandpa,

Annie Mae and Matthew W. Trahan.

I continue to stand on your shoulders.

CONTENTS

Foreword	ix
Preface	xiii
Acknowledgments	xvii
Introduction	1
1. Men of Color to Arms: Military Training and Service at Black Colleges in the Late Nineteenth Century	10
2. We Are All Louisianians and by That Sign All Americans: Negro Defense Training, Leadership, and War Activities at Southern University during World War II	30
3. Soldiering for Uncle Sam: Military Training at Southern University during the Cold War, 1946–1960	52
4. What the People Think: African American Attitudes toward Military Training and Service, 1950–1960	74
5. Our Uniform Hasn't Lost Its Prestige with Our People: Military Training and Service on the Bluff, 1960–1967	101
6. Keep Our Black Warriors Out of the Draft: The Antiwar Movement at Southern University, 1968–1973	139
7. Conclusion	168
Notes	179
Bibliography	207
Index	221

FOREWORD

In retrospect, I likely would have been a county agent working with farmers in Louisiana if I had not decided to enroll in Army Reserve Officer Training at Southern University. As a matter of fact, before I made up my mind to join the Army, I requested a deferment in January 1971 so I could apply to the Farmers Home Administration for a job processing loans for small farmers. In the meantime, I decided to return to Southern University a couple weeks after graduation and ran into one of the Army ROTC instructors, who said, "What are you doing here? You should report to Fort Benning next week." He looked at some papers and said, "Yes, you should be at Fort Benning next week to report to basic and airborne training." I had just been married for three weeks, so I immediately went home, wrestled-up my things, and on the 26th of January reported to Fort Benning, Georgia. Two weeks later I received my official notice approving my deferment from military service.

Vietnam was on the downturn and the letter would have given me a six-month deferment. I had decided to apply for a deferment because if you worked a couple months with the federal government before getting drafted or joining the military, you could serve in the military and then transfer back into federal service. So I thought that would be a great insurance policy when I came out of the military, because I did not plan to stay in the Army very long. But that obligation became a way of life and from one thing to the next—thirty-seven years, three months, and three days later, I left the service and retired as a lieutenant general.

My personal experience with the U.S. military started as a mandatory university requirement to participate in Army ROTC, much like other male students there. Once I began military training, the leadership attributes we learned were invaluable. The ROTC instructors were all Vietnam veterans who stressed that it was our obligation to receive our commission, serve in the Army, and be a part of the officer corps and leadership of the U.S. armed forces, because at that time you still had about 12 to 15 percent of the military that were African Americans. Since African Americans were drafted in disproportionate numbers, the likelihood of being sent to Vietnam was high. Until 1971 most Americans did not know the war was going to end soon, so a student graduating from college still faced the possibility of getting drafted. I thought, "Why wait to get drafted after I graduate?" The idea was to go in as a commissioned officer and place myself in a leadership position. I had no intention of seeking a career in the Army, so what started off as a temporary obligation became a way of life.

Despite the war in Vietnam, in the 1960s military service was still an attractive way for young blacks to improve their economic opportunities. You have to remember that the nation was one generation removed from World War II and most of us at Southern University came out of the baby boom of the post–World War II era. So, looking at the average age and demographics of the students, most of them knew someone that served in the war, such as their father, an uncle, or even a grandfather. That is the same generation that benefitted from the GI Bill, and it offered many African Americans the ability to attend school. Out of the eight male teachers I had in high school, six of them were military veterans who received higher education degrees by using the GI Bill. It allowed many African Americans the opportunity to complete school and to contribute economically to their families as well as society. African Americans who were able to take advantage of federal funding in the form of higher education and home loans were able to improve their personal lives as well as the lives of their children. This was also reflected in the fact that more of their children went to college because their fathers had had the opportunity to attend college. I am saying this not based on data but because that is what I experienced.

In fact, at Southern University, President Felton G. Clark was a staunch supporter of Army ROTC and military service. His father was an educator and many of black America's most celebrated scholars and leaders influenced Clark. He was not the type of person who had a lot of empathy for you just because you were poor. Being poor was not the exception at that time, it was the rule. Therefore, Dr. Clark attempted to express to us students that college represented an opportunity to raise ourselves and our families. But he also kept in perspective the values that we shared coming from rural south Louisiana and emphasized that there were people back home counting on us. He had a sincere desire to help us be successful. He was constantly challenging us and he embraced the idea of "Don't let where you came from be the measure of where you are going." He devoted a great deal of time in his public orations to individuals who were successful. Dr. Clark did not talk about failures. During the late 1960s there were still vestiges of white and black water fountains and other reminders of racial segregation, even though African Americans had made social and political progress. Dr. Clark insisted that students take advantage of every opportunity to achieve success.

That is why so many African Americans decided to participate in Army ROTC and pursue careers in the military. As a result, military training programs at historically black colleges and universities (HBCUs) have produced some of America's finest military officers and generals over the last fifty years. For instance, as a graduate of Southern University there was an expectation that when you reached the workforce you were not just representing yourself but you were representing Southern University. So, you needed to always do your best under the conditions you were placed. In many cases, you grew up in an environment that did not offer you many opportunities, but that was not an excuse. You were expected to get out there and earn your way. That was the attitude we left college with. When I left Southern University, that was the attitude that I had. Army ROTC cadets believed that we were just as good as lieutenants graduating from West Point, so go and demonstrate it! Take stock of your strengths and recognize what skills you need to improve and go and improve them! Many young officers that graduated from military academies appeared to be better prepared because they had more experience shooting weapons and studying military history. But that was no excuse for our not being able to compete with them. There was no reason why a guy from West Point should be able to outrun us. Our ROTC instructors, Dr. Clark, and the faculty taught us that difficult situations were only times for us to work harder. So, graduates from military colleges and academies might write better than us because they came from second- and third-generation parents that were well educated, but when the opportunity came for formal presentation, we should rise to the occasion.

Being black or poor was not recognized as an excuse at Southern University for not being successful. If anything, it was a reason to work harder. Being poor, we learned to adapt and overcome. In the military it is all about adapting to overcome. So, I think that has something to do with the number of men and women who were promoted to general officer that graduated from HBCUs. It is my opinion that a generation of African American cadets who became flag officers was taught that the only thing that could hold them back was themselves.

The virtues of military training and service are still relevant today, given the many social and economic problems facing society. For example, when you look at Junior ROTC programs at high schools, the main purpose is not to produce military officers for the armed forces. Instead, the focus is on leadership skills and other character attributes. There are several Junior ROTC programs in Chicago and around the country that I have visited which are very successful. I was amazed to see how well those cadets who come from disadvantaged environments plagued by crime and drugs respond to discipline, leadership, and physical training exercises. Junior ROTC programs do not judge a young cadet on where they come from, they focus on their natural abilities and on what they can do, much like the U.S. military today.

Segregated Soldiers is an important study because it documents the history and value of African American military training programs at historically black colleges and universities. Young people today need to know this history to better appreciate the fact that they too can overcome life's challenges and obstacles to success.

Lieutenant General Russel L. Honoré, U.S. Army (Ret.)

PREFACE

In 1941, Matthew Woodrick Trahan left Rayne, Louisiana, a small rural town in southwest Louisiana, and was inducted into the U.S. Army. Trahan, like most African Americans of the period, had few employment opportunities in the rural community from which he came. As a recent graduate of Armstrong High School, he worked as a general carpenter with his father constructing concrete and wooden structures. He was the oldest sibling in a family of seven, so his family quickly began to depend on his financial support. At this point, like many others, Trahan had never ventured far from home. Similar to his father and grandfather before him, he was destined to spend the rest of his life in the general area of Rayne, where he would marry, raise a family, and live a difficult but simple life with few options.

But like millions of African Americans of the World War II generation, Matthew Trahan found military training and service to be a life-transforming event. He spent the next thirty years as a professional soldier. In 1942, he was shipped out to the Southwest Pacific and Australia, where his engineering battalion spent over two years building bridges and constructing runways on various islands in support of the Allies. He returned to the United States near the conclusion of the war at the rank of sergeant and transferred to the 3379th Quartermaster Truck Company and was promoted to staff sergeant. During the war, Staff Sergeant Trahan served in several capacities as a draftsman, unit supply specialist, and truck driver. For a black man with limited options in a racially segregated army, those jobs reflected noncombat support roles and laborious tasks. In October 1945 Trahan received an honorable discharge, but he quickly reenlisted in the Army. By the end of Trahan's military career, he had reenlisted six times.

Throughout his tenure as a professional soldier, Matthew Trahan took full advantage of his ability to enroll in educational courses that had civilian applications. Beginning in 1947, he enrolled in clerical courses and courses on cooking, combat construction, supply chain management, auxiliary fire fighting, flight operations, and financial management. In addition, he received over four hundred hours of certified training in nonmedical personnel emergency medical care, general supply management procedures, educational teaching methods, noncommissioned officer administration procedures, and business management. In 1951, he received a certificate of excellence from the U.S. Constabulary Non-Commissioned Officers Academy, a commendation from the Office of Quartermasters Operations in 1960, and a Good Conduct medal for his service between 1948 and 1951. In 1965, Sergeant First Class Matthew Trahan received a certificate of achievement from Lieutenant Colonel A. L. Schalbrack for outstanding performance and exemplary work as manager of the EASCOM (Eastern Command) commissary in Seoul, Korea. The award read:

> SFC Trahan's initiative, devotion to duty, and efficient performance has greatly contributed to this activity's accomplishment of its mission. He has received many gratifying comments from many General Officers and Diplomatic officials of the American Embassy and various foreign embassies, who patronize this commissary. His initiative and concern has improved service rendered to these customers. SFC Trahan's supervision and guidance of the Korean National employees and the U.S. military personnel has been outstanding and has promoted harmonious and efficient operation. SFC Trahan's conscientious and outstanding performance of duty has brought much credit to this organization and the United States Army.[1]

Sergeant Trahan traveled throughout the world experiencing diverse cultures and gaining insight into vast opportunities. As a noncommissioned officer, Trahan lived in Germany with his wife and two daughters for over five years in a lifestyle that many African Americans back home would envy. In Frankfurt, Germany, the Trahans lived in a three-story home and employed a German maid. After leaving Frankfurt, Sergeant Trahan and his family returned to the United States for a year, then he was reassigned to Lenggries, Germany, where he entered Quartermaster School. Four years later, the Trahans returned to Western Europe to La Rochelle, France, for a three-year stay. In France, the family adjusted easily to its new surroundings in part because Trahan and his wife, Annie Mae, were both Louisiana Creoles and spoke French-Creole as their first language. In the United States, Sergeant Trahan and his family lived in Fort Slocum, New York; Fort Bliss, Texas; Fort Rucker, Alabama; and eventually returned to Louisiana. By the end of his remarkable military career, he had traveled to four continents, taken hundreds of hours of educational courses, expanded his employment opportunities, financed the education of his younger siblings, and moved his family well into middle-class social status.

Sergeant First Class Matthew W. Trahan in many ways represents the typical African American soldier during the post–World War II era. Millions of black men left the confines of rural and urban areas and were able to transform their lives and families through military service and training as soldiers and ROTC cadets at historically black colleges and universities. For me however, Sergeant Trahan is extraordinary. Matthew W. Trahan was my grandfather and the single most influential individual in my life. At an early age, my grandfather nurtured my interest in the U.S. military and would often spend hours answering my assorted questions. My grandmother, Annie Mae Alsandor-Trahan, would more than occasionally sit in her rocking chair in her bedroom and tell my brothers and me stories about when they lived in Germany, France, and throughout the United States. Always with a gleam in her eye and a smile on her face, my Nana would speak about the lifestyle of a noncommissioned officer in the U.S. Army with much pride and satisfaction. She would often refer to the hero's welcome that awaited my grandfather when they returned to her hometown of Opelousas, Louisiana. Family and friends would affectionately refer to my grandfather as "Sarge." My uncles would begin their reunion with a celebratory drink (usually several), and quickly prompt him to report details about life in Germany, France, or Korea and his responsibilities as an NCO. According to my mother, Grandpa was nothing short of a celebrity among my family in Opelousas. As a result, I quickly gained an elevated level of respect for and curiosity about military service and the benefits of being an African American soldier.

Of course, like most African American families of the period, many of my relatives also served in the military during World War II and the Korean War. My uncles Alexander Gourdine and Angelo Petite served in the Navy and Air Force. My Louisiana relatives, Alfred Norman, Albert Taylor, Bobby

Alsandor, Calvin Taylor, George Alsandor, Theophile Alsandor Jr., and Melvin Trahan, all served in the Army.

In many cases, the length of service for them was approximately three years. After a lengthy career in the Army, my grandfather retired and then served as a Junior ROTC instructor at Lee High School in Baton Rouge, Louisiana, before securing employment at Southern University and starting his own business.

As I matured, my level of interest about African American military service did not dissipate. Knowing more about African American history and legalized segregation and racism in America, I would often ask my grandfather why he and other African Americans would serve in the military for a nation that mistreated and devalued them. On the one hand, I clearly understood the economic and social benefits of serving in the U.S. military; on the other hand, from a political and ideological perspective, there appeared to be a contradiction in being a black solider in America. Later, I decided to finally seek the answers to many questions that puzzled me throughout my young adult life concerning African American attitudes toward military service.

ACKNOWLEDGMENTS

I am eternally grateful for God's blessings and the opportunity to complete this fantastic journey. I must first thank my wife, Rebecca, and our daughters, Callia and Leigha, for making this accomplishment possible. You are and will always be the inspiration for my work. I could never repay you for the love, happiness, and joy that you give me each day. There is nothing that I can achieve that can rival the pride I feel being your husband and father. Thank you for cowriting this book.

I am indebted to many people who touched my life in so many ways. My advisors at Northwestern University nurtured and encouraged me as I developed the idea and purpose of my research. Though it was many years ago, I still vividly remember the conversations and advice I received. Michael Sherry was more than the chair of my dissertation committee and advisor, he was my therapist, mentor, and friend. Nancy McLean and Adam Green were thoughtful and generous with their time as well. The late Charles Moskos Jr. was a living legend in my eyes and had a profound impact on the direction of my scholarly interest. On more than one occasion Charlie would autograph a copy of one of his books for me and I was so elated that I would leave his office nearly forgetting the purpose of my visit. Today I can better appreciate my professors at Northwestern University. They planted the seeds of my professional success.

Over the years I interviewed many individuals in preparation of this study, and I continue to be impressed by their accomplishments and wisdom. E. C. Harrison, Huel Perkins, Frank Ransburg, Henry L. Essex, L. F. Koons, Brigadier General Charles Honore (Ret.), James Lund, William O. Jones, my aunt and late uncle Reta and Al Norman, my mother- and father-in-law Larry and Josephine Dubriel, Tolar White, Oscar J. Braynon, Mickey St. Amant, Lieutenant Colonel Ralph Poole, my cousin Albert Taylor, and nearly one hundred Southern and Tuskegee University alumni who filled-out questionnaires provided important information. They spent hours of their time recalling events, individuals, and experiences in order to contribute to my understanding of the past. Lieutenant General Russel L. Honoré (Ret.) deserves special consideration for agreeing to write the foreword to this book and for being so generous with his time. In addition, I met with dozens of World War II, Korean War, and Vietnam War veterans from organizations such as the Knights of Peter Claver Council 112 at Immaculate Conception Church in Baton Rouge, Louisiana; the Knights of Peter Claver Council 110 from St. Patrick's Catholic Church in Charleston, South Carolina; and the brothers of Beta Kappa Lambda chapter of Alpha Phi Alpha Fraternity Incorporated.

I would also like to recognize the late Henry Bellaire for his tremendous influence on my life and my desire to positively impact my alma mater, Southern University. For me, Henry Bellaire represented a model of compassion, concern, devotion, and professionalism that many college administrators aspire to achieve. He was not only a husband to his wife, Elizabeth, and father to his daughters, Gaylyn and Gina, but a community leader, neighbor, true friend, and role model for countless students and individuals at Southern University and throughout the Baton Rouge community. My desire to write this book and to pursue a career in higher education is directly attributable to the life of Henry Bellaire and the lessons that he taught my siblings and me many years ago at Southern University. He will always be a special part of my life.

I certainly appreciate the support of the faculty and staff of the departments of history at Southern University and the Citadel. In particular, I would like to thank Michael Fontenot, Gregory Mixon, Gardel Fuertado, Judge Roberta Tracy, Bo Moore, David White, Sharon Parsons, Dena Davis, Jennifer Speelman, Paul Paskoff, Ronald Morazan, Jeffrey Pilcher, Marvin W. Dulaney, and Bernard Powers.

My research efforts would have not been possible if it were not for the generous support of the Citadel Foundation and a Marshall-Baruch Fellowship from the George C. Marshall Foundation. Funding allowed me to travel to several depositories and libraries throughout the United States. I am very grateful to librarians, archivists, and staff at the National Archives in College Park, Maryland; the Lyndon Baines Johnson Library and Museum in Austin, Texas; the Louisiana State University Library; the Citadel's Daniel Library; the Tuskegee University Library; and the Louisiana State Archives in Baton Rouge, Louisiana.

I owe a huge debt of gratitude to the administration and faculty at the Southern University Library and Archives. Specifically, I would like to thank Dean Emma Bradford Perry, the late Ledale Smith, and Angela Proctor. Over the last few years, I had the pleasure of working closely with Eddie Hughes, department head of the Camille Shades African American Heritage Collection, who devoted a great deal of time and care to my research requests and contacted me periodically with search updates and helpful information. The Southern University Library and Archives is a treasure and tremendous resource on the history of African Americans in Louisiana. I am very appreciative for my research assistants, Kathryn King, Nancy Turner, Elizabeth Hair, Theresa Sulkowski, and Michelle Smith, for their contributions and professionalism throughout this process.

I would also like to thank Rand Dotson, Lauren Tussing-White, Lee Sioles, Catherine Kadair, copy editor Derik Shelor, and the staff at Louisiana State University Press for embracing this project, offering advice, and encouraging my efforts. I am very fortunate to be associated with one of the leading academic presses in the United States.

My personal friends and colleagues that have encouraged and supported me also deserve recognition. Robert Pickering Jr., Troy Allen, Gayle Ward, Lena Rodriguez, Ian Johnson, Brigadier General Walter F. Johnson III (Ret.), Louis Waring, Keith and Donna Waring, Arthur McFarland, Robert Curry, Thaddeus Bell, Vernell Green, Clay Middleton, Sergeant Kenneth Greene, and my students at Southern University and the Citadel. I am blessed to call you my friends and colleagues.

And last but far from least, I have received continuous love and support from my grandparents, parents, brothers, and sister. No one understands my personal struggles and challenges better than my grandparents, the late Annie Mae and Sergeant First Class Matthew W. Trahan, my parents, Brenda and Michael Durham, and my brothers and sister, Brian, Randy, and Shannon. Throughout my life I have worked hard to be a testament to the sacrifices you made for my siblings and me. Thank you for making this dream a reality and maintaining the support and love that I needed to accomplish this monumental task.

SEGREGATED SOLDIERS

INTRODUCTION

Segregated Soldiers is about African American attitudes toward military service and how black higher education and military training programs worked in concert to advance the quest for citizenship rights. It also serves as the definitive history of military training programs at historically black colleges and universities (HBCUs). The book is unique because it examines why African American educators were supportive of military training as early as the late nineteenth century and how military training at black colleges and universities was used to improve the social, economic, and political state of black America. Historians rarely focus on blacks in the military when discussing the civil rights movement because they fail to recognize the importance of military service on the subject and the fact that it became a central part of the civil rights struggle by the eighteenth century.

CURRENT RESEARCH ON AFRICAN AMERICAN MILITARY TRAINING

Military service was at the core of the civil rights movement. It was a way for minorities to demonstrate their respectability and citizenship in the community and economically advance themselves into middle-class social status through enhanced financial and educational opportunities. During the late nineteenth century, when the movement to educate African Americans became essential to uplift the race, military training quickly became a fundamental component of black higher education. African American educators encouraged military activities in order to promote discipline, moral behavior, and patriotism in young blacks. All of these virtues were believed to impact the African American quest for civil rights and social progress. For much of the twentieth century, African American interest in military training and service continued to steadily rise. By the late 1960s and early 1970s, despite the growing unpopularity of the Vietnam War, the rise of black nationalism, and a expanding economy that offered African Americans enhanced economic opportunities, support for military training and service persisted because many African Americans continued to believe that military service represented the best way to advance themselves in a society where racial discrimination flourished.

African American attitudes toward military service were influenced by opinions on civil rights, the Black Power movement, social discrimination, Cold War domestic and international politics, and African American experiences during the Korean and Vietnam wars. Military training in conjunction with educational opportunities was used to confirm African American social and political legitimacy in civil society. This combination explains why black leaders and college administrators were adamant about supporting military service and why ROTC units were sought at nearly every black college and university throughout the twentieth century. The 1950s and 1960s was a turbulent period for HBCUs in that while many institutions and ROTC programs continued to grow and prosper, the civil rights movement and student activism threatened to negatively impact the future. The military tradition in the black community was vigorously promoted at African American institutions of higher learning, and at those schools racial uplift was the primary mission. In addition, military training became an integral part of the curriculum at black colleges and universities and survived the turmoil of the late 1960s and early 1970s, with many new ROTC programs established at HBCUs while predominately white institutions were terminating their military programs.

Retired Army lieutenant colonel and Morgan State University professor of history Charles Johnson Jr. wrote an extensive history of African Americans and military training. Johnson's monograph, *African Americans and ROTC: Military, Naval and Aeroscience Programs at Historically Black Colleges, 1916–1973*, makes a tremendous contribution to our understanding of the institutional histories of over a dozen ROTC programs at black colleges and universities. Because Johnson's book begins in the early twentieth century, it fails to discuss the social and political origins of those programs and does very little to illuminate our knowledge of why these programs were essential to the political and social progress of the black community.[1]

Rod Andrew's *Long Gray Lines: The Southern Military School Tradition, 1839–1915* and *Making Citizen Soldiers: ROTC and the Ideology of American Military Service* by Michael Neiberg are two works concerning the history of military training and the Reserve Officer Training Corps. Although Andrew's book devotes a brief, well-written chapter to military training among African Americans in the late nineteenth century, his study mainly focuses on the military tradition in the South among white Americans. By contrast, Michael Neiberg's study devotes only a few pages to ROTC programs at black colleges and universities in the late 1960s and early 1970s and does not explain the origins of those programs and why military training and service was so valuable to black educators and students throughout the Cold War.[2]

While numerous books have been published on the history of black colleges and universities in recent decades, many scholars have concentrated on institutional histories and avoided reference to the detailed study of broader social, political, and economic issues, and why military training programs were a vital part of the schools' missions. *Stand and Prosper: Private Black Colleges and Their Students* by Henry Drewry and Humphrey Doermann underscores the evolution of private black colleges and universities and their successful contribution to the black community and nation.[3] However, it only makes brief reference to World War II and reveals nothing concerning private black colleges and their relationship to military training programs for African Americans.

BENEFITS OF AFRICAN AMERICAN MILITARY TRAINING AND SERVICE

As early as the American Revolution, the War of 1812, and the Civil War, African Americans served in the U.S. military with the hope of acquiring freedom or the privileges of citizenship. During the late nineteenth century, education became the primary approach to socialize thousands of oppressed and subjugated individuals. Military training was introduced to further promote virtues of self-discipline, order, punctuality, and character that many white paternalists and black leaders believed was not only essential to African American youth but impacted their efforts to successfully obtain equal rights. Military training was also a way for African American males to assert their manhood in a society that often referred to them as "boy." In the South, definitions of masculinity were closely connected with military training in education.[4] Gender roles were strengthened by the distinction between those who protect and individuals who are protected. Military training reinforced aspirations for masculinity in addition to having educational benefits. As a way to confirm their social and political legitimacy, minorities sought active roles in local militias to demonstrate their respectability and citizenship in the community. Moreover, citizen-soldiers enjoyed the rights and privileges of full citizenship. Military service was indeed an indication of citizenship status.[5] Consequently, African American civil rights struggles were historically associated with the ability to serve in the armed forces as defenders of America's democratic institutions and to support the nation in times of war.

WHY HISTORICALLY BLACK COLLEGES AND UNIVERSITIES?

I examine African American attitudes toward military training and service at black colleges and universities using Southern University and Agricultural and Mechanical (A&M) College in Baton Rouge, Louisiana, as a case study. The campus of Southern University is located on Scott's Bluff, near the Mississippi River, approximately seven miles north of the state capitol in Baton Rouge. The institution represents most HBCUs during the late nineteenth and twentieth centuries because it possessed many of the same problems and challenges of other institutions. Between 1914 and 1969, Southern University had two presidents, Joseph Samuel Clark (also known as J. S. Clark) and his son, Felton Grandison Clark (also known as F. G. Clark). The Clarks were nationally recognized educators and black intellectuals who were well received among their peers. In particular, Dr. Felton G. Clark traveled extensively to other black colleges throughout the nation meeting with administrative officials, delivering speeches, and collaborating on countless initiatives as well as sharing ideas and strategies. Many of Southern's efforts were duplicated to the point they reflected general practices among HBCUs.

In addition to Southern University, Tuskegee University also figures prominently in this study. Tuskegee University is located in Tuskegee, Alabama, which is positioned thirty-five miles east of Montgomery, Alabama. Tuskegee is a private university founded by Booker T. Washington in 1881 and one of the best-known black institutions of the twentieth century. It is also home to World War II's most famous African American military unit, the Tuskegee Airmen.

During this period, African American administrators corresponded with one another on a regular basis to express support and offer advice on various matters. Black colleges and universities suffered the same financial problems, they were normally located in rural areas within the South, their presidents were considered key black leaders of the state, the faculties often moved between black institutions, and the primary mission of the institutions was racial uplift of African Americans. In addition, state and federal governments utilized these institutions to mobilize support from the black community in war and peace. Black colleges and universities became the primary focus of black political action because they were centers of intellectual and local community life. Efforts to educate and uplift the African American population were fundamental to the mission of HBCUs, and military training quickly became another way to accomplish those tasks. Also, Southern is an 1890 land-grant public institution, like many African American colleges located in the South. It was selected as the focus of this book because it reflects an HBCU with a distinguished history of military training and was one of the largest African American institutions of higher learning during the post–World War II era. With an enrollment of nearly five thousand students during the 1950s, the student body increased to over ten thousand by the early 1970s. Southern University's influence had national implications in the black community.

AFRICAN AMERICAN ATTITUDES IN THE POST-WORLD WAR II ERA

During the post–World War II era, African American attitudes toward military service were greatly impacted by the Selective Service System. Although thousands of African Americans volunteered for military service during that period, the vast majority of black and white servicemen were drafted into the armed forces. According to a June 1945 Gallup poll, nearly 70 percent of African Americans surveyed believed that the Selective Service System was fair. By 1948, as President Harry S. Truman called for a renewal of the draft, the Committee Against Jim Crow in Military Service and Training, led by A. Philip Randolph, lobbied for desegregation in the armed forces. Randolph, in conjunction with other black leaders, threatened the president with a boycott if their demands were not met. According to George Flynn, "polls showed over 70 percent of black college students supported Randolph's call for a boycott of any racial draft calls."[6] While Gallup polls of the 1950s suggested that African Americans were supportive of military service, the 1960s and the Black Power movement prompted young African Americans to question the equity of the Selective Service System and ask who was the real enemy? With every incident of racial violence, discrimination, and police assault on demonstrators, African Americans at black colleges and universities questioned the sensibility of African American support for military training and service and the legitimacy of ROTC programs.

As civil rights demonstrators and marches met repeated physical violence throughout the South, an increasing number of African Americans began to turn their backs on the U.S. military. In July 1965 the McComb, Mississippi, branch of the Mississippi Freedom Democratic Party (MFDP) was the first African American organization to formally condemn America's role in Vietnam.[7] Though the MFDP's declaration encouraged many African American college youths to support its agenda, on the campus of Southern University students still overwhelmingly supported the armed forces.

Although most students at Southern did not voice opposition to serving in the military in 1965, within three years student newspaper articles and public forums on black college campuses were continuously debating the merits of African American participation in the armed forces and America's role in Southeast Asia. By 1968 many college and university student organizations throughout the country were attempting to remove ROTC units from their respective campuses, while numerous HBCUs and Southern University students were calling for the abolition of compulsory ROTC. The unpopularity of the Vietnam War and reported claims of African American soldiers being killed in disproportionate numbers caught the attention of student leaders and civil rights organizations in the South. National leaders, such as Malcolm X, accused the U.S. government of genocide against people of color, and H. Rap Brown and Stokely Carmichael, leaders of the Student Nonviolent Coordinating Committee, spoke out against the draft in black communities and universities throughout the South. Thus, the Black Power movement was conceived during a period of deep suspicion and mistrust of the federal government and symbols of authority. Between 1968 and 1972, much like at Southern University, students at Jackson State, Texas Southern, and South Carolina State witnessed the death of unarmed demonstrators at the hands of the National Guard or local police. In each instance students charged that police indiscriminately fired into the crowd of protesters without cause. Military training programs at HBCUs that were once popular in the 1950s became sources of contention and criticism by the end of the 1960s. In 1973, shortly after these tragic events, the federal government abolished the draft and ushered in the beginning of the all-volunteer armed forces. This book will carefully analyze this shift in attitudes toward military service in the black community.

OUTLINE OF THE BOOK

Segregated Soldiers is organized in chronological order, beginning during the American Civil War. Chapter 1 highlights the historic connection of military training and service with the quest for citizenship rights, which quickly became an essential component of the African American civil rights movement and the struggle for social equality in America. In addition, it examines the military tradition in the black community and discusses why African American soldiers, educators, and leaders promoted the virtues of military training at HBCUs.

Chapter 2 describes the wartime contributions of black colleges and universities—in particular, Southern University—during World War II and the black community's desire to contribute to America's victory overseas while improving social and economic opportunities at home. Moreover, it discusses how Southern University's president, Felton G. Clark, and African American educators like him diligently worked with civil rights leaders and the black press to improve the university's educational standing within the state and region while vigorously seeking increased funding opportunities from federal and state agencies.

African American higher education and the Cold War is the subject of chapter 3. This chapter focuses on how Southern University officials participated in Cold War programs and encouraged African American support for military training and service at the beginning of the post–World War II era. Similar to other black colleges and universities, Southern University offered military training for the first time and vigorously promoted economic and social opportunities that military service offered African Americans as the armed forces led the nation in racial integration.

Chapter 4 argues that between 1950 and 1960, the black press encouraged, honored, supported, and admired African American men and women in military uniform and enthusiastically advertised the benefits of military training and service. This occurred while the first phase of the modern civil rights movement was gaining momentum with the Montgomery bus boycott and news of the landmark court case *Brown v. Board of Education* was making headlines. During this period, African American military veterans were involved in or leading dozens of civil rights protests throughout the South because their sacrifices as soldiers strengthened their demand for social and political equality. On the campuses of black colleges and universities, such as Southern University and the Tuskegee Institute, student newspapers devoted attention to military training and service in the same fashion as national black newspapers.

Chapter 5 discusses the importance of the civil rights movement and the Vietnam War on black college campuses, particularly Southern University. Between 1960 and 1964 the civil rights thrust incorporated innovative tactics and a wider support base that included young African Americans, white Americans, and sympathetic clergy throughout the nation. Much like during the 1950s, the armed forces played a major role in the civil rights movement in that national security and Cold War politics dictated the fair treatment of African American servicemen and citizens. African American ROTC cadets on black colleges and universities embraced the virtues of military training and service but also led many of the demonstrations and protests for enhanced opportunities and a greater voice in the same manner veterans did. After 1965, on black college campuses antiwar supporters and individuals who believed in the merits of military service became engaged in a verbal standoff concerning America's escalation of the war. Antiwar and promilitary advocates debated such issues as: "Should America remain in Vietnam?" and "Is military training necessary?"

Chapter 6 contends that despite strong opposition to the war by a vocal minority, African American interest in military training and service survived the turmoil of the Vietnam era, though with several alterations. Motivation for military service by African Americans shifted to involve less the uplift of the whole race and more the individual's advancement and economic opportunity. Similar to changes at white colleges and universities during the period, compulsory military training was abolished at nearly every HBCU, but not to the detriment of the ROTC programs. Military officials occasionally maintained that students that joined ROTC programs at black colleges from that point on were visibly more dedicated and motivated to embrace the demands of military training. By 1973, as the Vietnam War drew to a close and the draft was ended, the number of ROTC programs at black colleges and universities continued to grow with the addition of female cadets.

The conclusion will summarize the research and elaborate on major shifts in African American attitudes toward military service since 1973. It will also highlight how questionnaires, interviews, and quantitative data were used to support the book's main thesis.

1

MEN OF COLOR TO ARMS

MILITARY TRAINING AND SERVICE AT BLACK COLLEGES
IN THE LATE NINETEENTH CENTURY

Throughout American history, African Americans most diligently fought for the right to serve and fight in America's armed forces. The historic connection between military service and citizenship is well documented and provides the foundation to the African American quest for civil rights and the social movement that followed. While military training and service are linked to the fight for freedom and social equality, they also reflect how African American soldiers and proponents broadened this experience to include the pursuit of literacy and strengthened concepts of masculine identity. This multidimensional quest of citizenship and social equality became intertwined in the late nineteenth century and manifested itself in the establishment of military training programs at black colleges and universities.

African American soldiers during the Civil War established the link between military service and the communal pursuit of literacy in the black community as a way to empower African Americans in their claim for citizenship rights. In addition, military preparedness and training in the South challenged the docile stereotype of the black man and reinforced a masculine self-identity embraced through military discipline and notions of honor and civic duty. Historically black colleges and universities such as Hampton Normal and Agricultural Institute, Howard University, Wilberforce University, and the Tuskegee Institute were some of the first institutions to establish military training programs in the late nineteenth century and became models for subsequent training units as Negro land-grant institutions were being created throughout the South.[1]

THE MEANING OF CITIZENSHIP DURING THE CIVIL WAR

The American Civil War represents a decisive moment in U.S. military history. For the first time, the federal government enacted a compulsory draft call that forced the nation to rethink how it defined citizenship and who was eligible. According to Christian G. Samito, "the Union armed forces mobilized Americans from different classes, ethnicities, races, and states in unprecedented ways, on a national scale. Wartime experiences cut across people's different backgrounds and created stronger links between the federal government and the people. Politics pervaded the armed forces during the Civil War, turning the military into an institution that raised political consciousness with soldiers and sailors in the ranks."[2] In particular, this was true for Irish Americans and African Americans. Both groups made incessant demands during and after the war for enhanced social and political rights that each believed were earned through sacrifice and peril during the conflict.

Though African and Irish Americans had served the nation in previous military engagements, for the first time their numbers had reached into the hundreds of thousands and it was indisputably clear that Union military victories were influenced by their presence. Black and Irish soldiers also challenged the nation to redefine the notion of citizenship. Black soldiers en masse demonstrated their commitment to the egalitarian principles of the nation while highlighting that loyalty, not race, was a necessary component of national citizenship. The point was strengthened after the implementation of the Fourteenth Amendment and when discussing the treasonous acts of southern Confederates. For Irish Americans, national allegiance was more relevant to citizenship than ethnic considerations. For both groups, carrying the American flag into battle highlighted a personal connection to the Constitution of the United States. Participation in the Union Army spurred on a greater demand for inclusion into society as national citizens.[3]

THE AFRICAN AMERICAN CALL TO ARMS

African Americans did not serve in the U.S. military in significant numbers until 1863. Once the Emancipation Proclamation was signed on January 1, African American recruits began to filter into recruiting stations throughout the North. Rallies were held at which speakers urged blacks to enlist, and in Boston, New York, and Philadelphia blacks went to recruiting stations in large numbers. Black leaders such as Martin Delany, William Cooper Nell, John Mercer Langston, Frederick Douglass, and many others challenged free blacks to enlist into the Army and help champion the cause of African American civil rights. Douglass proclaimed, "Once you let the black man get upon his person the brass letters, 'U.S.,' let him get an eagle on his button, and a musket on his shoulder and bullets in his pocket, and there is no power on Earth which can deny that he has earned the right to citizenship in the United States."[4] During the Civil War nearly two hundred thousand African American servicemen participated in over 180 battles, and for the first time African Americans were commissioned as Army officers. Despite racism, discrimination, and ill treatment suffered at the hands of their white comrades, African American soldiers helped turn the tide of the Civil War.[5]

Many African Americans and black leaders such as Frederick Douglass believed that the Civil War was the opportunity to fight for their freedom and prove that they were indeed worthy of citizenship. Many soldiers also enlisted for a variety of social and economic reasons, including escaping servitude, obtaining regular wages, fighting to liberate their enslaved brethren, and eradicating prejudice and racism.[6] The Civil War was the first conflict that African Americans felt truly invested in and could view as a part of their own struggle for freedom.[7] Frederick Douglass embraced this philosophy and championed the northern cause like no other leader during this period. Douglass remarked, "To fight for the Government in this tremendous war is to fight for nationality and for a place with all other classes of our fellow citizens."[8] Like Douglass, military recruiters stressed freedom, social equality, citizenship, and heroism as inducements to encourage African American participation in the war. The message was clear and the link between military service and citizenship was quite potent. In 1863, "when African Americans in Kansas pushed for voting rights, they reminded whites that it is as necessary to make the black man a voter, as it was to make him a soldier. He was made a soldier to *restore* the Union. He must be a voter to preserve it."[9]

THE CONTRADICTION OF BLACK SOLDIERS FIGHTING FOR THE CONFEDERACY

Even the Confederacy acknowledged the link between African American military service and enhanced political rights and freedom. As early as 1863, General Patrick R. Cleburne, an Irishman and division commander of the Army of Tennessee, championed the cause of arming freemen and slaves to preserve the Confederate States of America (CSA). Though many Confederate officers supported Cleburne's plan initially, General Robert E. Lee and Confederate president Jefferson Davis did not. For many southern leaders and CSA military officers it was a practical response to a dire situation. They argued, "should the Union triumph, as it seemed poised to do, slavery would be dead away—it had been crumbling for years—so the white South might as well retreat to its last ditch. Such independence would allow the South to rebuild on its own terms and limit how much the war could undermine the Southern social order."[10] But in contrast, several vocal southern leaders retorted that the "arming of slaves [was] tantamount to abandoning the Confederacy's ideological underpinnings." They reasoned that, "the day you make soldiers of them [blacks] is the beginning of the end of the revolution. If slaves will make good soldiers our whole theory of slavery is wrong."[11]

Despite the vigorously argued debate, in the very late stages of the war Jefferson Davis and the Confederate Congress, with the support of General Robert E. Lee, authorized the recruitment of blacks who were already free, which only gained the attention of a small number of African Americans. On March 13, 1865, Jefferson Davis signed the Barksdale bill (authorizing the recruitment of African Americans) into law, only weeks before Robert E. Lee's surrender at Appomattox. The law did not free a single slave and was a controversial issue among southerners until the last days of the war. Although the Confederate president had endorsed the law, Davis, Lee, and many others acknowledged the contradictory nature of arming African Americans as soldiers while holding many more as slaves. Despite this fact, Davis refused to free a single slave against the wishes of his master, not even to save the Confederacy.[12]

Nevertheless, by this time the war had completely shifted in favor of the Union and African Americans had little doubt that their prayers would soon be answered. In addition, at this point in the war the Confederacy had little to offer and even the promise of freedom would have fallen on deaf ears. That is why, according to Bruce Levine, "only in Richmond, Virginia is there evidence of any units of black Confederate soldiers ever forming. Those units were recruited from two sources. One was the staff of two local hospitals and the other was the formal recruiting efforts of Lt. General Richard S. Ewell and his junior officers. In all, approximately 40–50 African Americans were enlisted under the new law."[13] By contrast, serving in the military under Union colors offered African Americans freedom, social opportunities, and educational prospects that were enhanced during the war and ultimately too great to ignore.

MILITARY SERVICE AND EDUCATIONAL OPPORTUNITIES

The African American quest for social improvement and economic opportunity during and after the Civil War is well documented. While many individuals are vaguely aware of the efforts of abolitionists, philanthropists, religious organizations, and white northerners to assist African Americans in their desire to obtain a formal education, there is little or no reference in history surveys to the vital role the U.S. military played in this endeavor. During the war, though the Union Army did not maintain an official policy or program of education for African Americans, it did not impede the efforts of white officers, their spouses, or educated African American soldiers to promote literacy among the black troops. Thus, thousands of African American servicemen, and in many cases their dependents, attended improvised schools sponsored by regiments of the U.S. Colored Troops.[14]

As the number of African American soldiers began to rise and they made their way further south in 1862, the hunger for education became more evident. When Colonel Thomas Wentworth Higginson took command of the 1st South Carolina Colored Volunteers (later the 33rd U.S. Colored Troops), he immediately witnessed how his soldiers eagerly gathered in the evenings as an African American woman read from a New England speller. In a short period of time African American soldiers quickly incorporated a period of formal education into their twenty-four-hour schedule between military training and evening bivouac duties. What is most impressive is that this behavior was common among African Americans soldiers throughout the eastern and western theaters of operations.[15] For African American soldiers who worked hard to excel in the rudiments of military life and culture, education became an essential prerequisite for promotion. Joseph T. Wilson, a member of the 2nd Louisiana Native Guards and later the 54th Massachusetts Infantry Regiment, wrote, "Each soldier felt that but for his illiteracy he might be a sergeant, company clerk, or quartermaster, and not a few, that if educated, they might be lieutenants and captains. This was not an unusual conclusion for a brave soldier to arrive at, when men no braver than himself were promoted for bravery."[16] Many individuals embraced the philosophy that an educated soldier was potentially a good soldier.

As the war pressed on, the link between military service and education was strengthened among African American soldiers. Black soldiers participated in educational programs sponsored by the collective efforts of men and women associated with the regiment.[17] In some cases, educational pursuits were even organized beyond the regimental level. At Fort McIntosh (Texas) in 1866 a conversation between soldiers ensued concerning the need for a school to continue the educational efforts of the soldiers who were recently honorably discharged. As a result, African American soldiers of the 62nd and 65th U.S. Colored Troops contributed over $6,000 toward the establishment of Lincoln University in Missouri. General Nathaniel Banks of the Department of the Gulf in New Orleans, Louisiana, was so adamant about the eradication of illiteracy among his black soldiers that he employed the services of the American Missionary Association to teach all 18,500 African American soldiers under his command.[18]

Before the end of the war many African Americans had come to believe that military service equated to educational opportunity and that the ability to read and write was an avenue to citizenship and full manhood. In fact, the transition of *slave to soldier to man* was what the nation needed in order to solve its most pressing social and economic challenges.[19] According to Heather Andrea Williams, "If the war provided pathways into freedom, enlistment in the military enabled black men to expand educational opportunities that they hoped in turn would improve their ability to intervene in civic governance. Military service combined with education, they believed, would enable them to claim and exercise the rights of citizenship."[20] First

Sergeant John Sweney is a clear demonstration of this philosophy and the desire of thousands of African American soldiers. Sergeant Sweney was so passionate about the virtues of education that he wrote a letter to the federal government requesting the establishment of a school for African Americans within his Union regiment and highlighting the desire of other soldiers. He specified that once educated, African American soldiers would return home empowered to petition for their rights and become community leaders as well as contributors to general society.[21] Sergeant Sweney's petition for formal education explicitly highlights the connection to citizenship under the auspices of military service. What may be implied also is the link between military service, citizenship, literacy, and the legitimacy of manhood.

MILITARY SERVICE AND THE DEFINITION OF MANHOOD

Much like the historic link shared between citizenship and military service, participation in militia units authenticated masculine images that resonated in the minds of Americans, especially southerners. "In the nineteenth century," Harry S. Laver believes, "being a man meant in part not being a woman or a child; in other words, not being effeminate or immature. In the slave South, most damning was the unmanly fault of dependency. Dependents lacked the ability to care for themselves, and nineteenth-century southern society branded women and African Americans as thus deficient, relegating them to the margins of the public sphere."[22] African American soldiers viewed participation in military service and a formal education as a way to eradicate the negative stigma of dependency that was placed on them as chattel property and to strengthen their claim to full manhood in society. In 1852, Martin Delany, the first African American to be commissioned as a field officer in the U.S. Army, wrote, "Black men in the United States had been shorn of their strength, disarmed of manhood, and stripped of every right." The only solution to this problem was the virtues of education.[23] For African American males, manhood required self-sufficiency, self-determination, and economic opportunity to support one's family.

As soldiers, black men believed that they had earned the rewards of full political participation. Actually, the military uniform alone gave black men an instant sense of empowerment that was easy for others to identify.

The white commander of the 59th U.S. Colored Infantry observed African Americans at a recruiting station when he remarked, "the men stripped off their old clothes, tossed them in a fire, and stepped into a bath. Then they buttoned up their new blue coats, and the metamorphosis was complete. Yesterday a filthy repulsive nigger, today a neatly attired man; yesterday a slave, today a freeman; yesterday a civilian, today a soldier."[24]

In addition, literacy had empowered them to compete with others in arenas of new economic opportunity and community involvement. A most profound example of this relationship is the life of a former slave named Elijah Marrs. In 1864, Marrs simply walked away from his master and decided to enlist in the Union Army in Louisville, Kentucky. While in the Army he learned to read and write and was quickly promoted to the rank of sergeant, which was no small feat for a former slave. As an educated African American noncommissioned officer in the U.S. military, Marrs fashioned a new identity for himself that quickly gained the respect of his peers and even some whites. This prescription for African American manhood was well publicized and embraced by black leaders of the day.[25] In his 1863 manifesto to black men, Frederick Douglass proclaimed, "Men of Color To Arms! Our enemies have made the country believe that we are craven cowards, without souls, without manhood, without the spirit of soldiers. Shall we die with this stigma resting upon our graves? Shall we leave this inheritance of Shame to our children? No! A thousand times No! Let us rather die freemen than live to be slaves. Decried and decried as you have been and still are, you need an act of this kind by which to recover your own self-respect. You owe it to yourself and your race to rise from your social debasement and take your place among the soldiers of your country, a man among men."[26]

African American soldiers such as Elijah Marrs, Alexander Newton, John Sweney, Henry McNeal Turner, Joseph T. Wilson, and James Henry Gooding represent only a few of the well-documented cases where black soldiers asserted their claim to manhood through military service, literacy, and the expectation of enhanced political rights.[27] Even after the Civil War, while a Negro militia movement was being launched in the South by Reconstruction governments, African American men continued to answer the call of recruiters and serve in these units as a reflection of social respectability and manly prowess.[28] African American militia units also served a more vital purpose, in that they allowed black men the ability to protect their communities and immediate family members from vicious and brutal attacks by former Confederate soldiers, Ku Klux Klan members, and white southerners.

AFRICAN AMERICAN MILITIA IN THE RECONSTRUCTION SOUTH

The level of violence perpetrated against African Americans in the Reconstruction south was unparalleled in American history. An unknown number of African American men were murdered, lynched, or attacked by organized mobs of whites for attempting to exercise their newfound rights as citizens, protecting their families, or demanding to be treated as men. In York County, South Carolina, in 1871, Major Lewis Merrill of the U.S. 7th Cavalry recorded in a four-month period over four hundred whippings and six murders of African Americans in addition to the destruction of several schoolhouses and churches.[29] Note that this was one county in one southern state.

During this period, African American women and children were sexually assaulted, abused, and routinely murdered by southern and northern white men in acts of white male dominance. Even though assailants in these crimes were often arrested, it was not uncommon for them to be acquitted at trial or receive minor punishment. In Shreveport, Louisiana, shortly before the war ended, three Confederate soldiers and a Union prisoner encountered an African American woman alone at a roadside. "They ordered her to come near. Each one of the trio in turn raped the helpless woman and after they finished their lustful desires they turned to the Union prisoner and remarked, now, Yank it's your turn." What was even more horrifying about the incident was that a white female watched with amusement during the ordeal and even clapped with gratification.[30] In another incident in Raleigh, North Carolina, Patrick Hickey of the 3rd New York Infantry Regiment climbed on board a wagon driven by two African American boys below the age of twelve. The white soldier directed one of the boys to walk behind the wagon while he forced the other to fondle him and perform oral sex. When the youth resisted, the soldier threatened to kill the boys. After the soldier completed his act he promised to return the next day with candy.[31]

Former black soldiers and freedmen quickly realized that local authorities and state officials would not be able to protect them from the cruelty and aggression of southerners and even white males from the North. As a result, African American militia companies were formed in nearly every major city throughout the South. "Negro militia companies assumed a high-profile presence in black communities. Exhibiting their firepower and occasionally discharging rifles into the air, the militiamen reassured the black community that the freedmen would not succumb to violence without putting up a fight."[32]

In the late nineteenth century, as white southerners regained social and political control of state and local governments, African American militia companies were disbanded and outlawed. African American men were quickly disarmed and forced at gunpoint and through terroristic acts to accept whatever treatment whites decided to impose. For white southerners, the fact that African American men allowed themselves to be attacked, murdered, and their vote taken away only reflected their lack of manliness and that they did not deserve the blessings of citizenship or equal rights.[33] Nonetheless, though much of the social and political progress African Americans achieved after the Civil War was quickly reversed by the rise of white supremacy and the Redeemers of the Democratic Party in the South, African Americans continued to make advances as historically black colleges and universities (HBCUs) were established throughout the nation.

MILITARY TRAINING PROGRAMS AT BLACK COLLEGES

During the Reconstruction era, efforts to educate African Americans in the South experienced a tremendous boost. Northern philanthropists, religious denominations, and African American politicians established a host of institutions of higher education for African Americans. During this period, a total of sixty HBCUs were established in fourteen southern states.[34] Universal education in the South had a far-reaching impact on the black community. Over two dozen black colleges and universities were established before 1870, with a faculty and staff of primarily former black military soldiers and officers.[35] Less than five years after the Civil War, African Americans had personally raised over $1 million and built nearly three thousand schools serving over one hundred thousand students throughout the South.[36] Hampton Normal and Agricultural Institute, Tuskegee Institute, Prairie View State Normal and Industrial College, and many other institutions offered formal instruction in scientific, classical, agricultural, engineering, and military training programs that were established with the hope of satisfying the educational needs of black southerners and lifting the veil of oppression.[37]

In particular, military training and service programs in conjunction with educational opportunities were used to confirm African American social and political legitimacy in the minds of African Americans even while they were being systematically disenfranchised. In 1868, a black member of the Arkansas Constitutional Convention defended the right of African Americans to vote when he proclaimed, "Has not the man who conquers upon the field of battle, gained any rights? Have we gained none by the sacrifice of our brethren?"[38] This union explains why black leaders and college administrators in the late nineteenth century were adamant about offering military instruction at nearly every black college and university. The military tradition in the black community was vigorously promoted at African American institutions of higher education, and at those schools racial uplift was the primary mission.

Hampton Normal and Agricultural Institute is considered to be the first African American institution to offer military training among HBCUs. In 1868, white paternalist and retired Union general Samuel Chapman Armstrong founded Hampton Institute with the desire to reverse the negative tendencies of laziness and sloth that he believed African Americans had acquired as slaves. He immediately organized the male students into a regiment equipped with uniforms and initiated a military training program of strict discipline, military drill, and a daily inspections. Though cadets had no official connection to the U.S. military and would never receive a commission, male students were expected to develop a manly presence from this unique form of educational instruction.[39]

General Armstrong took special pride in the rigorous training his students received at Hampton Institute. At 5 A.M. cadets were directed to the parade field by training officers to begin physical training. A strict honor code was established at the school, and Armstrong and cadet officers supervised student courts-martial and punished cadets for infractions of school policy and breaches of conduct. General Armstrong's motivation for this strict system of student oversight and control was reflected in his embrace of racial stereotypes and a low opinion of African Americans in general. By contemporary definitions, Armstrong would be considered a virulent racist or highly suspect concerning his views of the black race. In speaking of African Americans, General Armstrong remarked:

> His worst master is still over him—his passions. This he does not realize. He does not see the point of life clearly; he lacks foresight, judgment, and hard sense. His main trouble is not ignorance, but deficiency of character; his grievances occupy him more than his deepest needs. There is no lack of those who have mental capacity. The question with him is not brains, but of right instincts, of morals and of hard work.[40]

Nonetheless, the military system at Hampton had many redeeming qualities that many black leaders found socially valuable. In fact, in the late nineteenth century Hampton Institute's military program quickly became the model for other HBCUs and land-grant schools to emulate. Among those institutions were Wilberforce University, West Virginia Collegiate Institute, State Agricultural and Mechanical College in Orangeburg, South Carolina, Florida Agricultural and Mechanical College, Georgia State Industrial College in Savannah, Georgia), Talladega College, and Claflin College, also in Orangeburg, South Carolina).[41]

The military tradition at Tuskegee Institute was established on opening day in 1881. The Institute's first students marched in procession after inspection and were instructed in school policy and regulations. Similar to Hampton Institute, military training at Tuskegee was influenced by Hampton founder and former Union general Samuel Chapman Armstrong. Booker T. Washington, Hampton Institute's most famous pupil, believed that military-type training was considered necessary to school discipline and an integral part of the curriculum. Personally, Washington championed General Armstrong's educational philosophy of discipline, orderliness, and character building as a preferred vehicle of social uplift for African Americans.[42] The military department at Tuskegee was officially recognized in the 1887–1888 catalogue that reported, "the military system has been introduced for the reason that it cultivates habits of order, neatness and unquestioning obedience. Besides, the drill is good physical training, promoting, as it does, a graceful and manly bearing. Students are subject to the drill, guard duty and such other training as may be thought best."[43] The military department at Tuskegee was responsible for many functions at the institution.

Student officers were selected among the cadets and assigned specific duties. Once Major Julius B. Ramsey arrived from Hampton Institute in 1893 as commandant, his duties included administering a strict code of conduct to students, as well as judging all breaches of discipline and institute violations. The commandant also worked closely with the school principal and executive council on matters of student affairs.

Military training programs similar to those at Hampton and the Tuskegee Institute began to appear in greater numbers at HBCUs throughout the South as African Americans continued to uplift themselves from the heavy burden of racism and discrimination. In 1917, the Selective Service Act was responsible for the enlistment of thousands of black soldiers who happened to be illiterate. As a result, the federal government and the U.S. military established educational and vocational training programs at eleven black colleges:

- Atlanta University (Atlanta, Ga.)
- Howard University (Washington, D.C.)
- Tuskegee Normal and Industrial Institute (Tuskegee, Ala.)
- Western University (Quindaro, Kans.)
- Florida Agricultural and Mechanical College (Tallahassee, Fla.)
- Georgia State Industrial College (Savannah, Ga.)
- Hampton Normal and Agricultural Institute (Hampton, Va.)
- Negro Agricultural and Technical College (Greensboro, N.C.)
- Branch Normal School (Pine Bluff, Ark.)
- Prairie View Normal and Industrial College (Prairie View, Tex.)
- State Agricultural and Mechanical College (Orangeburg, S.C.)
- Wendell Phillips High School (Chicago, Ill.)
- Sumner High School (Saint Louis, Mo.)[44]

The success of vocational training programs at colleges and universities prompted the War Department to establish the Student Army Training Corps (SATC). SATC units were located at educational institutions to utilize the physical facilities as well administrative and teaching personnel. General Order Number 79 on August 24, 1918, stated that:

> Under the authority conferred by Sections 1, 2, 8 and 9 of the Act of Congress "authorizing the President to increase temporarily the military establishment of the United States," . . . the President directs that for the period of the

existing emergency there shall be raised and maintained by voluntary induction and draft, a Students Army Training Corps. Units of this Corps will be authorized by the Secretary of War at educational institutions that meet the requirements laid down in Special Regulations.[45]

Nineteen black colleges and universities were chosen to offer the SATC program. Practically all of them had established programs of military instruction. Those institutions included:

- Tuskegee Institute
- Howard University
- Lincoln University
- Fisk University
- Atlanta University and Morehouse College (combined)
- Wiley University and Bishop College (combined)
- Wilberforce University
- Virginia Union University
- Talladega College
- Meharry Medical College
- Hampton Institute
- Georgia State Industrial College
- North Carolina A&T College
- South Carolina A&M College
- Prairie View Normal and Industrial College
- West Virginia Collegiate Institute
- Alabama A&M College
- Tennessee A&M College
- Louisiana A&M College[46]

After World War I, in 1919, Special Regulations 44 established new guidelines for the instruction and governance of the Reserve Officer Training Corps (ROTC) at educational institutions. ROTC units were designated as either a Senior or Junior unit. In order to offer Senior ROTC, your institution must grant a college degree or be essential to the military. Initially, only eleven black institutions were selected to establish the ROTC program:

- Howard University
- Tuskegee Institute
- Wilberforce University

- South Carolina A&M College
- Hampton Institute
- Virginia Normal and Industrial College
- Prairie View Normal and Industrial College
- Tennessee A&I College
- West Virginia Collegiate Institute
- Branch Normal School
- Straight College (New Orleans)[47]

The growth and development of military training programs at black colleges and universities in the late nineteenth and early twentieth centuries reflect the African American effort to sustain its vigorous pursuit of first-class citizenship and social equality. This legacy of activism and determination was promoted and nurtured by black soldiers during the Civil War and was quickly embraced by African American leaders and educators in the years thereafter. Black military education at HBCUs aspired to maintain the extraordinary military tradition of soldiering in the black community, but also highlighted the level of African American self-sacrifice and patriotic support that demanded equal inclusion in civil society.

Though inferior to the education of whites, black education became a vehicle in which African Americans could attempt to escape the bonds of political and economic oppression. It was also an avenue to obtain democratic citizenship or at least vestiges of it. With the end of the Civil War, thousands of African Americans enrolled in colleges and universities, normal and industrial schools, and public school systems throughout the South. To most African Americans, this was their first opportunity to acknowledge to themselves and others that they were no longer slaves. During this period of turbulent race relations, Southern University and many other black colleges and universities were established with the hope of satisfying the educational needs of black southerners and lifting the veil oppression.

SOUTHERN UNIVERSITY AND A&M COLLEGE

Southern University was created by the Constitutional Convention of the State of Louisiana in July 1879. Not surprisingly, P.B.S. Pinchback, a former African American Union officer, Republican state senator, and delegate seated on the Legislative Committee on Public Education, championed the cause of Negro education in Louisiana and introduced a resolution for the establishment of "a university for the education of persons of color." The resolution easily passed on a vote of 81 to 28. Immediately, the only other African American member of the committee, T. B. Stamps, voiced his approval and offered an amendment to set a dollar amount for future funding for the institution. Although Stamps's amendment met some resistance, after rewording his passage it passed by a vote of 78 to 8.[48] Pinchback and Stamps's ability to garner Democratic support for the resolution represents a combination of skilled political wrangling and the assistance of a former Confederate general, influential Democrat and future governor Francis T. Nicholls. In a contested gubernatorial election in 1876, Nicholls had needed Republican support to be declared the winner, so he had approached Pinchback with a proposition. In a letter Nicholls wrote, "I will use my utmost endeavors, as governor, and with all the influence at my command as such to promote the educational and material interest of the colored people precisely to the same extent that I will those of white people. It will be my constant aim to promote kindness and sympathy, confidence and justice, between the two races in the State."[49]

Although Pinchback and Stamps were praised for their accomplishment, many African Americans criticized their efforts. Reportedly, a petition with the names of thirteen hundred African American citizens was signed in protest because there was a distinction made in the race of future Southern University students. Many individuals, including Henry Demas, a black convention delegate, argued that the resolution's wording represented an acceptance of "Jim Crow laws." Pinchback reasoned that Southern University was established for the educational welfare of African Americans throughout the state. Since African Americans were prohibited from enrolling in the state university (Louisiana State University), Southern University was to be the first state-supported institution for African Americans.[50]

The establishment of Southern University followed the history and trend of the promotion of education for African Americans in Louisiana and throughout the South. During the Reconstruction era, while African American politicians enjoyed a level of unprecedented political influence on a state and national basis, public and church-sponsored private institutions of higher learning were being established in rapid session. In Louisiana, Leland University (1870) was first located in New Orleans. It moved to

Baker, Louisiana, shortly after World War I. During that same year, Straight University was founded by the Congregational Church and offered former slaves the ability to study theology and the law. By 1873, New Orleans University developed from the Union Norman School and included a curriculum of courses on theology, medicine, and normal studies. Over two hundred students quickly enrolled at New Orleans University. In 1935, Straight University and New Orleans University merged to become Dillard University, which is still presently located in New Orleans.[51]

Though Southern University had a slow and tenuous start after relocating several times in New Orleans, enrollment and legislative support began to increase by 1887. Beginning with an enrollment of forty-three students in 1880, Southern University's student body numbered almost five hundred at the turn of the century. The university was then located in a Gothic-style three-story building at 5116 Magazine Street. In 1890 the agricultural and mechanical department was established by virtue of the 1890 Morrill Land-Grant Act. The federally sponsored bill mandated that Negro land-grant colleges, in particular, emphasize training in agriculture and mechanical arts and teach military tactics to their male students. Historian Rod Andrew argues, "African American southern land-grants schools that existed under these same guidelines in 1890 did not incorporate the military feature until after World War I."[52] In addition, the Act provided that, "states should either admit Negroes to white land-grant institutions or establish such institutions for Negroes. By 1900, all of the states in the South had organized land-grant colleges for Negroes or arranged with another institution to carry on the land-grant program."[53] Even though Southern University was organized as a liberal institution, it primarily taught courses in elementary education, domestic science, and industrial arts. For white Louisianians, Southern University's main purpose was to teach Christian values, how to be good servants, and how to be better farmhands. To do this, many white officials believed that the institution should be moved to a rural location and centrally located in the state. Scotland Plantation, located north of Baton Rouge, the state capital, was eventually selected for a new site for Southern University. In 1908, Louisiana governor Jared Y. Sanders Sr. declared, "In order to establish Negro education in the State upon a sane basis there should be a state institution organized to train colored teachers along the lines of agriculture, manual training, and domestic science. This institution should be located in the country, and not in a town or city. The town is filled up now with many worthless Negroes who should be earning an honest living in the country, and not in a town or city."[54]

JOSEPH SAMUEL CLARK, FIRST PRESIDENT OF SOUTHERN UNIVERSITY

After moving in 1914, Southern University welcomed a new leader and its first president, Dr. Joseph Samuel Clark, a well-known African American educator who is credited with leading Southern University for twenty-five years to national recognition as well as elevating an already capable faculty. Although administrator and faculty salaries were substantially less than those of their white counterparts, Dr. Clark made it clear that he was not interested in monetary rewards but in the opportunity to serve his people and state in the eradication of illiteracy. Usually hand-picked, his faculty was composed of men and women who were equally dedicated and ambitious instructors. Clark made numerous educational and physical improvements, including a Junior College and teacher-training curriculum, the establishment of a Cooperative Agricultural Extension Program, a summer normal school, the erection of six brick buildings for instructional activities, five brick dormitories, and eleven wooden structures for faculty needs. Even as J. S. Clark's professional career was coming to a close, he negotiated funding from the state and federal governments to build a library, a football stadium, an administration building, a gymnasium, and additional dormitories.[55] During this period, one of Southern's most promising graduates was Felton G. Clark, J. S. Clark's only son.

FELTON GRANDISON CLARK—THE EARLY YEARS

In 1938, Dr. Felton G. Clark became the second president of Southern University and A&M College and served longer than any president to date, thirty years. There is no question that Felton. G. Clark was hand-picked and groomed by his father to one day take the mantle of leadership. After leaving Baton Rouge in 1922, Felton G. Clark traveled to Beloit College in Wisconsin, where he received a Bachelor of Arts degree. Shortly thereafter, he was accepted to Columbia University, where he completed a Master of

Arts and became the eighth African American to receive a Ph.D., in 1933. More impressively, young Clark distinguished himself by becoming the first black man to specialize in college administration in the doctoral program.[56] Clark was articulate, deeply religious, and nearly always impeccably dressed. As a teacher-trainer, Clark was employed at Wiley College in Marshall, Texas, and returned to Southern University in 1927 as a professor of secondary education. While completing his doctoral studies he worked at Howard University in Washington, D.C., and received a fellowship from the General Education Board. Within a year of receiving his Ph.D. from Columbia University, once again Clark returned to Southern University and was appointed as dean of the college and director of instruction. By 1938, when Clark was offered the presidency, university enrollment reached nearly fourteen hundred students.[57]

Although Felton. G. Clark's educational philosophy was not extraordinary in comparison to his peers and black leaders of the day, he truly believed that African American leadership was essential to the progress of black higher education. Clark's doctoral dissertation, "The Control of State Supported Teachers Training Programs for Negroes," argued that white leadership of black educational institutions was often predicated on unsupported opinions or tradition. He further stated, "schemes for the control of state supported institutions for the higher education of Negroes should provide for direct representation of the Negro group."[58] Like other African American intellectuals, Clark believed that education was the key to personal and collective progress as well as social and economic prosperity. This explains why Clark worked tirelessly at improving the university to ensure its longevity. On September 23, 1938, Clark addressed the faculty, emphasizing his understanding of the school mission and his personal philosophy on the importance of education:

> ... today, more than ever before, public education is our major process identified with making people lead and live a happy life. We are Negroes in America. This very expression serves as a release for associations that are identified with unhappiness, inadequacy, dissatisfaction, and many other conditions identified with a life deprived of richness and fullness. In view of these three observations, each varying in degree of cruciality, the work of those of us engaged in the educational enterprise, especially where Negroes are concerned, can be considered in anything but a light vein.

In the scheme of things, there is no place for bitterness. There is no place for jealousy, there is no place for selfishness, there is no place for favoritism. . . . If there are those in this room whose characteristic personality trait is identified with one or a combination pattern of the attributes set forth in this last sentence, they cannot foster the Southern University program.[59]

Felton G. Clark understood that higher education excellence starts with a dedicated and talented faculty. If Southern was to reach his level of expectation, then the faculty must not waver in their role as facilitators of the school mission. Clark was insistent that faculty and staff be competent, ethical, and loyal to Southern University. If they demonstrated behavior to the contrary, that was grounds for immediate dismissal.

By the end of the 1930s, Jim Crow laws and the economic depression served to confirm the importance of higher education. In addition, America's call to arms in the First World War gave African Americans hope that military service and patriotic sacrifice would ultimately equate to obtaining citizenship and improved social opportunity. The emergence of civil rights as a national issue combined with political pressure on the Roosevelt administration helped publicize African American dissatisfaction with military racial policies. Black leaders and newspapers launched campaigns directed toward the African American public in an effort to encourage interest in military equality. The *Pittsburgh Courier*, under the leadership of its publisher, Robert Vann, began attacks on the federal government and its discriminatory racial policies. Citing the war record of black Americans, Vann declared, "The traditional loyalty of the American Negro remains unchanged. He wants to continue and to add to the service which has distinguished him in all our country's wars."[60] Thus, historically black colleges and universities placed special emphasis on military training and service. Though formal military training was not offered at Southern University until 1948, wartime support for America during the 1940s could have similar benefits.

2

WE ARE ALL LOUISIANIANS AND BY THAT SIGN ALL AMERICANS

NEGRO DEFENSE TRAINING, LEADERSHIP, AND WAR ACTIVITIES AT SOUTHERN UNIVERSITY DURING WORLD WAR II

During World War II, African Americans made tremendous sacrifices in an effort to trade military service and wartime support for measurable social, political, and economic gains. As never before, local black communities throughout the nation participated in wartime programs and intensified their demands for social progress. The struggle for African American first-class citizenship was primarily waged in the workplace and training facilities throughout the nation.[1] In particular, black colleges and universities made vital contributions to the defense program and, on a state level, directed training facilities and organized the African American war effort.[2]

The wartime contributions of Southern University in Louisiana reflected the black community's desire to contribute to America's victory overseas while improving African American social and economic opportunities at home. In addition, Southern University's president, Felton G. Clark, carefully worked with civil rights leaders and the black press to improve the university's educational standing within the state and region, while seeking increased funding opportunities from federal and state agencies. As Louisiana's most prominent African American academic administrator, Clark was placed in the difficult position of seeking to improve the quality of education for African Americans under the oppressive restrictions of Jim Crow laws and with meager resources. Negro defense training programs quickly became a way to demonstrate African American patriotism and loyalty while promoting the economic welfare and political outlook of Southern University and the black community.

BLACK COLLEGES AND UNIVERSITIES JOIN THE WAR EFFORT

During the war, African American leaders achieved many political victories while black colleges and universities trained and helped blacks secure employment opportunities in the defense industry. Southern University's contributions to the national defense program during the war reflected similar experiences of black colleges and universities throughout the South. Soon after the war began, training for African Americans was offered at black land-grant institutions such as Tuskegee Institute and Prairie View Agricultural and Mechanical College, in addition to numerous vocational training schools. Black leaders in cities with a substantial minority population, such as New Orleans, Houston, Dallas, and Atlanta, petitioned the federal government to establish regional training facilities to offer black Americans access to training programs essential to national defense.[3] In total, seventy-five black colleges and universities with direct links to the federal government, or as sub-contractors, participated in the national defense program. Southern University was one of the first African American institutions designated as a regional defense training center for blacks in the South.[4]

During World War II, the U.S. Office of Education was primarily responsible for soliciting wartime support at colleges and universities, including African American institutions. J. W. Studebaker, commissioner of the U.S. Department of Education, believed that higher education and citizenship intersected during the national crisis. "As a Nation we must move forward on this general front of citizenship education as a practical measure of national defense."[5] The intersection between African American support and the national defense program was echoed by President Franklin D. Roosevelt's establishing several departments within federal agencies, such as the Negro Employment and Training Branch, the Negro Manpower Service, the Minority Groups Branch in the Office of Production Management, and the National Defense Advisory Commission.[6]

By 1942, African Americans in the thousands began to enroll in preemployment courses at black colleges and universities throughout the South. Nearly thirty black colleges offered fifty new courses that ranged from mechanic arts, radio engineering, tool engineering, welding, electronics, and boat building to nursing, sheet metal work, photography, internal combustion engines, production management, and nutrition. Students received training in occupations that reflected a shortage of personnel in regional areas.[7] Sixty-five black colleges, including Southern University, participated in federal programs such as the Engineering, Science, and Management War Training (ESMWT) program. Twelve of those institutions had direct contracts with the federal government and offered a total of seventy-four courses in physics, mathematics, management, engineering, and chemistry. Eighty percent of black colleges and universities changed their curricula to offer defense-related courses and training for the war effort.[8]

The federal government vigorously solicited the support of HBCUs in numerous programs, such as the Defense Savings Bond and Stamp Program and the Army Enlisted Reserve Corps, a precursor to the U.S. Army Reserve.[9] In addition to thousands of Africans Americans, more than fifty thousand students throughout the South were registered in defense-related training programs. African Americans received valuable training in skilled and unskilled occupations that qualified them to work in numerous war-related industries. Though African Americans eagerly sought these defense training program opportunities, many local and state employers avoided hiring blacks for fear of social unrest and mass strikes.[10] In response, black trainees in Louisiana and throughout the Southwest were directed by the War Manpower Commission regional office in Dallas, Texas, to seek employment at shipyards and defense plants located in the North and the West.[11] The Fair Employment Practices Committee (FEPC) did, however, influence a small increase in the number of blacks employed in defense industries once the pool of white laborers began to decline by 1944. Between 1940 and 1950, approximately ten thousand African Americans were employed in Louisiana's wartime industries.[12]

SOUTHERN UNIVERSITY DURING WORLD WAR II

In Louisiana, Southern University provided valuable training and support for black men and women associated with the war industry. F. G. Clark, along with his administration, held important appointments and supervisory roles at the state and national level within the black community. National black leaders, such as Claude Barnett of the Associated Negro Press, Robert C. Weaver, director of the Negro Employment and Training Branch, and Judge William O. Hastie, civilian aide on Negro affairs to the secretary of war, called upon Clark and men and women like him to galvanize support for federal and state programs associated with the national defense program, while they lobbied the Roosevelt administration and the Department of War for equal inclusion of African Americans in national defense.[13]

Historian and writer Rayford W. Logan and the bureau chief of the Negro Newspaper Publishers Association, Louis R. Lautier, both of the Committee on Participation of Negroes in the National Defense Program, best described what many black leaders believed was at stake: "The success of our combined efforts will determine in a large measure not only the equitable integration of the Negro into this program but will perhaps provide the pattern of the Negroes' post-emergency status."[14] At a conference of black educators in 1942, an anonymous black representative from the Office of War Information reiterated this philosophy when he remarked, "There is a vital job to be done in interpreting to our people the enormous implications of this struggle for us as Americans and as members of a racial minority."[15] Clark embraced this viewpoint and understood the implications of his wartime leadership.

Although President Roosevelt's Executive Order 8802 prohibited racial discrimination in the defense industry, the order did not include state defense training programs. African Americans in the South received defense training and exposure to war-related educational programs and opportunities at black colleges and universities and some high schools because segregation laws prohibited them from attending state training centers established for white Americans.[16] Felton G. Clark, along with other educational leaders, made genuine efforts to ensure the success of these programs and encourage optimal participation by the black community.

At Southern University the national defense program was a serious matter in which President Clark and the black community participated. In the fall of 1940, Clark began receiving circulars from national organizations such as the National Urban League, the National Association for the Advancement of Colored People (NAACP), and the Council for Democracy soliciting support for African American participation in the armed services and defense program.[17] The federal government also developed a plan to enlist the help of black colleges and universities in the training of men for the Army, Navy, war industries, and essential civilian services. The plan included not only able-bodied young men but also those not physically qualified for military service.[18] In addition, the Department of War sponsored conferences at black colleges and universities to introduce the national defense program agenda.[19]

Once Southern University was designated as a regional center for national defense by the U.S. Department of War in October 1941, Clark received a federal grant worth $4,000 to purchase war-related training equipment for its sheet metal and welding division and to expand the number of courses offered at the college for the defense program.[20] Southern already offered eleven defense-related courses to nearly three hundred students. Administrators expected student enrollment to increase as new courses were added to the curriculum. Under Clark's authority, the university operated on a twenty-four-hour shift with its defense-training program and the production of sweaters, socks, and other accessories for black military personnel in the home economics department.[21]

In November 1941, U.S. Treasury Department official Jesse O. Thomas wrote Clark and requested his assistance in the Defense Savings Bond and Stamp Program. He asked Clark to appoint a committee to encourage the sale of war bonds throughout the African American community.[22] Eight weeks later, Thomas again wrote Clark and insinuated that he was prohibiting teachers and students from fulfilling their patriotic duty by not responding to his earlier correspondence. Understanding the severity of the accusation, Clark immediately replied and articulated his resentment at being labeled disloyal and unsupportive of the war. Clark began his letter with a hint of sarcasm, "I am very sorry that because inadvertently you have not received a statement concerning our local Defense Savings Staff Committee, that the inference had been made that we of the Southern University community are not interested in Defense Savings, that we are doing little or nothing about the matter, and that we are otherwise disloyal."[23] He added:

> Even before your correspondence came, asking us to appoint a local committee, whose acts would be credited to your suggestion, we were at work on De-

fense Savings. Of course it did not have the type of emotional publicity that it might have been given because this is not our policy. We think that the main thing is to do something rather than, "whooping it up." One of our teachers bought a thousand dollar Defense Bond. As yet, no publicity has been given it and in all probability none will be given it in the future.

When I bought my first Defense Bond of five hundred dollars, I even stood in line in order to get into an office to purchase it. There are more than these instances on our faculty, reflecting interest and participation in our Government's Defense Savings efforts.[24]

Clark ended the verbal skirmish by noting, "Thus we are hoping that you will at least mentally retract the thought that Southern University and its President are the one exception when it comes to being loyal and patriotic with reference to the Defense Savings Program. I am assuring you that we will go our limit to express our loyalty not only in the Defense Savings issue, but everything else."[25] Thomas's comments concerned Clark a great deal. Although Thomas mistakenly suggested that Clark was unpatriotic, Clark believed that neither he nor Southern University could afford such a slanderous label. Clark encouraged all Southernites to buy defense bonds and requested that everyone employed at the university write a brief statement telling him if he or she had purchased bonds, the amount, date, and source of purchase. He also retorted, "Southern University least of all [could] afford to have the taint of disloyalty tagged on any of its teachers or staff members."[26] Clark sincerely believed that African American social and political progress rested on expressions of patriotism, wartime service, and support.

WAR MORALE IN THE BLACK COMMUNITY

Clark's enthusiasm for supporting the war was well grounded in overt expressions of patriotism throughout the 1940s. During the war, Americans routinely sang "God Bless America" and the "Star Spangled Banner" and posted signs and American flags in support of troops and war-related programs. Americans enthusiastically urged the participation of war bond drives and encouraged everyone to comply with government regulations.[27] Fervent displays of patriotism, however, did not include the support of black troops. During this period racial violence against African American soldiers was common near military installations in the South. Shortly after the Japanese attack on Pearl Harbor, a race riot ensued between African Americans GIs and the local police as well as civilians in Alexandria, Louisiana.[28] That is why Clark, along with F. D. Patterson, president of the Tuskegee Institute, Howard University's President Mordecai W. Johnson, other black educators, and the black press believed that building morale in the black community and African American support for the war was even more essential.[29] Not only would the black community benefit socially and politically from training programs and increased employment opportunities, but Southern University, like other institutions, would also receive much needed financial and technical support from the federal and state governments. Loyal support and participation in the national defense program was a theme that Clark continuously promoted among faculty and staff at Southern throughout the conflict.

Within forty-eight hours of the Japanese attack at Pearl Harbor on December 7, 1941, F. G. Clark wrote Louisiana governor Sam H. Jones and requested an active role in state wartime programs and offered an assurance of African American loyalty and support. "Through you as Governor of Louisiana, Southern University hastens to offer its entire resources to the service of the Country in this crisis. Faculty and students want you to know that they stand loyally for all programs to defend the United States. Please remember us in your plans. We are all Louisianians and by that sign all Americans."[30] Nine days later, Clark wrote the Coordinator of Louisiana Civilian Defense, Roland Cocreham, and again emphasized African American loyalty and a history of wartime support:

> Please permit me to state that it will be a joyful duty to work as a part of our State organization of Civilian Defense. Of course, you probably know that the Negro people have always aggressively rallied to their Country, especially during a crisis. This is a part of history that occasions much pride in the hearts of members of our group. I mention these things to you merely to have you know that now, as always, we stand ready and anxious to serve.[31]

NATIONAL DEFENSE PROGRAMS AT SOUTHERN UNIVERSITY

In 1942, as a key center for information and training, Southern University was charged with the responsibility of informing the African American public about war related programs and opportunities.[32] In addition, F. G. Clark was appointed state coordinator of the Negro Division for Louisiana Civilian Defense. Southern University Defense Council responsibilities included civilian morale services, counseling speakers, writers, teachers, and librarians in the use of war information materials, and assisting producers of radio programs on national defense, publicity, and first aid instruction. The university also offered a program in civilian defense training for the African American general public. Interested students and civilians were able to receive training in many subjects, such as high explosive bombs and fire defense, the use and care of the gas mask, fires and explosions, emergency medical services, blackouts, the civilian air raid warning system, and espionage and sabotage.[33]

As state coordinator for Negroes in Louisiana civilian defense, Clark helped organize a statewide Civilian Defense Exposition that was held in New Orleans in March 1942. Clark planned the program to be an elaborate demonstration of African American patriotism and wartime support. The exposition included the participation of more than twenty organizations and groups, such as the Boy Scouts of America, Junior and Senior Red Cross workers, U.S. soldiers, National Youth Administration workers, the Veterans of Foreign Wars, air raid wardens, and auxiliary policemen. There was a demonstration by African American soldiers from the Jackson, Mississippi, barracks and the New Orleans Air Base affectionately called the "Bronze Warriors in action." Felton G. Clark served as the keynote speaker and delivered a moving address, followed by the national anthem and the pledge of allegiance by the assembly.[34] This was indeed an impressive exhibition of African American loyalty and wartime support that received the attention of the governor and numerous state officials. Within weeks after the Civilian Defense Exposition, Hugo Weidmann, director of the St. Tammany Parish Louisiana Civilian Defense Commission, wrote to President Roosevelt commending Clark for his efforts and informing the president what African Americans were doing in Louisiana for the civilian defense program.[35]

In another related demonstration of patriotism and wartime support on March 20, 1942, Southern University sponsored a parade and campus ceremony titled "Agriculture, the First Line of Defense." The celebration included a livestock contest, marching bands, floats, and over three hundred marching soldiers. T. N. Roberts, special assistant to the director of personnel in the U.S. Department of Agriculture, delivered an address, "Food for Freedom," and "urged students to pioneer in the field of Agriculture stating that there [were] more than 1300 jobs open to Negroes in governmental service."[36]

In 1942 the Department of War contacted Clark with an offer for Southern University to participate in a preinduction training program. The Enlisted Reserve Corps (ERC) accepted men between the age of eighteen and forty-five who did not have a bachelor's degree and could pass a physical exam.[37] However, all colleges and universities involved in the program would be subject to a preexisting quota. Clark enthusiastically responded and requested additional information. By late summer Southern and Xavier Universities, with the largest quota among African American institutions in the state, had 120 enrolled in the program.[38] Southern University's interest in the ERC coincided with the desire of other African American institutions to participate in the joint Army-Navy initiative. By December 1942, one hundred African American colleges and junior colleges throughout the nation were accepted by the Department of War for the ERC program.[39]

Though Southern University was already heavily involved in numerous wartime programs and serving in many support roles, F. G. Clark was always eager to find additional ways to contribute to and benefit from national defense. In August 1942, under the direction of Clark, J. B. Cade, the university's dean, wrote West Virginia State College president John W. Davis requesting literature on its Small Rural Industries Program.[40] In addition, Clark made a formal request for an Army Air Corps unit to be established at Southern University. A few months later, Army Air Corps officials visited Southern University for the purpose of ascertaining whether the existing facilities were adequate for the location of a ground training school similar to those located at Tuskegee, Alabama, and Chanute Field, Illinois. After a tour of inspection, federal officials concluded that the only feature that could prohibit locating the school in Scotlandville was the lack of housing for officers.[41]

In 1942 the "Win the War Campaign" was in full stride throughout Louisiana. The Louisiana Colored Teachers Association, with the support of F. G. Clark and his father, J. S. Clark, published a series of articles in the *Louisiana Colored Teachers Journal* relating to African American wartime support. The articles referred to services rendered by state libraries for national defense, the Victory Book Campaign, the United Service Organization (USO), and thought-provoking articles titled: "What Are We Fighting For?" "Blunt Speaking on Negro Attitudes toward the War," and a nationally syndicated column by Cornelius King titled "National Defense and the Negro."[42]

In particular, the *Louisiana Colored Teachers Journal* described a show called *Freedom's People Radio Program* that was aired over the National Broadcasting System. The U.S. Office of Education sponsored the program in conjunction with national African American educational leaders. The radio program featured African American entertainers such Count Basie, Cab Calloway, Paul Robeson, and Dorothy Maynor. It was designed to highlight African American contributions in national defense, American history, education, science, and music and to improve morale in the black community. *Freedom's People Radio Program* was considered a monumental success. Shortly after the initial broadcast, the Office of Education began receiving requests from southern educators and faculty, both white and black, asking for additional information to distribute to their students. Even white radio stations in Louisiana offered surprisingly positive feedback concerning the quality of the show after it was determined that the program would not disturb southern social customs.[43] Serving on the program committee were such noted black leaders and educators as Mary McLeod Bethune, educator and director of Negro affairs in the National Youth Administration, Carter G. Woodson, editor and publisher of the *Journal of Negro History*, Charles S. Johnson, president of Fisk University, Ambrose Caliver, specialist for higher education of Negroes at the U.S. Department of Education, F. D. Patterson, president of Tuskegee Institute, and F. G. Clark. The committee believed that "If more programs of [that] nature were given, probably a mutual understanding of all groups and races of people in the United States would be understood and the Negro, especially, would be more appreciated in his own American country."[44] Clark not only worked closely with black educators to implement similar national programs, but also promoted the same principles on a statewide basis.

SUPPORT FOR THE WAR IS EVERYONE'S RESPONSIBILITY AT SOUTHERN

During the first eighteen months of the war, Clark spent enormous amounts of time and energy promoting national defense and soliciting federal and state agencies to establish wartime programs and invest in the campus. His efforts paid off in the fall of 1942 when the federal government listed Southern University as a major training center for civilian defense and the largest Vocational Education for War Production Workers program in the region for African Americans.[45]

Though Clark's commitment to the war effort was difficult to match, he expected Southern employees to make similar contributions. He distributed a university-wide memorandum requesting that faculty and staff put in writing what they were doing to assist in winning the war. While many individuals made note of their financial contributions and the various committees that they served on, several employees remarked that they were especially concerned with student morale. One professor announced, "My War effort has been to tell and keep the young men reminded that it is their duty and obligation to serve in the armed forces of the nation. If a nation is good enough to make a living in, it is good enough to fight for, and if necessary, to die for, I served in the first World War as a volunteer. Why there is so much 'ADO' trying to escape the draft in this war is something that puzzles me."[46] Dean of Men A. P. Pertee also wrote, "Since the United States entered the war I have tried to organize and direct a program for men students to meet the challenge of a general lowered morale. This condition, which became felt throughout the country during the first quarter of 1942, could be detected in every activity on the campus where men students were concerned."[47]

POOR WAR MORALE ON CAMPUS AND THE BLACK COMMUNITY

The fact that several individuals mentioned poor morale on the campus of Southern University suggests that Clark may have been aware of and especially concerned with this dilemma. In addition to Clark, many black leaders and organizations such as the NAACP were acutely aware of and concerned about African American disaffection for the war. Rightly so, black Americans were unenthusiastic, considering that many of them were barred from civil defense training programs and jobs, Jim Crow philosophy permeated the Army, Navy, and Marines, and African Americans that suffered from maltreatment and assaults at the hands of whites had no recourse in the justice system.[48] Huel D. Perkins, a former student and the dean of Arts and Humanities, later remarked, "nobody resisted serving the country, even though we were second-class citizens. Nobody openly opposed going into the military. I remember distinctly 90 percent of the males at Southern were drafted in 1942, they all left the school."[49] But clearly, many faculty and students held mixed emotions about their uncertain future and supporting the war effort. Poor morale among African Americans was no surprise at black colleges and universities or on the campus of Southern University.[50] In fact, this attitude was representative of the mood in the black community throughout the nation. To combat this pessimistic atmosphere, the Research Branch of the Special Service Division, Army Service Forces, released a report titled "Attitudes of the Negro Soldier" that suggested that the following measures were needed to combat low morale in the black community:

a. An increased flow of news about Negro military achievements both in combat and in training.
b. A special effort to assign colored troops to important military duties, including combat, so that there may be more positive news of effective war participation for release and less evidence of overlong training and inconsequential domestic duty in support of the view that Negro soldiers are not really to be used for serious work.
c. A steady flow of information concerning enemy racial doctrine and practice should be developed as a means of emphasizing to the Negro the importance of winning the war.[51]

Pittsburgh Courier war correspondent Frank E. Bolden made a special plea to African American soldiers that was circulated in military post newspapers where they were stationed:

I sometimes wonder if the men serving in this combat unit are aware of the great responsibility that rests upon their shoulders. In making my trips around the camp during the Division's activation, I have been impressed by those who are aware of the magnitude of responsibility and the opportunities that this Colored army unit affords. THEY ARE SOLDIERING FOR AMERICA AND THEIR RACE. As far as Colored citizens are concerned, they are duty bound to do their bit. AS THEY ALWAYS HAVE WHEN THIS COUNTRY'S LIBERTIES WERE IMPERILED. This is YOUR COUNTRY AND IT IS WORTH FIGHTING FOR BECAUSE YOU WOULDN'T TRADE IT FOR

ANY OTHER WHEN THE CHIPS ARE DOWN. You have never had another military opportunity in race history as you have now. Get in on the gravy train with biscuit wheels! BE A SOLDIER.[52]

While many students did not publicly voice opposition to the war, privately they were not eager to join a military that not only mistreated them, but also was known to employ them in the most menial and laborious tasks. The contradiction of fighting to sustain democracy throughout the world while experiencing the humiliation of Jim Crow laws, second-class citizenship, and exclusion from wartime job training programs at home understandably proved too great for many African Americans.[53] Although antiwar and antimilitary sentiment did not reflect the rhetoric of many mainstream black leaders, the feelings of individuals such as socialist C.L.R. James represented how many black soldiers and civilians felt. James proclaimed:

> Why should I shed my blood for Roosevelt's America, for Cotton Ed Smith and Senator Bilbo, for the whole Jim Crow, Negro-hating South, for the low-paid, dirty jobs for which Negroes have to fight, for the few dollars of relief and the insults, discrimination, police brutality, and perpetual poverty to which Negroes are condemned even in the more liberal North? When the working Negro asks this question, what can the warmongers say to him? Nothing. Nothing but lies and empty promises of better treatment in the future. Why must I die for them? I am not afraid to fight. Negroes have been some of the greatest fighters in history. But the democracy that I want to fight for, Hitler is not depriving me of.[54]

Many of these individuals resisted supporting the war by refusing to support national defense programs or to contribute to the national war chest. At Howard University many students linked wartime support and the civil rights movement and began to participate in sit-ins and demonstrations that protested segregationist policies of restaurants, department stores, and drugstores throughout the Washington, D.C., area. In the minds of many young African Americans the notion of fighting for freedom and democracy in Europe as second-class citizens only angered and insulted them.[55]

A. P. Pertee and F. G. Clark worked to improve the morale of young blacks on the campus of Southern University, who were asked to make extreme sacrifices and turn their heads from public lynchings, physical assaults, and other injustices. In 1943, the Office of War Information confirmed this attitude when it revealed that nearly 70 percent of African Americans believed that racism and discrimination prohibited them from adequately contributing to the war effort.[56] Despite this telling fact, most African Americans continued to enroll in national defense training programs, even if reluctantly, and to seek employment opportunities related to the war. In particular, African Americans in the South attempted to use military training and service as a vehicle of social uplift. Prior to the war, the average income for an African American was $371 per year. In the military, the average soldier could earn between $2,000 and $2,600 annually.[57] Black men in Louisiana, Georgia, Alabama, and Mississippi who could only find employment in local sawmills or cotton fields like Clevester Jordan were eager to become a soldier when given the opportunity. In many respects, military service was a ticket out of the South, away from a life of daily injustices, humiliation, and the constant threat of assault and even death. Once black soldiers lived outside of the South in the North or overseas, it was very difficult to return home for an extended period. Upon returning home after leaving the Army, Jordan told his father, "I'm leaving for Cleveland, Ohio, next week. I can't stay around here anymore. I've seen too much. A black man will never get justice in the South. To stay out of trouble, Papa, I'm leaving."[58] World War II veterans Nelson Perry and A. William "Bill" Perry suggest that military service offered them secure employment in addition to a sense of respect in the black community. Even though racism and discrimination existed in the military, they believed that it was worse in civilian society.[59]

WARTIME ILLITERACY AMONG AFRICAN AMERICAN SOLDIERS

Another motivation to serve in America's Jim Crow Army was the fact that many African Americans in the South were functionally illiterate or had very little formal education, which was by design. African American men had only a few employment options to choose from, such as agricultural and semiskilled labor. Unfortunately, as black inductees poured into recruiting stations, the Army equated the lack of education with low intelligence. Upon taking the Army General Classification Test (AGCT), which was used to determine what military occupation a soldier was best suited for, nearly

80 percent African Americans from the South consistently scored in the two lowest categories, Class IV and Class V.[60]

The lack of African American enthusiasm for the war was nothing new and, quite frankly, understandable given the social and political state of black America in the 1940s. It is not clear whether some employees at Southern purposely resisted Clark's request for information about their contributions to the war effort or if they were just tardy in their response, but when more than a month transpired and Clark had not received an answer to his original request from each employee, he drafted another letter that emphasized his agitation with the remaining staff:

> Virtually all of the letters are in except yours and one or two others. Please let me know if I am to take your "no response" as an index that you are expending no extra effort in connection with the war situation. If this were the case, it would be appropriate to make a statement in this respect. In any event, let me have some statement from you. Such commitments as have been requested will be made a matter of record. It is necessary that there be such record be it positive or negative.[61]

Clark's office compiled a list of Southern employees, and a check mark was placed by individual names of people who had not forwarded their letters. Clark wanted to record and remember those among the Southern family who did not make a genuine effort to support the university or the national defense program. During the national crisis, Clark was placed in a precarious position. To gain or continue to receive the political and economic support of white state officials and federal agencies that he deemed essential to Southern's future, he had to galvanize support among African Americans throughout the state but especially at Southern University. On the other hand, Clark's reputation and standing the black community was predicated on his ability to represent the needs and desires of African Americans and advocate for their social progress.

HIGHER EDUCATION—
THE KEY TO AFRICAN AMERICAN PROGRESS

F. G. Clark's support of the national defense program reflected African American wartime patriotism and the desire to advance the social progress of the black community. To Clark, the livelihood of Southern University was at stake and the institution's traditional mission was African American social progress through the promotion of higher education and the ultimate eradication of racial discrimination. In the July 1942 edition of the *Journal of Negro Education*, Clark stated, "it would seem that any inroad against the practice of racial discrimination would be beneficial, to the extent that this gain serves as a bulkhead for continued assault in a campaign for the ultimate objective of true democracy for the Negro. Most assuredly, the foregoing should be a desideratum in the formulation of any and every program of Negro Higher Education!" Clark believed that alterations in university facilities and curriculum during the national crisis reflected the institution's adaptation to changing societal conditions for the betterment of the black community.[62] He also embraced the philosophy that black colleges and universities should work to instill social values in their students and that African American institutions had a responsibility to address social and communal issues that plagued the black community.[63] Clark was so adamant about this subject that in 1934 he wrote his doctoral dissertation on the premise that African Americans should have greater administrative control and influence on Negro colleges. He suggested that the function of black higher education was to address various needs of the black population.[64]

Clark's faith in the value and positive influence of higher education was not innovative. At the turn of the twentieth century it was not uncommon for black leaders to embrace the view that "the Negro problem could be solved through the training of southern black youth."[65] Because Clark did not feel that the state government was addressing Southern's needs adequately, he, like President Rufus E. Clement of Atlanta University, believed that federal support of HBCUs was essential to the future progress of black higher education. According to Clark, "for Negro higher education, the problem is not so much that of federal allocation of funds as it is one of the disposition of state and local authorities to assume their full responsibility for the adequate support of education for the Negro."[66] Though President Clark energetically worked to establish federal funding opportunities at Southern University during World War II, he continued to humbly work to appease the all-white governing board of higher education in Louisiana, which was a price of survival and a necessity for an African American college president at a public institution in the South.[67] Still, while Clark was never considered a political militant or social activist, he publicly embraced the philosophy of African American equality even in the company of white southerners. During a speech hosted by a white Methodist Church in Baton Rouge, Clark boldly remarked, "Out of one blood, God created all men equal, which refutes the old belief of a superior race."[68]

ARMY SPECIALIZED TRAINING AT SOUTHERN UNIVERSITY

In the final weeks of 1942, Clark attempted to establish two additional wartime training programs at Southern University. He answered a preliminary questionnaire for the location of an Army Engineers Training School at Southern and initiated steps for the establishment of an Army Specialized Training Program (ASTP). The ASTP was designed to increase the number of qualified technicians and specialists in the U.S. Army. Clark believed that these programs would not only benefit the university but would also make a viable contribution to the war effort. The ASTP in particular appealed to Clark because it had postwar implications. According to Colonel Herman Beukema, director of the Army Specialized Training Division, "The Army Specialized Training Program [was] designed primarily to furnish technically-trained manpower needed to prosecute the war. In addition, it [would] respect the best interest of the men themselves and prepare them for citizenship in the reconstruction period after the war."[69] Clark's interest in the ASTP coincided with the response of sixteen hundred other colleges and universities throughout the nation. But for Clark this program held the key to Southern's first step in securing formal military training on the campus. The Department of War had determined that institutions with existing ROTC units would receive special consideration in the selection process. Since the military had refused to establish any new ROTC units during the war, an established ASTP would increase an institution's chances of receiving an ROTC unit after the war.[70]

By 1943 Clark began making additional inquiries about the status of the Army Specialized Training Program. He contacted Ambrose Caliver for an update and suggested that his superiors on the Louisiana Board of Education were interested in the reasons why Southern did not offer Army Specialized Training:

> Members of our Board and our Director of Higher Education have asked me why something has not been done to enlist the services of the Negro college in the Army Specialized Training Program. Believe it or not, these persons, though white Louisianians, are just as anxious to see Southern, its Negro college, become a part of the cooperating scheme as the white colleges which it directs. In view of this, it seems rather strange that as yet no announcement has been made by the Joint Committee of the War Manpower Commission concerning the negotiation of contracts with Negro colleges, other than in those instances where R.O.T.C. units previously had been established. I find myself writing to you because you can probably give me the insight as to why the Negro colleges appear to be "out of the picture."[71]

Clark also wrote J. W. Studebaker and explained that Southern had completed the necessary questionnaires and had received government officials on several occasions to review campus facilities and he did not understand why a qualified university such as Southern was not selected for the program.[72] Weeks later the Joint Committee for the Selection of Non-Federal Educational Institutions assured Clark that careful consideration would be given to Southern University. Eventually the War Manpower Commission informed Clark that the Army Specialized Training Programs would be divided among colleges and universities that received both white and black students, and therefore Southern was ineligible.[73]

Although discouraged, Clark did not give up. In June 1943 he received a boost when the American Council on Education stated that additional colleges and universities would be added to the list of participants in the ASTP.[74] He immediately wrote Fred J. Kelly, chief of the Division on Higher Education, and asked, "can you tell me what is the probability of any of us Negro Land-Grant Colleges, in addition to the few that have been chosen, being authorized to negotiate contracts for the ASTP? Along with numerous other presidents of Negro colleges, I am still wondering if it is that, apparently, in a systematic way, so many of the Negro colleges are continuing to be excluded from this program."[75] Four months later, with an obvious degree of frustration and displeasure, Clark fired off a rare accusation of racial discrimination:

> I come to the point directly by stating that Negro higher education in general is very disappointed over the operation of the Army Specialized Train-

ing Program as it affects them. In other words, we feel definitely that racial prejudice has been exhibited with reference to Negro higher education and a prejudice, which is negative. This is reflected not only in the failure to choose Negro colleges in a consistent manner for the Army Specialized Training Program, but also in the statements coming from Negro members of the Armed Forces.[76]

Clark's disappointment with the War Manpower Commission was evident. His desire to participate in the Army Specialized Training Program was reflected in his numerous written requests and at least two personal visits to Washington, D.C., attempting to persuade federal officials to add Southern to the short list of black colleges that already participated in the program, such as, Prairie View Agricultural and Mechanical College, Howard University, and North Carolina Agricultural and Technical College.[77] Although the official criteria for participation in the ASTP were "transportation factors, manpower quotas, and facilities available at accredited institutions,"[78] colleges and universities with established Reserve Officer Training Corps units appeared to receive preferential consideration. That would at least explain in part why the above mentioned black colleges were selected to receive the training program and Southern was not.[79]

THE "WIN THE WAR CAMPAIGN" AT SOUTHERN UNIVERSITY

Throughout the duration of the war, F. G. Clark continued to respond to America's call to arms by actively pursuing every opportunity to contribute to the "Win the War Campaign." He wrote hundreds of letters to federal and state officials requesting opportunities to contribute and participate in the national defense program and encouraged involvement on the campus of Southern and among the black community. Clark worked tirelessly to promote democratic principles, in which he was a firm believer. In a symbolic effort to raise money to purchase war bonds, Clark authorized a program sponsored by the senior class to charge a penny to each student who was tardy for class. The proceeds were collected and used to purchase war bonds on behalf of Southern University.[80]

In the process of soliciting support for the national war chest at the university, Clark included an anonymous poem that he believed was applicable to African Americans during America's wartime crisis, but which also symbolized his attitude toward racial discrimination and indifference:

> If you think you are a thing abused
> and by the government are being used
> Then consider the boys out Pearl Harbor way
> Who were on land that fateful December day.
> If you think your salary is not enough
> And you should get more of that green stuff,
> Think of that Buck Private at Luzon
> with not even a drop of water to fight on.
> If you think the way you are treated
> Is just the same as being cheated,
> Then think of the Manila hero
> Who was blasted to bits by a Mitsu Zero.
> If you don't like your boss,
> And you think your job a loss,
> Then think of the Marines at Wake
> and their bones in the sun that bake.
> So when you start to fuss and gripe,
> Remember the boys who carry the fight
> And battle the Nips day in and day out—
> Hell, Mister—You ain't got a damn thing to kick about![81]

F. G. Clark understood African American frustration with racism and discrimination during the war. African Americans throughout the South lived in a segregated society where they experienced violence and indignities on a regular basis. An Office of War Information poll reported that "resentment at Negro discrimination [was] fairly widespread throughout the Negro population."[82] To Clark, the war chest poem reflected the belief that although life was difficult for many African Americans, the "real" fight was happening overseas.

HBCUS AND WARTIME SUPPORT

During World War II, black colleges and universities became the focal point of African American defense training programs. Tuskegee Institute, Howard University, Prairie View Agricultural and Mechanical College, and Southern University were the larger institutions that offered an extensive list of skilled and unskilled training courses designed to enhance the occupational opportunities of black Americans while contributing to an Allied victory. Though HBCUs had never played such a significant role in national defense prior to this point, wartime activities at black colleges were not new. During World War I, much like F. G. Clark, President John Hope of Morehouse College believed that "black social progress rested on the ability of African Americans to continuously demonstrate their patriotism through unqualified support of the war." Hope sponsored a list of activities at Morehouse College that included purchasing war bonds, promoting a campaign to "support our boys in uniform," and using African American support for the war to advance the political fight for black equality.[83]

CONCLUSION

Southern University, however, was unique in the sense that as a small, obscure black college emerging from the economic depression in the late 1930s, it quickly seized the opportunity to enhance its visibility within the state of Louisiana and the nation. During the war years, Clark corresponded with numerous black national leaders, African American newspaper publishers, and prominent educators at black colleges and universities. He sought the support of white philanthropists at the Rockefeller Foundation, of Louisiana state officials, such as Governor Sam H. Jones, and even of President Roosevelt's wife, Eleanor.[84] He wrote hundreds of letters during the 1940s soliciting state and federal support to improve the facilities of the campus as well as to promote the social welfare of African Americans throughout the South.

The university received funding from federal grants, authorization to administer numerous federal and state wartime programs, and was even named a vocational guidance center for returning veterans in 1945.[85] This allowed Clark to qualify for additional federal funding for new construction projects and to enhance the university's current facilities and programs under the Lanham Act for returning veterans.[86] By the conclusion of the war, F. G. Clark had redefined Southern University as a regional beacon of social uplift and economic opportunity and had placed the institution on the level of black America's premier institutions, such as Hampton Institute and Fisk University. While the Second World War represents a benchmark in the modern civil rights movement, it also marks a decisive moment for the future of Southern University and highlights Clark's ability to cleverly navigate his way through Louisiana racial politics and federal "red tape" with the intent of making Southern University a vital part of black higher education within the nation.[87]

3

SOLDIERING FOR UNCLE SAM

MILITARY TRAINING AT SOUTHERN UNIVERSITY
DURING THE COLD WAR, 1946-1960

In the post–World War II era, African Americans challenged racism and discrimination in pursuit of equal rights and better opportunities. World War II created improved social and political conditions for African Americans and provided political organizations considerable influence with the White House. In addition, the Cold War had tremendous implications for African Americans. American racism and discrimination became a source of international embarrassment for U.S. president Harry S. Truman, and African American support for military service became essential in order to protect America's interests around the world. As 10 percent of the U.S. population and military manpower, African Americans became a crucial part of defense planning.[1] During this period, many African American leaders supported America's Cold War agenda while pursuing civil rights gains, and they pressed Truman to address America's race problem or suffer international humiliation and loss of credibility.[2]

DESIRE FOR MILITARY TRAINING AT SOUTHERN UNIVERSITY

On the campus of Southern University and other HBCUs, officials and students participated in Cold War programs and encouraged African American support for military training and service. F. G. Clark regarded military training as a patriotic duty as well as a badge of citizenship. Just as he worked diligently in the "Win the War Campaign" throughout World War II, in 1945 he began efforts to establish an ROTC unit at Southern University. With the help of the *Afro-American* newspaper publisher, Carl Murphy, Clark made numerous informal requests to the War Department that were generally ignored. In a telegram to Murphy, Felton Clark expressed his frustration: "Informal request for ROTC made as early as 1941. War Department claims official request not made until 1946. Have exchanged at least 50 communications with War Department in effort to get unit plus support of members of Louisiana's Congressional delegation. All war communications received, courteous but indefinite or evasive. General idea was to continue requesting unit but more or less hopeless."[3] Murphy responded and asked whether Clark was prepared to accept an ROTC unit immediately. Murphy and Clark agreed that Southern should request the first available unit be assigned to the Baton Rouge campus. On May 7, 1946, Clark made a formal request to the War Department for an Air ROTC unit like Tuskegee Institute's. Clark wrote, "In terms of facilities we think we can offer all that will be necessary for such a successful unit. Harding Field, formerly an army air base, is within a mile of our campus. Our ability to furnish personnel that would want the program and whose training should be a great investment by our Country, is available for the asking."[4] Clark's request, however, was denied on the basis that the air program was currently in the developmental stages and expansion of that program was uncertain. A few months later, Major General Terrell C. Holliday of the Fourth Army, at Fort Sam Houston, contacted Clark and explained that the Army had no plans to establish any new Army ROTC units where there was no preexisting unit. Holliday emphatically reported, "from the above you will see that there is little or no chance of your obtaining a ROTC unit in 1946, but it is the plan of the War Department to expand the present ROTC within the next two years."[5]

BENEFITS OF MILITARY TRAINING

Although Southern's president did not have military experience, he did embrace the virtues of military training for African American males and recognize its importance to America's Cold War agenda. Clark believed that Southern University had a moral obligation to provide military training on the campus, considering the increasingly volatile situation overseas as a result of the Cold War tensions between the United States and the Soviet Union. He declared that "the constant pleas of the War Department for military training and the daily international 'incidents' plus the paucity of trained Negro military leadership at the outbreak of the last World War, make us feel that in these federal and state-supported land-grant colleges we have a moral responsibility to operate such a program as the ROTC; now and in the future."[6]

When two of Clark's former colleagues were asked why Clark was so supportive of military training, Huel D. Perkins remarked, "Dr. Clark was extremely supportive of ROTC. He thought it was excellent training for students, it was a means of increasing support (financial) for students, and good training in terms of leadership."[7] Elton C. Harrison, a former student and the vice president of academic affairs, reported, "Clark saw military training as increasing the stature of the university. He saw it as an honor. At that time, Prairie View had an ROTC unit and Clark was in competition. But ultimately, he saw it as an achievement or recognition. He was always supportive of military training at Southern."[8] As early as the 1920s, shortly after the university relocated to Scott's Bluff in Scotlandville, Louisiana, military cadence and discipline was a regular feature when the small student body assembled for convocation or campus presentations. Harrison confirmed that, saying, "When time came to dismiss we marched out of the chapel like a military unit, the men on one side and the ladies on the other. The ladies would march out first, and then the men would follow loudly in step."[9] Clark's attitude toward military training was shared by many African American administrators at HBCUs during the period. At Tuskegee, a former student remarked, "In the 1950s, I think educators thought military training was a way to instruct males in the art of self-discipline. It gave structure to one's life. It was a paternalistic attitude but nonetheless a strong one."[10] James Evans and Albert Parker believed it was more than a military program: "ROTC provided to educational institutions a means for practical training in organization, leadership, and discipline which [would] be of value to their graduated students in an industrial or professional career."[11] In particular, ROTC was understood to offer African American youth essential character attributes that reflected favorably on the black race.

EXPANSION OF ROTC AT HBCUS

In 1948, the Executive Committee of the Conference of Presidents of Land-Grant Colleges of Negroes appeared before the Committee on Civilian Components of the Armed Forces and stated that members of the Conference of Presidents were particularly concerned with the following issues:

> Increasing the number of ROTC programs in colleges for Negroes and in high schools for Negroes in states where separate educational institutions exist for Negro and White people to the end that more Negro youth may receive the military training and acquire leadership benefits from such training. Increasing the pay, benefits, grants-in-aid to be provided to ROTC and NROTC students of all groups.
>
> Pointing up the military and citizenship obligations of persons involved in the total ROTC and NROTC program.[12]

The Executive Committee also suggested that African Americans viewed their lack of participation in ROTC as a direct result of institutional racism and discrimination:

> The morale of our people is important in peace and in war. We urge this day that steps be taken in the operating areas of the civilian components of the Armed Forces to eliminate the tensions, fears, and misgivings on the part of Negroes with respect to their training, limited or narrow use, opportunities and outlook in the civilian components or regular Armed Forces of this nation.
>
> Racism is probably the weakest link in our democracy and it is time in our own interest as a nation to do something about it. Fortunately, something can be done—even, today, by the Honorable Members of the Committee on Civilian Components of the Armed Forces.[13]

The establishment of military training programs on black college campuses during the post–World War II era also strengthened the link between military training and service as a citizenship obligation and the quest for African American civil rights. In addition, the economic benefits of military service helped expand a growing black middle-class that played a significant role in the civil rights movement of the late 1950s and the 1960s.[14] These important developments were greatly influenced by many wartime contributions of black colleges and universities during World War II and their desire to positively impact the lives of African Americans.[15]

When the National Association for the Advancement of Colored People petitioned the Human Rights Commission of the United Nations to investigate human rights violations in the American South, President Truman became distressed. He realized that communist propaganda made it imperative that he address African American pleas for equal rights as Third World countries watched intensely.[16] For the Truman administration, military segregation was a logical place to address African American political grievances. The black community had long established its desire to serve in the armed forces on an equal basis with other Americans.[17] As a result, in December 1946 Truman formed a special civil rights committee charged with submitting recommendations on the matter. The committee produced a landmark document titled "To Secure These Rights," which advocated integration of the military in addition to a federal anti-lynching law, prohibition of discrimination in defense industries, the elimination of state poll taxes, and federal protection of voter registrants.[18]

FELTON G. CLARK WORKS TO ESTABLISH ROTC PROGRAM

In June 1947 Clark wrote Howard C. Petersen, assistant secretary of war, regarding Southern's application for an Army ROTC unit. Clark admitted that he made a formal request to the War Department in December 1946, but as early as 1941 he had inquired about establishing a unit and visited the War Department in Washington. He listed additional factors that he believed the War Department should be aware of, and in the process demonstrated his growing impatience with the agency's position: "First the general interest and desire of our male students for ROTC. Second, the fact that incessantly, calls are being issued to increase the strength of the Armed Forces of our Country. Third is the fact that a primary reason for the creation of Land-Grant colleges is to provide military training," asserted Clark. He concluded with a bit of sarcasm: "it may seem a bit absurd for us to be trying to convince you and your good office of our desire to have an ROTC in the light of these conditions. But, our interest is just that great."[19]

To increase his chances of receiving an ROTC unit, Clark sought the advice of other black college administrators who operated successful military training programs. He wrote to South Carolina State College president M. F. Whittaker:

> The War Department, specifically, Assistant Secretary of War, Honorable Howard C. Petersen, is giving us a consistent run-around on the matter of our desire to have a ROTC at Southern University. The alleged reasons are that our application was rather late and that the applications are being taken in order and that no expansion in the program is contemplated at this time.
>
> Please, with the background of the above, and adding anything, which is pertinent, tell me how you succeeded in getting the Unit at your school. Any help that you may give will greatly be appreciated.[20]

Clark also contacted Louisiana native Major General Edward S. Bres, chief of staff for Reserve and ROTC Affairs, and made a personal appeal for assistance: "Although I could write at great length, General Bres, everything would point to the conclusion that, as one of the seventeen Negro Land-Grant colleges and incidentally the third largest in the United States, we hope that we will be able to do our part by our Country and by the principle upon which Land-Grant education is founded by having the sort of program that we believe only an ROTC can give."[21]

General Bres responded six days later and informed Clark that Southern University's application was being considered in connection with the 1948 schedule and that Southern was one institution among 180 that had applied for a unit.[22] Clark also contacted various citizen organizations throughout Louisiana, such as the American Legion and the Veterans of Foreign Wars, and requested their support.[23] Throughout 1947, Clark continued to press the War Department and request support from all individuals who could influence the speed and process of Southern receiving an ROTC unit.

In November of 1947, the Committee Against Jim Crow in Military Service and Training, chaired by A. Philip Randolph and Grant Reynolds, invited Clark to join their efforts to protest racial segregation in the U.S. armed forces. The committee forwarded a memorandum that voiced its opposition to the recommendations of President Truman's Commission on Universal Military Training. Randolph and Reynolds cautioned black leaders to be aware that segregation would prevail in the Regular Army and discrimination in college ROTC units would continue if military segregation was not challenged. Black leaders, including F. G. Clark, were encouraged not to support the federal government's military policies if they did not include desegregation of the U.S. military.[24] Despite Randolph and Reynolds's appeal, Clark was undaunted in his efforts to receive an ROTC unit on the Baton Rouge campus.

FELTON G. CLARK SOLICITS THE SUPPORT OF MILITARY OFFICIALS

Clark contacted Brigadier General Wendell Westover of Reserve and ROTC Affairs and voiced his desire to have ROTC training at Southern University. He suggested that if America found itself in another global conflict, Southern University would be there to contribute in the form of military leadership and manpower.[25] General Westover responded to Clark on March 8 and suggested that the fact that Southern would accept any type of ROTC unit simplified the problem, but nonetheless would not guarantee favorable results. He was impressed at the desire and determination Southern demonstrated to train citizen soldiers.[26]

During F. G. Clark's quest to establish an ROTC unit at Southern, the black press, in particular the *Afro-American*, initiated an elaborate campaign to provide valuable support and advice to black colleges and universities in their quest to offer military training. In an article titled "ROTC Drive Bears Fruit," the periodical exclaimed, "The *AFRO's* campaign to obtain Reserve Officers' Training Corps (ROTC) units for more land-grant colleges bore its first fruit last week. Colored Presidents of land-grant colleges, who were not represented when the Gray Board [the federal board that recommended the merger of the National Guard and the United States Reserves] held hearings last week, are now being given an opportunity to file written statements or to appear before the board. Quick action on the part of the *AFRO*, working in concert with officers of the Colored Land-Grant College Presidents' Association, resulted in the board's announcement."[27] Carl Murphy informed Clark that the *Afro-American* newspaper would print an article displaying a list of applications on file with the War Department for ROTC units. Murphy reported the number of applicants and the type of unit they requested. He also suggested that Southern revise its request and ask for a unit with a small number of applicants on file. Murphy noted that while there were fifty-three white colleges with Naval Reserve Officers Training units (NROTC), there were no African American colleges that had applied for one. He believed that Southern should also apply for an NROTC unit.[28] Murphy and other black newspaper editors were also successful in applying political pressure to the Truman administration and War Department to establish additional ROTC units at HBCUs. In a memorandum from the War Department's public relations office, Special Consultant L. Eugene Hedberg wrote the deputy director of public relations:

> The Army is currently confronted with a problem having definite public relations aspects. My informant believes that the Air Force may anticipate having this same problem soon.
>
> The problem is that of pressure from negro institutions and their supporters, particularly newspapers, to have ROTC units established in them. (NOTE: Refer to (for example) Washington Afro American, February 17, 1948—main headline and leading article, page 1; same paper, February 21, 1948, front page box article).
>
> The President of Afro American Newspapers has addressed letters to General Eisenhower and to General Westover (Army Exec. For Res. And ROTC Affairs) within the past two weeks. A telegram has been sent to General Westover from the Conference of Colored Land Grant College Presidents in Atlantic City last week.[29]

In March 1948, A. Philip Randolph and the Committee Against Jim Crow in Military Service and Training met with Truman and asserted, "Negroes are in no mood to shoulder a gun for democracy abroad as long as they are denied democracy at home."[30] Two months later Randolph formed the League for Nonviolent Civil Disobedience Against Military Segregation, which received the support of many black political organizations. In a poll taken by the NAACP, 71 percent of African American college students were supportive of Randolph's efforts, while 15 percent were opposed.[31] After Southern Democrats formed the Dixiecrat Party, Truman and his advisors believed that the time was right to draft an executive order that would incorporate the recommendations of "To Secure These Rights." Executive Order 9981 declared that "there shall be equality of treatment and opportunity for all persons in the armed services without regard to race, color, religion, or national origin."³² Although Truman and his administration were adamant about the directive, the U.S. military was slow and reluctant to implement the order.

SOUTHERN UNIVERSITY RECEIVES A SENIOR ROTC PROGRAM

After two years of relentless determination, President Clark was getting closer to realizing his dream. James C. Evans, civilian advisor to the secretary of defense, contacted Clark and reported, "There is increasing evidence that your perseverance will soon yield results. Don't give up the ship."³³ Southern was getting closer to receiving an ROTC unit and Clark felt that to increase his chances he would amend Southern's original application to say "military training will be compulsory for freshmen and sophomore students."³⁴ F. G. Clark had worked for several years to bring formal military training to Southern University, but most importantly he wanted to instill in young male students the virtues of discipline and integrity that he believed represented Southern University, the state of Louisiana, and the Negro race. Less than a month after amending Southern's application to include compulsory military training, the War Department informed Clark that "the Reserve Officer Training Corps unit at Southern University would be activated on July 15, 1948."³⁵ Southern was the only African American institution in the nation to be assigned a Transportation Corps unit, and the school immediately began preparations to offer formal military training.³⁶

BLACK HIGHER EDUCATION AND THE COLD WAR

America's colleges and universities were enlisted to help fight the Cold War.³⁷ Although colleges and universities enjoyed increased funding and support in the first decade of the post–World War II era, students, faculty, and administrators were closely scrutinized for radical political beliefs or alternative lifestyles. It was commonly believed that violation of traditional gender roles or societal sexual mores created familial chaos and threatened the moral fiber of the nation.³⁸ Female premarital sex and homosexuality were unacceptable behaviors that were condemned by the church, anticommunist crusaders, and relationship experts of the day.

During the Cold War, many college presidents and administrators micromanaged their institutions and took a personal interest in the lives of faculty and students in an effort to reflect the highest standard of patriotism and Cold War conformity. African American college presidents such as F. G. Clark, F. D. Patterson of Tuskegee Institute, and many others were concerned with everything from student dress, conduct, and behavior to university finances and faculty hiring. For example, if students at Southern wanted to get married they were required to have a conference with President Clark at least three months before the wedding date.[39] Clark's influence on campus affairs supports Lionel Lewis's belief that during this period "academic administrators were managers of institutions that marketed conformity and security."[40] In addition, African American college administrators linked the civil rights movement to higher education and believed that through educational opportunities, moral and dignified behavior, and unwavering support for democratic ideas and principles African Americans would eventually obtain equal rights.[41] In an address to university faculty, Clark articulated this belief when he declared:

> We are Negroes in America. This very expression serves as a release for associations that are identified with unhappiness, inadequacy, dissatisfaction, and many other conditions identified with a life deprived of richness and fullness. In view of these observations, each varying in degree of cruciality, the work of those of us engaged in the educational enterprise, especially where Negroes are concerned, can be considered in anything but a light vein. I cannot point out to you the countless implications of the above facts for our work here at Southern University. But, I can say to you that to effect a program that will deal with the conditions so outlined calls for the finest type of human character, a thorough-going philosophy of education, a functional possession of real knowledge and a belief in divine consideration.[42]

At Southern, the Discipline Committee policed the conduct of students and on a regular basis dismissed individuals who "failed to adjust to college life." In 1952, a female student was suspended for one year because she was accused of exhibitionism, being nude in the halls, and leaving campus without permission. Another female student "left the campus and returned to the dormitory under very suspicious circumstances." The committee reported, "This lady is too illusive in her movements for us to give her proper protection."[43] She was subsequently placed on probation. Dr. Clark received numerous letters from married women in the community who accused female students of being involved in extramarital affairs with their husbands. These women wrote detailed letters of how their husbands met young ladies on and off campus and asked Clark to expel the co-eds for immoral behavior.[44] Two male students were also suspended for sexually "deviant" behavior, having been accused by another student for "engaging in homosexual acts and acts of perversion."[45]

Felton Clark's professional reputation as an educator and scholar was enhanced further when President Dwight Eisenhower appointed him to the Board of Foreign Scholarships in 1956. Clark joined an elite group of higher education administrators from institutions such as the University of Alabama, Catholic University, Harvard Law School, the University of California Medical Center, and Radcliff College. Clark was the only member representing a historically black college or university. Being asked to join the board was an honor that reflected his standing among African American educators of the period and how well he was received among state and national officials.[46]

THE U.S. STATE DEPARTMENT RECRUITS BLACK COLLEGES AND UNIVERSITIES

The role of higher education during the Cold War was also described by J. Thomas Schneider, chairman of the Department of Defense Personnel Policy Board, in a speech at a conference of the American Council on Education. Schneider's talk discussed the importance of education to the modern Army and also pronounced, "It is the job of the schools and the colleges and universities of America to provide the men of knowledge and of learning. It is the job of America's educators to supply the professionally trained manpower by providing the opportunity for every youth to equip himself for a place in the defense of his country, as well as contribute to increasing the standards of life in America."[47] Thus, the Cold War had long-term effects on the American social, political, and cultural landscape.

Academics who voiced opposition to American foreign policy or mainstream racial politics ran the risk of being fired or labeled subversive. In 1955 eleven African American college administrators from Atlanta University,

Fisk University, Kentucky State, Alabama State, Virginia Union, Morehouse College, and Tuskegee Institute were labeled "pro-communist" by a New York newspaper.[48] During this period, civil rights activist A. Philip Randolph remarked, "Being red was too great a handicap for people already handicapped by being black."[49] In the midst of the "Red Scare" of the 1950s a survey was conducted to determine whether African American colleges and universities forced their employees to take loyalty oaths. According to R. Grann Lloyd, "Of the Negro colleges and universities in the United States 10, or 9.6 percent, required their employees to sign a loyalty oath or pledge of allegiance to the American way of life as a condition of employment."[50] The ten state institutions were Georgia's Albany State College, Alcorn A&M College in Mississippi, Florida A&M College, Grambling College in Louisiana, Mississippi's Jackson College, Miners Teachers College in Washington, D.C., Maryland's Morgan College, Prairie View State College in Texas, Southern University, and Texas State University for Negroes.[51] Although Lloyd included Southern University in his survey, no evidence has been found that loyalty oaths were required as a condition of employment.[52]

During the same period, the Truman administration sponsored a program hosted by Secretary of State Dean Acheson for several black colleges. In addition to Secretary Acheson, the small conference was composed of "five Virginia Union University faculty members, two students from Storer College [an HBCU in West Virginia], one student from Hampton University and 15 students from Virginia Union, all of whom were also scheduled to meet with United States Vice President, Alben Barkley."[53] According to one of the faculty members present, the forum was designed to answer why African Americans should support American democracy and reject communism and how the Round-the-World study project would assist African Americans in their struggle for social equality.[54] Shortly after the Korean War began, the U.S. secretary of agriculture addressed college presidents at the annual meeting of the Association of Land-Grant Colleges and Universities. As keynote speaker, Charles Brannan discussed how land-grant colleges could contribute to the Cold War and help defeat communism. Secretary Brannan stated that international communism prevented world peace and that military aggression in Korea should be met with overwhelming military power.[55] Like many other land-grant institutions, Southern signed a contract to participate in a federal program to train foreign students in agricultural advances.[56] From the American perspective the Cold War included a series of policies established to contain the Soviet Union's power and the spread of communism in Europe and Asia, both regarded as serious threats to American democracy and national security.[57]

MILITARY TRAINING PROGRAMS EXPAND THROUGHOUT THE NATION

During the first decade of the Cold War military training was infused with campus life at colleges and universities throughout the nation. University administrators viewed ROTC training as an essential component of national security and a vital contribution to the Cold War. In addition, the presence of ROTC units encouraged students to embrace their civic duty while promoting order and discipline on campus.[58] For these reasons, the number of ROTC applicants rose considerably among HBCUs and white universities located in the South, where the military tradition was firmly in place.[59] In Louisiana, McNeese State College in Lake Charles was awarded an ROTC Infantry unit and Northeast Louisiana State College in Monroe was approved for a Military Police ROTC unit on September 7, 1950. Both were white colleges.[60] In Pineville, Louisiana, on June 25, 1952, Louisiana College officially applied for an ROTC unit and remarked, "Because we do not have a military unit, we are having a steady decline in the enrollment of men. With the establishment of a unit, we are assured that the enrollment of male students will increase from twenty-five to fifty per cent in a period of two years."[61] Two months later, the president of historically black Grambling College, Dr. R.W.E. Jones, wrote the adjutant general of the Army, Major General William E. Bergin, to request a face-to-face meeting to discuss establishing an ROTC unit on the north Louisiana campus. Similarly, a representative from Southeastern Louisiana College in Hammond wrote the Office of the Executive for Reserve and ROTC Affairs to inquire about the college's application for a unit. The letter dated February 19, 1953, also highlighted the number of eligible male students (574) who were qualified to receive commissions in the U.S. Army.[62] Prior to 1948, when Southern received its ROTC program, the only higher education institutions in Louisiana with Senior ROTC units were Louisiana State University, Loyola University in New Orleans, and Tulane University.[63]

AFRICAN AMERICAN MILITARY TRAINING UNITS AT HBCUS

During the years following World War II, the desire to establish military training programs at colleges and universities was nearly universal throughout the nation. Southern's ROTC program received the support of the university employees and black colleges throughout the South. A number of African American institutions immediately contacted President Clark and inquired how they could receive a military training program as well. By 1952, twelve black colleges and universities in nine different states had submitted applications to the Department of Defense for the establishment of senior military training programs.[64]

TABLE 3.1. Black Colleges and Universities that submitted Senior ROTC program applications to the U.S. Department of Defense.

Institution	Location	Date of application
Alabama A&M College	Normal, Ala.	August 20, 1952
Arkansas A&M College	Pine Bluff, Ark.	August 20, 1949
Delaware State College	Dover, Del.	August 20, 1949
Atlanta University	Atlanta, Ga.	May 26, 1952
Fort Valley State College	Fort Valley, Ga.	June 12, 1952
Kentucky State College	Frankfort, Ky.	June 30, 1952
Grambling College	Grambling, La.	June 30, 1952
Xavier University of Louisiana	New Orleans, La.	July 8, 1952
Alcorn A&M College	Alcorn, Miss.	July 15, 1952
Jackson College	Jackson, Miss.	June 30, 1952
Lincoln University	Lincoln University, Pa.	June 30, 1952
Texas State University	Houston, Tex.	September 30, 1948

Source: Memorandum, Office of the Assistant Secretary of Defense to Major General Hugh M. Milton, Executive for Reserve and ROTC Affairs, December 22, 1952, File: Educational Institutions, Civil–General, General Correspondence, 1948–54, Entry 149, Box 6, Record Group 319, National Archives Building, College Park, Md.

The National Urban League also encouraged the development of military training at black institutions of higher learning when the organization sent a bulletin to schools located in the southern region requesting a list of African American students who received college scholarships and were involved in NROTC.[65]

GROWING POPULARITY OF MILITARY TRAINING AT SOUTHERN UNIVERSITY

Southern's ROTC program quickly became noted for its highly motivated cadets. During the unit's first ROTC Camp at Fort Eustis, Virginia, Major B. W. Johnson informed Clark that three Southern cadets stood out among the trainees. "For the Final Parade on Friday one of our men Louis Wilson was chosen as Color Guard and another Esau Lewis was chosen as orderly for General Muller. Leonce Gaiter was one of the outstanding students here this summer and Southern as a whole has done a swell job."[66] Clark was indeed grateful to receive such encouraging news. He immediately sent a congratulatory dispatch to Major Johnson and praised his efforts for making the program a success: "So I finally do hear from you. Anyway, I shall try to appreciate the fact that you have had no time to write because you have been so busy soldiering for Uncle Sam. I must say congratulations, and to give you a special pat on the back for beginning the leadership in our ROTC Program which makes everybody justify proudly what has taken place."[67]

Within the first year of the program, Southern University's Reserve Officer Training Corps unit established itself as a university hallmark. As the student population increased, so did the number of male cadets receiving military training. President Clark instructed the university dean, John B. Cade, to circulate a university-wide memorandum to all freshman and sophomore males explaining military training attendance requirements. Clark was in fact fulfilling an earlier pledge he made to the War Department to make ROTC training mandatory for all underclassmen. The directive read, "It is required that all able bodied non veteran Freshman and Sophomore men pursue courses in Military Science. Freshman and Sophomore men who have *not* registered for Military Science must do so or clear their exemption, with *proof* of their eligibility to be excused. *All* freshmen and sophomores not so cleared will be carried on the roll of the Department of Military Science and Tactics."[68] Within weeks, the university registrar issued a notice to Dean Cade listing the names of ninety-one freshman and sophomore males who had not registered for ROTC classes. Two hundred copies of the list were posted on campus. Although it is not determined whether students deliberately did not register for ROTC or were not aware of Clark's new directive, Huel Perkins later claimed that "military training at Southern never received 100 percent of male support." He added, "I don't remember anybody talking down the military or talking it up either. It was just sort of . . . it came to Southern and some people gravitated toward it and some did not."[69] Elton C. Harrison believes that "there were always a minority of students that were critical of military service and training."[70] Former Southern student Frank S. Ransburg remembers little resistance to military training on campus: "During the 1950s there was not very much opposition to military service and training. You have to understand, during the post–World War II era, the best jobs were through the U.S. government. Many postal workers and teachers who were military veterans were supported through the G.I. Bill. Military service provided economic opportunities to African Americans that were not available in the South or the black community."[71] Ransburg's remarks coincide with the results of a survey conducted in relation to this study. When former Southern and Tuskegee students and faculty read, "Blacks were in no mood to shoulder a rifle abroad so long as they were denied democracy at home," nearly 70 percent disagreed.[72]

Although Southern's ROTC program was only a year old, recent success and popularity prompted Clark to petition Fourth Army headquarters for the establishment of an Infantry unit. After Clark received an unfavorable response by acting Army Chief of Staff Colonel F. T. Dodd, who indicated that new Infantry units would receive low priority in future planning,[73] he waited two weeks and made a formal request to Brigadier General Hugh Hoffman for an Antiaircraft Artillery unit for several reasons:

> The second largest oil refinery in the world is located in Baton Rouge less than three miles from Southern University campus. For this reason I herewith request that an Antiaircraft Artillery ROTC unit be added to our Department of Military Science as it is believed that such instruction would be of

extreme value in this industrial area. It is anticipated that after the present school year we will have at least five hundred cadets each year in our ROTC program, a figure that, it is hoped, will justify the addition of a second unit.⁷⁴

Though Southern University did not receive authorization for the Infantry or Antiaircraft Artillery units, Southern University ROTC commander Major Thomas B. Taylor and F. G. Clark continued to promote the ROTC program and the virtues of military training to the state and surrounding community. In November 1949 Major Taylor invited James C. Evans, civilian assistant to the secretary of defense, to visit Southern University in the coming spring semester.⁷⁵ During the same month, Clark wrote American Legion Posts 505 and 502 in Baton Rouge and requested that they honor outstanding cadets during the upcoming Commencement Day ceremony.⁷⁶ Clark was elated when Post 502 commander Raymond P. Scott answered:

> We as Legionaries and citizens of our community are extremely proud of the Reserve Officers Training Corps at Southern University. It is our hope that out of this unit will come some of our most efficient leadership, which is of invaluable consequence in the accomplishment of the many problems that must be dealt with in our community, state and nation.
>
> The men of our Post consider it a privilege to be able to express our appreciation to grateful and deserving men who are striving toward that goal of making for our communities and the world———BETTER CITIZENS.⁷⁷

KOREAN WAR

By the summer of 1950 America found itself once more engaged in war on foreign soil. The communist-backed North Korean People's Army, in a surprise attack, crossed the 38th parallel and overwhelmed American-supported South Korean forces. President Truman responded by calling for the assistance of the United Nations and ordered counterattacks by the U.S. Air Force and Navy. The Korean War gave black colleges and universities another important reason to promote military training on their campuses.⁷⁸

In 1951, however, Clark became worried that misinformation concerning the Selective Service Extension Act of 1950 would adversely affect attitudes toward military training and service on campus. Rumors quickly circulated about the eligibility of college students for the draft. Subsequently, many students and ROTC cadets became worried that they would be drafted into service without the opportunity to complete their education or receive a commission in the Army. He assembled a small committee of administrators and faculty to conduct an open forum with male students. Clark wrote committee members, "I am asking you gentlemen to constitute a panel for discussing current issues in the deferment of students with particular reference to the executive order of President Truman last week. The purpose of this discussion will be to clear up misunderstandings that our men students might have with reference to the issue at hand. My belief is that the approach suggested will make a valuable contribution to the Southern University enterprise."[79]

RACISM AT ROTC SUMMER CAMP

Although ROTC training at Southern was experiencing enormous success, the cadets were confronted with racism during their annual training camp at Fort Eustis, Virginia, in the summer of 1951. Clark wrote the civilian assistant to the secretary of defense, James C. Evans, and expressed his displeasure and disappointment with the situation:

> Major Taylor has informed me that he has received a letter from Major Fernandes at the Camp concerning the problem of the separate dance for Negro Cadets. You will remember that this problem has occurred twice before. Conferences on this matter, which members of my staff have had with Cadets returning from the camp, indicate that many of them consider problems in connection with the dance as being humiliating to them. In fact, a recent graduate, Richard Francis Johnson, now a Regular Army Second Lieutenant, told a member of the Military Staff that the members of his class went to the 1950 Camp with a group desire to be outstanding and that group morale appreciably suffered after the group was denied the right to attend the dance with their campmates and were offered a dance with attendance restricted to Negroes.[80]

Clark added, "Camp authorities will find that year after year a separate dance or other social activity for Negro Cadets on a United States Army Post will be unacceptable to many of those attending the Camp from Southern University."[81] He further suggested that segregated functions were undemocratic and should be discontinued in order to prevent future embarrassment and humiliation of African American cadets, which he believed could affect Army efficiency.[82]

SOUTHERN UNIVERSITY ROTC REACHES NEW HEIGHTS

In December 1951, the number of ROTC cadets was increasing and U.S. military officials recognized Southern as an institution making great contributions to the nation's defense program. Major General Hobart R. Gay, deputy commanding general of the Fourth Army, reviewed the ROTC program and reported: "The Fourth Army extends to you and your staff the seasons warmest greetings. During the past year it has been most gratifying to witness the very material contributions your institution has made to the National Defense effort through your support of the Army ROTC program. We are counting on the men you are training in this relentless fight against the forces which would destroy our very freedoms."[83]

Letters such as General Gay's and the steady improvement Clark witnessed made his efforts to acquire a military program worthwhile. Clark believed that military training at black colleges held numerous benefits for the cadets as well as the institutions. The U.S. military had taken the lead in racial integration, and African American soldiers were some of the first to experience living among whites on an equal basis. Though the transition was not embraced by everyone, it was indeed progress. Clark and many African Americans believed that the U.S. military provided a successful model for the general public to follow.[84]

Military training at Southern University was popular among the male students from the very beginning. In the first two graduating classes, the program produced approximately 140 second lieutenants. Initially, Southern's ROTC cadets were assigned only to the Transportation Corps, but because of shortages in other military occupations, some of the school's graduates were directed to serve in the armored and ordinance branches. Southern University alumni took such special pride in the enthusiasm and success of the school's military graduates that the Shreveport Alumni Association committed to purchasing the insignia of the newly commissioned officers.[85] This event happened in part due to the extraordinary service and positive publicity provided by ROTC officers and cadets during a recent flood emergency suffered by the residents of south Louisiana. State officials commended the ROTC unit for their well-coordinated evacuation of residents throughout East Baton Rouge Parish. E. A. Bauer of the Baton Rouge City Police Department reported, "This was smoother than any operation we've had in Baton Rouge. The cooperation and efficiency of the men from Southern University was excellent."[86] SU cadets used two amphibious vehicles and were successful in rescuing three hundred individuals trapped by flood waters. The cadets and other university students began operations by rescuing a busload of children in the Zachery/Chaneyville area and were able to reunite them with their parents. After working tirelessly for three days and nights throughout the metropolitan area, the cadets were asked to initiate relief efforts sixty miles away in Opelousas, Louisiana.[87]

In 1954, Brigadier General John Weckerling, assistant to the commanding general of the Fourth Army Area, visited Southern University for the purpose of a formal inspection. After the review and meetings with Major Robert F. Tarver, professor of military science and tactics (PMS&T), and President Felton Clark, the general praised the unit for a most impressive showing: "I wish to speak for myself and my whole staff when I say that the S.U. Regiment has made an excellent showing. I extend congratulations to your PMS&T and his entire staff. This performance shows that a great deal of work was required in order to make this Regiment reach such a high degree of perfection."[88] Two weeks later, the ROTC department proudly reported that eighty-five cadets were scheduled to receive their commissions as Army officers in the spring graduation ceremony. Also, the men were assigned to a growing number of military occupations. Besides the transportation, armored, and ordinance branches, newly commissioned officers would also serve in artillery, infantry, the medical service corps, and the signal corps. The ability to serve as Army officers in numerous service branches was further indication that ROTC training at Southern University had progressed and become so extensive that it offered cadets the opportunity to pursue a number of options that in many cases were not available to African Americans a short time earlier.[89]

BLACK WOMEN AT SOUTHERN UNIVERSITY EMBRACE ROTC ACTIVITIES

Although female students could not participate in ROTC during the 1950s, the ROTC department reached another milestone in 1957 when it organized a girls' drill team, known as the Marching Cavalettes. The Marching Cavalettes performed in homecoming parades, community festivals, and other university functions wearing khaki skirts, white blouses and gloves, gold scarves, and brown loafers. Organized in four squads of ten individuals, the team numbered approximately forty-five members. Sergeant First Class Harold J. Turner was the drill team instructor and organizer. Members of the Cavalettes practiced six days a week to master the precision steps and formations.[90]

According to Major John R. Reaves, PMS&T, "the purpose of this team is to stimulate the interest of the young women in the ROTC program, with the hope that some will take the tour that the Women's Army Corps (WAC) is offering. It is felt that it will help to develop leadership traits in the young ladies."[91] On the first day of tryouts for the elite squad, over two hundred young women responded. Ultimately, only fifty were selected. Similar to the boys' drill team, the girls' drill team was taught to march with precision timing and perform maneuvers. Both drill teams took center stage at the annual Military Day community celebration, which included a formal inspection by President Clark, presentation of the ROTC Queen and Court, drill squad competitions, a platoon drill competition, a military band performance, and presentation of awards. The girls' drill team and Military Day celebration and activities were expected to bring further prestige to the university in the same fashion as the ROTC unit.[92]

MILITARY TRAINING AT SOUTHERN UNIVERSITY REACHES HEIGHT OF POPULARITY

In the fall of 1957 the enthusiasm and popularity for ROTC training at Southern University continued to grow among male students. Members of the Marching Cavaliers drill team were installed as charter members of the newly formed chapter of the Pershing Rifles National Honor Military Society at Southern University. The purpose of the Pershing Rifles was to "encourage, preserve, and develop the highest ideals of the military profession, to promote American citizenship, to create a close and more efficient relation, and to provide appropriate recognition of a high degree of military ability among the cadets."[93] A total of 981 male students were enrolled as cadets, and as the regiment grew, so did the number of student organizations associated with military training. In addition to the Pershing Rifles, other organizations included the Scabbard and Blade, the girls' drill team, Rifle Team, the Non-Commissioned Officers (NCO) Club, the Association of the U.S. Army, and Cadence Call.[94]

Throughout the 1950s, Southern University's ROTC program experienced much success. In May 1950 fourteen commissioned officers graduated, and by 1952 over seventy individuals from Southern were commissioned as second lieutenants in the U.S. Army.[95] In 1954 the program was changed from a Transportation unit to a general military science unit. This meant that ROTC cadets were able to train for various military occupations as opposed to only the Transportation Corps. Between 1948 and 1961 Southern's military program commissioned over two hundred Army officers and achieved national acclaim.[96]

4

WHAT THE PEOPLE THINK

AFRICAN AMERICAN ATTITUDES TOWARD MILITARY TRAINING AND SERVICE, 1950–1960

> Those Valiant doughboys had it made when they entered the Korean Conflict and those who by the blessings of God make it back to their home, will still have it made. They know they'll be welcomed by one of the best military leaders in the field—Col. Harry F. Lofton—and they know they'll be welcomed by the 170,000 residents of Gifu and 15,000 in Naka. They are right.
> —ALEX WILSON, *Chicago Defender*, November 18, 1950

This passage from an American newspaper may sound typical of popular sentiment in 1950: America's finest soldiers, under the capable leadership of a high-ranking officer, welcomed by grateful overseas residents. But it was not typical. The valiant doughboys in question, including Colonel Harry F. Lofton, were African Americans stationed in Gifu, Japan. The article in the *Chicago Defender* described Colonel Lofton as "a popular and brilliant Tan American that holds and wisely exercises the power of a Touiassant L'Overture."[1] Although it was rare for African Americans to have such authority in the U.S. military in 1950, newspaper articles that reflected general African American sentiment and praised black men and women in uniform were not.

Civil rights activism influenced attitudes toward military training and service in the same manner that military training and service impacted desires to fight for civil rights and social equality. This explains why many African American military veterans were some of black America's most militant and determined civil rights leaders and why college administrators and many black college students embraced the virtues of military service and ROTC training. Black World War II and Korean War veterans represented the vanguard of grassroots civil rights leadership in the war against white supremacy and social oppression during the 1950s and 1960s.[2] Contemporaneously, African American ROTC cadets at Southern University and other black institutions throughout the South adopted the same philosophy as war veterans and led or actively participated in local demonstrations and campus protests to equally claim their citizenship rights and sense of manhood.

THE BLACK PRESS SUPPORTS MILITARY TRAINING AND SERVICE

Throughout the 1950s, many individuals in the black community, including black leaders and the black press, encouraged, honored, supported, and admired African American men and women in military uniform. Military training and service reflected African American social progress, economic opportunity, and black manhood and was further indication of why African Americans deserved full citizenship rights in the South. During this period black Americans serving in the armed forces received tremendous attention from the most influential black newspapers and magazines in the form of human interest stories, pictures, and weekly features. Consistently, black America's most successful periodicals, such as the *Pittsburgh Courier*, *Chicago Defender*, and *Afro-American* newspapers, as well as *Ebony* magazine, voiced overwhelming support for African American participation in America's armed forces.

Newspaper articles and stories celebrating the black soldier demonstrate how to a large extent African Americans viewed men and women in uniform as courageously leading the community and nation in breaking down racial barriers while achieving personal success.[3] Much as it did during World War II, in the 1950s the black press was critical of racism and discrimination against African Americans while it supported national ideals and encouraged the community to embrace U.S. Cold War ideology.[4] Though the fight for the right to fight had been won by 1950, black leaders vigorously lobbied the federal government for military integration as the first step toward the ultimate goal of equal opportunity and social equality throughout American society.

Among the various types of newspaper articles relating to African Americans in the armed forces, human interest stories accounted for the vast majority. Most national African American newspapers had a weekly feature devoted to the general welfare of military personnel. The *Pittsburgh Courier*'s weekly feature was called "At Home and Overseas with Our GIs." The *Chicago Defender* had "Along the Korean War Front," and the *Afro-American* labeled its feature "Up Front with Hicks" (it was named for the paper's war correspondent, James Hicks). Articles and short excerpts highlighted everything from military assignments and marriages of military personnel to educational accomplishments and the status of military units. Weekly features normally included a small picture and short commentary about a soldier.

Scores of human interest stories were designed to emphasize advances made by black men and women in the armed forces. The *Pittsburgh Courier* reported, "The attendance of Negro enlisted personnel doubled in schools of the armed forces during the past year since the racial quotas have been removed, according to the former Secretary of Defense, General George C. Marshall. He pointed out that opportunity for enlistment, promotion, and advancement is being provided on an individual basis without regard to racial quotas."[5] A similar article, "A Break for Korea Vets," included news concerning the new GI Bill. Highlighted in the story were five significant benefits that would assist African American veterans making the transition to civilian life. Included were education and training, guaranteed or insured home, farm, and business loans, unemployment compensation, mustering-out pay, and employment relocation assistance. Veterans could also expect a $110 monthly stipend to enroll in training programs in schools and colleges and an additional $25–$50 for dependents.[6]

Newspapers' editorial sections were frequently used to accentuate racial progress in the armed forces. In 1952, a letter appeared in the *Pittsburgh Courier* signed by "an interested reader":

> I have noticed frequent headlines and front page stories deploring the injustices done Negro servicemen, but few articles, which indicate the great strides that have been made in improving race relations notably with the Army. In Denver there is a junior ROTC unit at Manual High School, the senior instructor is a Negro sergeant. Working under him are a white sergeant and a Spanish-American sergeant, both of whom accept his orders unquestioningly. This Negro sergeant has made an enviable record since he was

first assigned to our school system two years ago. The school has developed a drill team that is perhaps the most famous high school unit of its kind in the nation.[7]

The theme of military integration was a popular subject with mainstream black newspapers during the period. Newspaper stories served to highlight social progress of African Americans and the reality that if racial integration was possible in the military, it was possible in civilian society. "In the Heart of Mississippi: Integration Complete at Keesler Air Base" was written to highlight that desegregation was possible even in the Deep South. E. W. Kenworthy, executive secretary of the President's Committee on Equality of Treatment and Opportunity in the Armed Forces, toured several military installations in addition to Keesler Air Force Base and remarked, "the commander at Keesler thought it best not to have two standards on the base." After close inspection, Kenworthy was pleasantly surprised to learn that racial integration existed even in the living quarters and mess hall.[8]

The Committee on Equality of Treatment and Opportunity in the Armed Services's eighty-two-page document acknowledged that the U.S. Navy and Air Force had made significant strides in a relatively short period of time. From 1945 to 1950, the Navy went from a policy of African American exclusion to near complete integration. Similarly, nearly 75 percent of African Americans in the Air Force were assigned to integrated units throughout the United States and as far South as Mississippi. Concerning the Army, the article exclaimed, "All Army jobs are now open to Negroes. All Army school courses are open to them without restrictions or quota. For the first time Negroes no longer are limited in assignment to Negro overhead (housekeeping) units, but are assigned according to their qualifications."[9]

BLACK STUDENT NEWSPAPERS CELEBRATE ROTC CADETS

On the campuses of Southern University and other black colleges and universities the student newspapers devoted attention to military training and service in the same style as national black newspapers. Newspaper articles paid tribute to current and former students who participated in ROTC or served in the military, to ROTC balls and beauty pageants. The *Southern University Digest* regularly printed pictures and stories that announced the achievements of cadets and recently commissioned officers, ROTC social functions, Selective Service information, military competitions, and the social and economic benefits of military service. A regularly featured column called "Uncle Sam's Southernites" appeared throughout the 1950s that was designed to acquaint the Southern family with the many accomplishments, updates, and casualties of alumni in the armed forces.[10] In fact, it can be argued that student newspaper articles that focused on military training at Southern reflected the majority of human interest stories in the *Southern University Digest*. Personal letters from former students serving in the military were common and often described their experiences or desire to serve in the armed forces. In 1952, Stacy T. Williams Jr. wrote President Clark:

> As you can see by the letter heading, I am a member of the 73D Engineer Combat Battalion, previously a member of the 24th Infantry Regiment until deactivation. Enclosed you will find the last edition of the "Eagles Forward" Regimental Newspaper. This paper gives a brief sketch of the History of the 24th Infantry Regiment and a Speech of Commendation by Colonel Gillis, Regimental Commander. I would like for the student body to read about the progress made by this unit, which I personally feel was not publicized enough.[11]

Clark responded with, "How good it is to hear from you with reference to what is happening to you as you are doing your big bit to keep democracy alive. We shall take the liberty to print your letter in THE DIGEST and a copy of EAGLE FORWARD will be placed on the bulletin board of the ROTC."[12]

Southern University's ROTC department not only received the support of students, faculty, and staff on the Bluff, it also enjoyed the encouragement of various organizations throughout the state as well as local businesses. During an ROTC awards ceremony, the president of the New Orleans chapter of the National Defense Transportation Association presented an award to the most outstanding senior and junior cadets. The Royal Furniture Company, a local business, presented a loving cup to the cadet with the highest academic average, and a representative of the Twilight Masonic Lodge presented an engraved trophy to the most outstanding freshman cadet.[13]

RACIAL INTEGRATION IN THE U.S. ARMED FORCES

As President Truman's Committee on Equality of Treatment and Opportunity in the Armed Services met to discuss racial integration in the U.S. military, black newspapers praised the Army's recent efforts. The *Chicago Defender* declared, "Like we predicted here last week, [the] Army took a plea in its racial segregation policy. While reported policy changes don't let down the flood gates to racial integration, Army mules are at least headed in the right direction."[14] Even as the armed forces continued to desegregate, stories in support of integration and military service appeared more frequently. The *Afro-American*'s war correspondent, Ralph Matthews, asserted: "Although few colored soldiers are seen in the immediate vicinity of the Advance Headquarters of the 24th Infantry Division, integration is making phenomenal progress on the higher levels. Unprecedented in the annuals of the United States Army was the appointment of Captain Ordie P. Taylor. Taylor is to the Headquarters Command what the boss canvas-man is to a circus, in that it is his responsibility to select a proper site for the command post and supervise the location, erection and distribution of all the components of the organization."[15]

AFRICAN AMERICAN HEROISM IN KOREA WAR

When the U.S. military engaged North Korean troops in the summer of 1950, black newspapers closely followed the performance of African American military units. In particular, the famous 24th Infantry received national attention. Less than a month after arriving in South Korea and having experiencing numerous setbacks, the 24th Infantry had achieved one of America's first major victories against communist forces. Black newspapers throughout the United States printed large, bold, front-page headlines with detailed coverage of the battle. "COLORED TROOPS WIN FIRST VICTORY FOR U.S. IN KOREA," one newspaper boasted. The *Afro-American* wrote, "Tan Yanks Push Back 'Reds' in Furious Battle." "The 24th Infantry Regiment, which moved into South Korea as a part of the 25th 'Tropic Lightning' Division to reinforce the battered 24th Division, last Friday scored the most sizable victory that American Ground Forces have yet achieved in the fighting in Korea."[16]

Much like throughout American history, black military units in Korea proved their valor and military competence by receiving numerous awards and citations. African American newspapers regularly reported on the outcome of battles that involved African American units. The 503rd Field Artillery Battalion, stationed in South Korea, caught the attention of L. Alex Wilson, the *Chicago Defender* war correspondent, when it was commended for exemplary battle performance: "Big gunners—officially known as artillerymen—who can get off three rounds [shots] a minute from 155 mm howitzers, sticking fear in the heart of the enemy by effectively placing the exploding death, rate tops in honors. The 503rd Field Artillery Battalion is in line for these honors because it is one of the fastest and most deadly accurate big gun outfits in the Second Division."[17]

In addition to honoring the 503rd collectively, the newspaper printed the names and addresses of black officers as well as enlisted men in C Battery. On the same day, the *Afro-American* printed a 3x5-inch photograph, titled "Integration in Korea," of two marines, one white and the other black. In the caption, the white marine exclaims, "Hell, when a guy is good enough to get in the marines he is good enough to be accepted anywhere. Making a fuss about integration is a lot of hooey." The black marine responds, "we need every man we can get in the present crisis and it's no time to fool around about where he is going to serve."[18]

MILITARY SERVICE—A MODEL OF SOCIAL PROGRESS

Although in many cases the armed forces fell short of providing equal opportunity to its black personnel, during the 1950s many black leaders felt that military service held great promise. Men and women in uniform were leading the way in the total integration of American society. Louis Lautier of the *Afro-American* wrote, "The most important single factor affecting integration of colored soldiers in the Army was that they had to carry the burden of race prejudice in addition to all of the other problems faced by white soldiers. If race segregation is completely abolished at military installations, action will have to be taken to end jim-crow practices in civilian communities."[19] Lautier's contention was in part correct. Historian, Lee Nichols argues:

Men leaving service were taking back to civilian life at least some of their new experience. Part might "wear off" among men returning to rigidly segregated communities; some might have acquired or increased a dislike of Negroes in service and retained this attitude afterward; but from all available evidence the great majority of men in integrated units took home a fresh slant on race free from the basic concept of segregation that once dominated the American scene. This type of experience was certain to influence not only the men themselves but also their families, friends and casual acquaintances.[20]

Through increased personal contact among white and black soldiers, many African Americans hoped that integration would naturally spill over to other institutions, such as education, religion, housing, and public accommodations.

MILITARY SERVICE OFFERS ENHANCED OPPORTUNITIES

Career and educational opportunities in the U.S. armed forces and the ability to secure federal jobs upon separation from the military were attractive to men and women in the black community. According to John Modell and Timothy Haggerty, "unlike whites, black veterans attained more postwar education than nonveterans and held higher-status jobs, having emerged from their service with relatively enhanced or intact ambitions for the near-term future."[21] Women as well as men were encouraged to pursue the higher wages and educational opportunities that military service offered. Professors of military science at HBCUs actively recruited women for Officer Candidate School (OCS) upon graduation since they were not eligible to participate in ROTC. At Tuskegee Institute, where the famed Tuskegee Airmen trained during World War II, Lieutenant Colonel Campbell, professor of air science, highlighted the monetary advantages and employment benefits of pursuing a career in the Women in the Air Force service branch (WAF) as a lieutenant. "A WAF Second Lieutenant living off base receives $338.58 per month plus medical and dental care, liberal retirement benefits and $10,000 life insurance policy. Automatic salary increases are given with each two years of service, and an automatic promotion to First Lieutenant at the end of 18 months active duty."[22] An annual salary of approximately $4,000 in addition to health care benefits and life insurance were very attractive inducements for a black man or woman during a period when the average African American male earned around $2,000 yearly.

The *Pittsburgh Courier* applauded two female soldiers for successfully completing their training in the Women's Army Corp (WAC): "Howard University graduate, First Lieutenant Dorothy R. Parks of Philadelphia is receiving a certificate of achievement from Lieutenant Colonel Ruby E. Herman, Commanding Officer of the WAC Training Center at Fort Lee, Virginia. The certificate commended her for superior work. Honored at the same parade was Captain Eleanor B. Wilson of El Monte, California. Lieutenant Parks is the daughter of Mrs. Thelma Peterson of Philadelphia."[23]

In 1953, when Captain Mary W. Wilborne received a Bronze Star for outstanding service in Korea, the *Pittsburgh Courier* ran a half-page story congratulating her and highlighting her military career. In large, bold print the headline stated, "Nurse Earns Bronze Star!" The citation read, "Capt. Mary W. Wilborne, ANC, of Halifax, Va., has returned from duty in Korea with double honors—winning a Bronze Star Medal for her own outstanding service, and contributing to the record that earned a citation for the Eleventh Evacuation Hospital where she served."[24]

AFRICAN AMERICAN FEMALE SEXUALITY OVERSHADOWS MILITARY ACHIEVEMENTS

Although African American newspapers celebrated the achievements of black women in the military, women in uniform only occasionally appeared in weekly issues. By contrast, black females appeared regularly throughout major newspapers in photographs that revered the sexy figure and bustline of bathing suit contestants and campus queens. Not only did these pictures appear in the society column, but on the front page and in the sports section as well. The *Pittsburgh Courier* featured a cartoon strip of a little sister/big sister feature called *Patty-Jo 'n' Ginger*. The little girl was a politically aware gifted youngster and the young woman a sexy pin-up who was almost always clad in eye-catching, form-fitting shorts or dresses with a visible bustline or cleavage.[25] While the black community supported females in the military in nontraditional roles, female soldiers were overshadowed in newspapers by the sexual attributes and feminine appearance of women in traditional gender roles. Maureen Honey explains, "An improved image of black women emerged in mainstream popular culture, one that helped move aside the stock loyal maid so entrenched before the war. The erotic pinup that trivialized white women's representation in popular culture was in black magazines and newspapers connected to this new glamorous image of African American entertainers, who redefined black womanhood to include sexiness, romance, beauty, courage, and passion."[26]

Shortly after World War II, traditional gender roles became incorporated into Cold War ideology. In *Homeward Bound*, Elaine Tyler May declares: "The ideological connections among early marriage, sexual containment, and traditional gender roles merged in the context of the cold war. Experts called upon women to embrace domesticity in the service the nation, in the same spirit that they had come to the country's aid by taking wartime jobs. To meet the challenge of this postwar era, women were to marshal their energies into a 'New Family Type for the Space Age.'"[27]

Cynthia Enloe believes that this gendered process was essential to military manpower acquisition. "Military forces past and present have not been able to get, keep and reproduce the sorts of soldiers they imagine they need without drawing on ideological beliefs concerning the different and stratified roles of women and men. Without assurance that women will play their 'proper' roles, the military cannot provide men with incentive to enlist and re-enlist."[28]

African American female soldiers during the 1950s paved the way for subsequent generations of female recruits. Although they received a small portion of the attention black males received, their accomplishments were just as substantial. While black newspapers chose to devote limited attention to black women in the military, they could hardly overlook the importance of traditional gender roles and the popularity of the African American female sex symbol.

CAMPUS BEAUTIES COVET ROTC HONOR

At Southern University, the student newspaper placed the same emphasis on the beauty and physical attributes of female students as the dominate African American press. Many of the most popular co-eds on campus were young ladies who were chosen to represent various student organizations and clubs associated with the ROTC, such as the Pershing Rifles and the

Scabbard and Blade. Miss ROTC was an honor that was second only to Miss Southern University. Young ladies chosen as Miss ROTC reigned at the annual ROTC Ball, considered the most popular social event of the year. University administrators, faculty, staff, and students attended the gala each spring and were treated to an evening of ballroom dancing in the most elegant surroundings. In addition, the queen of the ROTC Ball enjoyed the honor of being featured in a front-page article of the *Southern University Digest* that included a detailed biography and a large picture. In 1954, Geraldine Jones was described as an "attractive and popular young lady who is known for her brilliant smiles."[29] Jones competed against sixteen other women for the coveted title.

MILITARY RACISM IS CRITICIZED IN BLACK COMMUNITY

Although black newspapers throughout the United States published articles that celebrated military integration, racism and discrimination in the armed forces were still emphasized and condemned. In some cases the success of integration at one military installation served to underscore needed progress at another. The *Chicago Defender* maintained: "Abuses and rank discrimination against a special mess unit at West Point have been highlighted by opposite conditions at a nearby air base, where complete integration has taken place. It was charged that the requests of Negro GIs to be sent to school to learn a trade have been refused on the grounds that their services could not be used by the unit upon completion of the courses."[30]

Occasionally, African American soldiers wrote to black newspapers and voiced their contempt for the racist behavior of fellow white soldiers. In the *Pittsburgh Courier*'s "What the People Think" column, a soldier wrote, "Negro inductees are being made the victims of rank discrimination. This began on the date of our arrival here, January 21st. On that date they began forming companies. Even then I could see tears of disgust forming in the eyes of some of the fellows."[31] Black leaders and civil rights organizations were so alarmed at the number of military arrests and courts-martial that the National Association for the Advancement of Colored People (NAACP) Special Counsel, Thurgood Marshall, made official inquires with the Eisenhower administration. Marshall noted that the number of courts-martial of white soldiers had not increased during the war and "the NAACP is ready to defend, with all of its resources, any of these [black] service men upon determination that they are victims of racial discrimination."[32] Incidents like the cases of Captain Silas Jenkins and Lieutenant Wilbur Dixon of Elmendorf Air Base in Anchorage, Alaska, were fairly common. Both officers were recommended for discharge from the Air Force when they objected to discriminatory treatment by the air base group commander, Lieutenant Colonel Prentiss C. Jones. Captain Jenkins claimed that after a junior officer was chosen over him to take command while the commanding officer was on leave, he made an official complaint to Lieutenant Colonel Prentiss and was charged with inefficiency of duty. Lieutenant Dixon had an altercation with a white enlisted airman in the mess hall. After filing a complaint with his commanding officer, he was assigned to the bachelor officers quarters for nine weeks.[33]

Although articles about discrimination were common in black newspapers, few letters were printed that voiced the emotions of men and women in their own words. As the racial policy of the armed forces began to change, the U.S. Army was described as the "New Army" in many publications. In response, an offended black soldier proclaimed: "I have been reading reports of the Chicago Daily newspapers about the Army, the new Army, they call it. Maybe your newspaper has been letting the people know about conditions—no food in Negro mess halls, white officers call us insulting names restricting Negroes from areas because it is classified as 'white areas.' What kind of a war are we supposed to be training to fight?"[34]

Many stories relating to social injustice occupied the front page or appeared in headlines. Despite this fact, very few editorials or features in major newspapers appeared that were intended to specifically discourage African American men and women from entering the armed forces. In fact, articles, weekly features, and photographs overwhelmingly supported the presence of blacks in the military.

AFRICAN AMERICAN ANTIWAR LEADERS

The contradiction between America's democratic principles and systematic oppression of African Americans prompted many black antiwar advocates to reject America's call to arms and to attempt to discourage others as well. Various organizations and leaders, such as the Socialist Workers Party, the

Civil Rights Congress, Paul Robeson, W.E.B. Du Bois, C.L.R. James, and William Patterson voiced their opposition to African Americans fighting in the Korean War. According to Gerald Horne: "When the war came, U.S. rulers would have to 'gag . . . peace-lovers' and squash civil liberties in order to prosecute it. Thus, [the] Civil Rights Congress (CRC) had no choice but to fight the warmongers with all the resources they could muster. Weeks later, William Patterson was chairing an eighteen-thousand-strong rally in Madison Square Garden that resolutely denounced the U.S. intervention in Korea. Soon after that were headlines throughout the Afro-American press claiming 'The war with Korea is not the Negro's war.'"[35]

During a press conference in New Orleans, Louisiana, Patterson further remarked, "I am preparing a white paper on the atrocities committed against Negroes in the United States which I shall submit to the United Nations, and I will avail myself of any Government willing to bring these charges to the floor."[36] Concerning racial integration in the armed forces, Patterson retorted, "Certainly the United States will abolish Jim Crowism in the Army because it wants the use of Negroes in the fight to reduce other colored people to the same status as Negroes."[37] William Patterson, like other black critics, held unfavorable views of U.S. State Department advisor Ralph Bunche, U.S. delegate to the United Nations Edith Sampson, and William Hastie, a U.S. court of appeals judge. Patterson believed that as federal appointees, these African Americans were careful not to criticize the federal government concerning social conditions of black Americans.[38]

While many African Americans justifiably choose not to support the war effort, more demonstrated their loyalty or were drawn to the social and economic benefits of military service. This was the view of most black newspapers. An *Ebony* magazine editorial responded to Paul Robeson's antiwar rhetoric:

> Periodically hysterical white folks have been sucked in to believing scare stories about the Negro's lack of loyalty to this land. In more recent years they took a fright when Paul Robeson sounded off with his 'Negroes-won't-fight Russia' propaganda. *Ebony* honestly feels that it is reflecting the heart-felt love of country of most Negroes when it speaks of the loyalty of the race to America. *Ebony* has said it before and says it again: The Negro in America is better off by far than most peoples in other countries around the earth.[39]

THE PERSHING RIFLES AT SOUTHERN UNIVERSITY

Because ROTC training was mandatory for all male students during their freshman and sophomore years at Southern University, ROTC organizations were popular and well supported. The Pershing Rifles was an organization that only accepted academically proficient cadets. These young men were almost always cadet officers that had previously demonstrated leadership skill and the ability to excel in a military environment. Though membership in the Pershing Rifles was open to all ROTC cadets, the organization was more reflective of a fraternity than a social club. Potential pledgees were required to attend a smoker, a social event where members of the organization could socialize with perspective members to determine whether a formal invitation to join would be extended. The Pershing Rifles were so well received on the Southern University campus that honorary members included Dr. Felton G. Clark, president of Southern University, Lieutenant Colonel John R. Reaves, professor of military science and tactics, Captain David D. Powell, officer-in-charge of the Pershing Rifles, Sergeant First Class Harold J. Turner, noncommissioned officer-in-charge of the Pershing Rifles, and Cadet Colonel Cleophus C. Lewis, brigade commander of the ROTC unit. During the pledge program the Marching Cavalettes were officially recognized as the sister organization to the Pershing Rifles.[40]

Less than twenty-four months after receiving their charter, the Pershing Rifles appeared at festivals, parades, and public celebrations. In April 1959, the unit appeared with the ROTC band at the Breaux Bridge Centennial celebration in Breaux Bridge, Louisiana. A few weeks later, the Pershing Rifles traveled to New Orleans to appear at the annual national Pershing Rifles meet with other units representing Tulane University, Louisiana State University, Centenary College, Loyola University, Spring Hill College, and Florida State University.[41]

SOUTHERN UNIVERSITY OFFICIALS VISIT ROTC SUMMER CAMP

In 1959, ROTC seniors traveled to Fort Hood, Texas, to participate in the annual summer camp, where cadets are exposed to simulated battle situations and training in military tactics. According to the *Southern University Digest*, "An overall achievement record of the cadets at summer camp of 1958 excelled all previous records. This was accomplished as several of the cadets emerged in the top third of their companies and their respective platoons."[42] During camp activities SU cadets were greeted by Martin L. Harvey, Southern's dean of students. Southern University administrators such as President Clark and other campus leaders frequently made appearances during the camps to encourage and boost the morale of the SU cadets.[43]

AFRICAN AMERICAN "FIRSTS" ARE CELEBRATED

During the 1950s, social and racial progress was also celebrated in the black community. Newspapers highlighted the achievements of African Americans in the armed forces in addition to black attorneys who passed the bar, black police officers who were promoted or received awards, and black men and women who graduated from predominately white universities. Sport greats such as Jackie Robinson, Joe Louis, and Sugar Ray Robinson captured the attention and admiration of the black community for their accomplishments on the baseball diamond and in the boxing ring. Lena Horne, Eartha Kitt, Eddie Anderson, and Nat King Cole were entertainers who routinely appeared in practically every issue of black newspapers. Many of these stories represented African American "firsts" or recognized individual achievements in the black community as well as the nation. In the same fashion, African American newspapers intently watched these historic events unfold and celebrated the collective and personal achievements of black military personnel.

The movement to integrate the military was spurred on by African American newspapers and publishers such as John H. Sengstacke of the *Chicago Defender* and Claude Barnett, director of the Associated Negro Press. Black leaders who worked closely with the Truman administration to provide African Americans equal opportunity in the armed forces formed a Cold War consensus that worked to demonstrate African American patriotism and loyalty. As a trade-off, the black press supported Truman's political and Cold War agenda and the president made civil rights a national priority. To be sure, while social advances were made by black soldiers during the Korean War, Brenda Plummer contends, "Afro-American disaffection mirrored, and amplified, a general public distaste for Korea. More southern blacks than whites saw Korea as a civil conflict that did not involve Americans. They felt that U.S. participation was a mistake. In spite of the fickleness of public opinion, this view persisted from January 1951 to May 1953, at the close of the hostilities."[44]

MILITARY INTEGRATION INFLUENCES EMPLOYMENT OPPORTUNITIES

African American newspaper editors and publishers were in many cases aware of discontent about the war in the black community and therefore decided to focus on social and economic benefits of military service, which accounted for a large percentage of newspaper stories, rather than discussing the politics of American foreign policy. By 1954 the black and white press reported that the U.S. military led the nation in race relations. In fact, military integration was leading to the desegregation of other federally controlled agencies. In the summer of 1953, President Dwight Eisenhower reported that his "administration is pursuing its policy of eliminating racial segregation in veterans hospitals, naval shipyards and federally-supported schools on Army posts." In a letter to Congressman Adam Clayton Powell, the president remarked, "we have not taken and shall not take a single backward step. There must be no second class citizens in this country."[45] Similarly, in Washington, D.C., public restaurants were mandated to end racial segregation by order of the U.S. Supreme Court. In a vote of 8 to 0, the high court upheld an 1873 law that decreed that any well-behaved person be served in restaurants or other accommodations in the District of Columbia.[46] For African Americans, the armed forces held the promise of a better lifestyle and opportunities than the average black man could receive in civilian society, especially in the South. In *Time* magazine an African American GI emphasized, "A Negro begins to see the fellows getting along in the Army and begins to say to himself, it would be so goddam nice if it could be like that all over."[47]

MILITARY SERVICE AS CIVIL RIGHTS ACTIVISM

Military service during World War II and racial integration in the armed forces had a direct impact on African American attitudes toward military service as well as heightened expectations for social progress in general society. Black men and women returned from World War II with more than a sense of entitlement to the benefits of first-class citizenship. In many cases they held a new determination to lead their communities in the quest for civil and equal rights. An African American Army corporal returning from the war in 1945 best described how many black veterans felt: "I spent four years in the army to free a bunch of Frenchmen and Dutchmen, and I'm hanged if I'm going to let the Alabama version of the German kick me around when I get back home. No sirreee-bob! I went into the army a nigger; I'm comin out a *man*."[48] Historian Glen H. Elders Jr. confirms the corporal's sentiment when he argues, "Combat veterans emerged from the war with a lessened sense of helplessness, and with an enhanced sense of assertiveness and resilience. After the war, many of these combat veterans were more capable, more active, and more in control of their own lives."[49] The long-standing connection between military training and service and black manhood that can be traced from the eighteenth century continued to resonate among African Americans in the 1950s as they served the nation in the armed forces and returned to civilian society eager to claim citizenship rights and seek new opportunities.

Very similar to the Reconstruction era and the decade after World War I, when black America's most militant and tenacious African American leaders were former soldiers and officers who challenged white supremacy and terrorism in the South, thousands of black veterans of World War II and the Korean War led local and state civil rights struggles throughout the South and in many cases became staunch supporters of armed resistance and self-defense activism.[50] For many of these men and women, they returned home to fight another war. A war for democracy in a familiar place called home. This was reminiscent of French veterans of the American Revolution who returned home to lead their compatriots in the revolution to form a new government in France. African American veterans were hyper-sensitive to political conditions and were eager to correct social inequality in the South.[51] These men resisted racism and discrimination in the hope of claiming self-respect, to maintain their dignity, and to assert the manly qualities of courage, strength, and fortitude. As former soldiers, they had already experienced a basic level of equality with white men in the military. This condition empowered them and created a source of pride and confidence that many white southerners found threatening.[52] For instance, World War II veteran Amize Moore, upon returning to Mississippi, led voter registration drives. In South Carolina, William Saunders, a Korean War veteran, became a well-known community activist and one of the chief organizers in the 1969 hospital strike in Charleston, South Carolina. Georgia native Hosea Williams served in Patton's Third Army during World War II, and in 1965 he was appointed by the Southern Christian Leadership Conference (SCLC) to organize the now famous Selma to Montgomery March in Alabama.[53] World War II veteran Walter Greene returned to Detroit, Michigan, filled with an energy and passion to fight for social equality after fighting for his life in the Pacific and against racism and discrimination within his unit. Greene explained why black soldiers were often at the forefront of the civil rights struggle: "The Negro soldier is going to be militant because he is looking for something—he expects something better than the status quo when he gets home or the public will have a severe problem on its hands."[54] Two of the more noteworthy local civil rights leaders were former marine Robert F. Williams from Monroe County, North Carolina, and Earnest "Chilly Willy" Thomas from Bogalusa, Louisiana, who served in the Air Force as a radio operator during the Korean War.

Robert F. Williams not only became the leader of the local NAACP branch in Monroe County, he encouraged other military veterans to become active members and resist pressure from the white community. It was not long before Williams began to initiate his own brand of leadership that many liberal whites and African Americans in Monroe County thought dangerous and antagonistic. Williams and many of the war veterans began to arm themselves and openly confront Ku Klux Klan members who routinely terrorized the black community by means of intimidation and assault. In one such case in late 1957, after an African American physician and his family received death threats, Williams and his fellow war veterans organized the community into listening posts to alert them when a heavily armed Klan motorcade was approaching. In preparation the men dug foxholes, stacked sandbags, and met the onslaught with automatic weapons, shotguns, and German-made rifles. Once the hooded terrorists began to fire their weapons, they encountered a steady barrage of bullets from several vantage points. From that day on in Monroe County, North Carolina, the Ku Klux Klan was afraid to enter black neighborhoods for fear of reprisals.[55]

In Bogalusa, Louisiana, the local police force was composed of white officers and a small contingent of African Americans. The black policemen were able to curtail incidents of white police brutality in addition to discouraging Ku Klux Klan caravans from committing terroristic acts in the black community. In 1964 the police chief decided to fire all of the black policemen at the request of local white community leaders. In response, Earnest Thomas, with the aid of other black war veterans, established an armed self-defense organization called the Deacons for Defense and Justice. According to Lance Hill, "the name reflected the group's desire to identify with traditionally respected symbols of authority, peace, and moral order in the black community. The Deacons were attempting to wed two contradictory symbols: Christian pacifism and violence. They hoped to identify with Christianity while defying its pacifist teachings."[56] By 1965, the Deacons for Defense and Justice had become so popular that chapters were started in Texas and Arkansas and plans were implemented to organize additional ones in Florida, Georgia, and North Carolina. The Deacons for Defense and Justice became a major deterrent to white terrorism in the South and Klan activity in the black community. Chapters also provided security and protection for local civil rights leaders and marchers. During the Meredith March Against Fear in Mississippi in 1966 the Deacons gained national attention.[57]

THE BATON ROUGE BUS BOYCOTT

While Southern University enjoyed the honor of promoting nationally recognized military and Cold War programs, many faculty and students began to concentrate on local civil rights causes. Students at Southern were encouraged to become more involved by several black and white faculty. In particular, it was a way for many of the white faculty members from the North to bond with students while voicing their contempt for segregation laws.[58] In the final weeks of the Korean War, in June 1953, former World War II veterans and local civil rights leaders in Baton Rouge organized and led the Baton Rouge bus boycott that became the model for other black leaders across the South to emulate.

The city of Baton Rouge is located roughly eighty miles northwest of New Orleans, directly adjacent to the Mississippi River, and serves as Louisiana's capital. During the early twentieth century it became a focal point for a rapidly growing business community and for industrial corporations such as Standard Oil, Solvay Process, Consolidated Chemicals, and Ethyl Corporation. As many of the chemical and manufacturing plants expanded during the 1940s to meet the growing demand of wartime production, so did the general population seeking employment opportunities and better living conditions. "In 1930, approximately 68,000 people lived in the East Baton Rouge Parish vicinity [Louisiana is organized into parishes, not counties]. By 1940, the number increased to 88,500, and five years later it topped 107,000. A decade after that the parish boasted more than 158,000 residents. Throughout this period of expansion, African Americans made up approximately 35 percent of the population."[59]

Jim Crow laws necessitated the development of a thriving, cohesive black community that witnessed dozens of black-owned businesses—restaurants, barber shops, drugstores, beauty parlors, funeral homes, medical practices, service stations, churches, and a hotel. Scotlandville, Louisiana, where numerous black businesses operated, served as a central point of the black community. Many African American entrepreneurs and church pastors understandably became some of the community's most vocal black leaders on the subject of racism and discrimination because their livelihoods were not dependent on white patronage or support. As second-class citizens in a staunchly segregated society, African Americans were constantly reminded of their inferior position in society.[60]

The boycott was initiated by a bus driver walkout in response to a new city council ordinance that provided that "Negroes seat from the rear and white passengers from the front" and that "bus drivers can request members of either race to move forward or backwards in the bus to prevent having aisle standees and empty seats."[61] The white bus drivers' union wanted to revert back to the old system that reserved ten seats in the front for white customers and ten seats in the back for African Americans. All seats in between those twenty seats were open on a first-come-first-serve basis.

At the beginning of the strike, the city council reminded the Baton Rouge Bus Company (BRBC) and bus drivers' union that in 1949, at the insistence of the bus company, the city council had passed an ordinance immediately removing from operation over sixty African American independent buses and giving exclusive rights of operation to the BRBC if the company agreed to "provide fair and adequate transportation to all segments of the population." This exclusive franchise also came with a wage increase for the bus drivers that was mitigated by the increase in business. The city council charged that for many prior months "because of the preexisting seating arrangements, the buses were operating only partially loaded buses on three main bus lines and at the same time passing up numerous negro passengers."[62]

In an effort to solicit public sympathy and support, scores of bus drivers' wives and children marched to the parish courthouse to apply pressure on city council members to rescind their vote. The women stated that "they and their children were suffering because of the strike and urged the Council to overturn the seating ordinance which played a central role in the work stoppage."[63] On the next day, the fifth day of the strike, the Louisiana state attorney general reported that the new seating ordinance was in direct conflict with state segregation laws requiring separation of the races. At the close of business, the strike was to end and the old seating system was to be renewed. In response, Raymond Scott, secretary of the United Defense League, urged African Americans not to ride city buses until a new system could be agreed upon by all parties. Scott added that transportation would be provided to all former bus riders, free of charge.[64] Later that evening, Raymond Scott and Reverend T. J. Jemison, the president of the United Defense League, held a mass meeting at Hebron Baptist Church with a couple hundred African American organizers and supporters in attendance. When Jemison was asked whether the black community was boycotting the bus company, knowing that Louisiana state law prohibited boycotts, Jemison remarked, "It's illegal to boycott, we're just not riding."[65]

The Baton Rouge bus boycott enjoyed the full support of the black community. In addition to well-attended mass meetings, the participation of 150 cars and drivers, and the cooperation of black bus riders, African American gas station owners sold fuel to car pool drivers at cost. It didn't take long for the Baton Rouge Bus Company to feel the negative impact of the boycott. The company called the African American effort 100 percent effective. A bus company spokesman reported that although the company had not fired any drivers as a result of the lack of customers, the number of bus lines was decreased in order to reduce company expenses.[66] In Baton Rouge, nearly 80 percent of the bus riders were African American.

The black community's desire to challenge segregation laws pertaining to public transportation not only had political ramifications. The boycott was designed to negatively impact the bus company. The bus line was losing $1,600 per day.

Within seventy-two hours of the first mass meeting, the United Defense League had collected over $1,500 in contributions to defray fuel costs and maintain the fleet of cars associated with the boycott. In addition, at a subsequent mass meeting held at McKinley High School the following evening with over one thousand attendees, organizers agreed that if the city council did not alter the bus seating policy, they would ask for a separate bus franchise that would service the black community exclusively. During the mass meeting, Jemison exclaimed, "Negroes are not going to pay 15 cents to ride buses and stand-up." He outlined two possible solutions to the problem:

1. If the Baton Rouge Bus Company bus drivers don't want to drive on buses with predominately Negro passengers, then the League will be pleased to name Negro bus drivers.
2. If the company doesn't want Negro bus drivers, we will ask the City Council for a Negro bus franchise.

Jemison further electrified the audience and sent a clear message to the bus company, drivers, and city council when he retorted, "This is not the fight of an individual or a group of individuals, but this is the onward march of people who desire to be totally free. We will not retreat one inch. We have sounded forth the trumpet and we shall not sound retreat."[67] African American bus riders were strongly encouraged not to ride the city buses under any circumstances. A police officer reported seeing a black man reluctantly enter a bus, but before he could take a few steps a car load of African Americans passed by jeering and hooting at the man, at which point he immediately exited the bus.

On the third day of the protest the United Defense League raised over $4,000. The *love offering*, as Reverend Jemison put it, was growing larger, and the number of black attendees to the community meetings was also. Over four thousand individuals participated in a meeting held at Capitol High School on June 22, and there, Reverend Jemison told the audience, "we have $260,000 waiting on the side for a franchise if they don't do what good people ought to do, and Christian people should do."[68] Reverend T. J. Jemison was not your ordinary small town black preacher. He was pastor to one of Louisiana's largest black Baptist congregations, with the state's most influential African Americans as members. In fact, Southern University president Felton G. Clark was a member of Jemison's church. Moreover, Jemison was the son of one of the most prominent African American pastors in the United States. His father was Dr. D. V. Jemison of Selma, Alabama. Dr. Jemison was the president of the National Baptist Convention, with over 4.5 million members and $10 million in real estate property.[69] Reverend Jemison was not making idle threats concerning his ability to raise the capital to purchase a franchise. On the contrary, he was one of the few black men in Louisiana who could acquire large amounts of money without the permission or support of white politicians. Before the meeting at Capitol High School concluded, Jemison remarked, "When this is over, we're not going to stop. We're going to vote. You're going to vote, you're going to register and if you can't read or write, we'll teach you."[70]

On June 24, the *Morning Advocate* newspaper reported that a compromise proposal would be discussed during a city council meeting that evening. City council members, bus company officials, bus drivers, and United Defense League leaders were urged to attend the meeting. The meeting was also open to the public and many officials expected the possibility of violence. In response, United Defense League officials encouraged African Americans to not attend the meeting en masse. Reverend Jemison and Raymond Scott did not want anything to happen that could jeopardize their position to broker the best possible solution.[71] The new city ordinance amended the original law by "reserving the two side seats up front for whites and the long rear seat for Negroes, with the rest on a first come basis. The old law had no reserved seats for whites or Negroes, which, the attorney general said, was contrary to state segregation laws." Even though the new city ordinance did mandate complete integration on city buses, it did allow African Americans the right to seat wherever they pleased on the bus with the exception of the two front-row seats. The chairman of the United Defense League, T. Roosevelt Smith, in response remarked, "We're law abiding citizens and can understand the council's position. That doesn't mean we think this new proposal is necessarily right. We're willing to go along with it however until we can prove our point."[72] Although the United Defense League suggested that the National Association for the Advancement of Colored People (NAACP) planned to file a lawsuit challenging state public transportation segregation laws in the near future, the organization claimed victory. In a letter addressed to the city council the UDL explained, "we have had one objective and only one . . . that every passenger who boards a bus and pays the fare be permitted to occupy a seat if one is available, and provided part of that seat is not occupied by a person of another race."[73]

After the city council voted to implement the new bus seating ordinance, Reverend Jemison addressed over seven thousand African Americans at a mass gathering at Memorial Stadium the following evening. Jemison told the enthusiastic crowd that although the seven-day bus boycott was officially over, he understood if individuals in the community decided not to ride the buses. It was clear by the crowd's shouts of "Stay off, stay off" that many individuals had chosen to maintain the protest on a personal basis. According to Reverend Jemison, the Baton Rouge bus boycott was a sign of things to come for African Americans and Baton Rouge at large. Jemison proclaimed, "Little by little, round by round, we are going to make Baton Rouge the Utopia of the South. You cannot change traditions and customs overnight; it takes patience, prayer and downright, rock-bottom common sense. Justice is on our side . . . and brother, it's on the way."[74] Indicative of Cold War politics of the period, Reverend Jemison also used the opportunity to deny rumors that he or his father were communists or had ties to communists. The following day, though African Americans began to reappear at bus stops across the city, many individuals were more than reluctant to ride buses that were filled with white passengers. A bus driver told a local reporter, "Negroes gather at the bus stops, but stand back a ways to inspect the situation carefully." Another driver "pulled up to a bus stop and opened his door, hoping they would get on. An old man ventured out, peered up and down the bus intently, spied a Negro in the back seat and decided to hop on. The rest followed him."[75]

The success of the Baton Rouge bus boycott was made possible for at least two reasons. First, Reverend Jemison and the United Defense League were well organized, received the cooperation and support of the black community, and were able to raise thousands of dollars fairly easily. Aldon Morris believes that the protest demonstration could have lasted much longer if necessary. Second, and probably most important, the bus drivers received very little support from the Baton Rouge Bus Company, local white politicians, and business leaders. Therefore, the effort of the bus drivers was not sustainable.[76] Nevertheless, the Baton Rouge bus boycott reflected significant progress in the struggle for social equality and equal rights in the postwar period. In a few short years, black leaders throughout the South would use those same tactics to challenge segregation laws in their local communities.

STUDENT ACTIVIST ARE ENCOURAGED BY BOYCOTT SUCCESS

While there is no evidence to indicate that Southern University employees or students held leadership roles during the protest, it is believed that a large number of black bus riders attended or were employed at the university during the bus boycott and that not a single one rode the bus to the university during the demonstration.[77] In fact, it can be argued that the Baton Rouge bus boycott raised the political consciousness of students at Southern University and encouraged them to take on a more active role in the civil rights movement from that moment forward. According to Reverend T. J. Jemison, "in the period between 1953 and 1960, African Americans in Baton Rouge made some attempts to desegregate eating establishments in the downtown areas, and these efforts were often led by students from Southern University. Students who trained at his church would arrive at a lunch counter individually or in small groups in the afternoon after the lunch time rush and sit in the 'whites only' area and try to get served. In some instances after the police had been alerted, the students were served and then were asked to leave."[78] So, even before the sit-in demonstrations of the early 1960s in the South, African American students at Southern University and other institutions, such as Alabama State College and Florida A&M College, assumed the role of civil rights activists in their local communities.

In 1954, the *Brown v. Board of Education* Supreme Court case overturned the *Plessy v. Ferguson* decision and made the doctrine of "separate but equal" unlawful. This prompted local civil rights leaders to actively challenge racial segregation laws throughout the South. Patterned after the Baton Rouge bus boycott, the Montgomery bus boycott of 1955 received national and international media attention. Shortly after that monumental civil rights victory,

Reverend T. J. Jemison invited Reverend Martin Luther King Jr. to speak at Mount Zion Baptist Church in Baton Rouge. In a standing-room-only venue, Southern University students and members of the black community listened to King exclaim, "we must continue to struggle against segregation and injustice," but then add, "we must do no violence. Right now, the colored peoples of the world are rising up against oppression. This new equality is nothing to be smug about, rather it should be prepared for by becoming better and better in every undertaking."[79]

By the late 1950s, as the American South became the national arena for civil rights struggles, black campus newspapers began to devote coverage to many local events. Though Southern University president F. G. Clark attempted to refocus student attention on educational pursuits, black college students were taking a deep interest in the world around them and effecting social change in their communities. In December 1955, a chapter of the NAACP Youth Council was formed at Southern University by twenty-six students with the support of the dean of students, Martin L. Harvey. Felton G. Clark was already a member of the organization, and he encouraged others to join as well.[80] By 1960 the NAACP Youth Council had already participated in several protest demonstrations in the Baton Rouge area. Not surprisingly, the first president of the chapter selected to lead the organization was ROTC cadet officer Donald Delandro. Delandro graduated from Southern University in 1956 and ultimately retired from the U.S. Army as a brigadier general.[81]

CONCLUSION

Even as America fought a war of ideas and political principles against communism, military integration and Cold War rhetoric encouraged African Americans to make greater social and political demands on American society. The postwar period reflected significant achievements in the struggle for equality in the federal justice system and U.S. armed forces that further motivated and empowered African Americans and students at black colleges and universities. As a result, many faculty members and students believed that military service represented the best opportunity for personal advancement as well as a vehicle for social change. All of these events impacted attitudes toward black ROTC programs such as Southern University's military program and had far-reaching influence on the future of black higher education. By the late 1950s, as the civil rights movement ushered in a new phase of youth-inspired activism, the African American quest for equal rights would become entangled with the war in Vietnam and place the virtues of military training and service in the heart of a political debate.

Dr. Felton G. Clark. He served as president of Southern University from 1938–1968. Courtesy of John B. Cade Library/Archives and Manuscripts Department/Southern University and A&M College.

Members of the State Police Unit and East Baton Rouge Parish sheriff's deputies in front of the Academic Building. Courtesy of John B. Cade Library/Archives and Manuscripts Department/Southern University and A&M College.

State Police disperse from gas as sheriff's deputies continue to move forward and prepare to launch tear gas. Courtesy of John B. Cade Library/Archives and Manuscripts Department/Southern University and A&M College.

Commencement exercise held outside on the campus of Southern University. Courtesy of John B. Cade Library/Archives and Manuscripts Department/ Southern University and A&M College.

First girls' drill team. The team made its first public performance at a homecoming football game in 1957. Courtesy of John B. Cade Library/Archives and Manuscripts Department/Southern University and A&M College.

Military cadets in uniform. Photographed just before commissioning. Courtesy of John B. Cade Library/Archives and Manuscripts Department/ Southern University and A&M College.

Matthew W. Trahan leaving class. United States Constabulary, Second Brigade and NCO Academy. Jensen Barracks, Munich, Germany.

Matthew W. Trahan and family. The family photo was taken *circa* 1950 in Frankfurt, Germany. In the photo are (*left to right*) SFC Matthew W. Trahan, Brenda J. Trahan, Theresa Alsandor-Petite, and Annie M. Alsandor-Trahan.

5

OUR UNIFORM HASN'T LOST ITS PRESTIGE WITH OUR PEOPLE

MILITARY TRAINING AND SERVICE ON THE BLUFF,

1960-1967

Support for African American service in the armed forces persisted in the 1960s despite the upheavals of civil rights protests, the Black Power movement, and disillusionment with the war in Vietnam. Between 1960 and 1967 the civil rights thrust incorporated innovative tactics and a wider support base that included young African Americans, white Americans, and sympathetic clergy throughout the nation. Much like during the 1950s, the armed forces played a major role in the civil rights movement in that national security and Cold War politics dictated the fair treatment of African American servicemen and citizens. Within the black community, military service continued to offer greater benefits and opportunities for advancement than most civilian jobs. As a result, military training and service remained a popular career choice on black college campuses throughout the South.

After 1965, however, many individuals in the black community began to question America's motives and presence in Vietnam and linked the struggle for African American civil rights and social equality with the Vietnamese fight for self-determination. Many black leaders and student activists openly criticized the federal government for perpetuating what they believed to be racial imperialism in the United States and throughout the world. Jim Crow laws in the South and the presence of U.S. armed forces in Vietnam were clear indications of white America's desire to exert its will upon people of color. The conflict in Vietnam not only divided civil rights organizations on issues concerning the war, but tended to place African American students in three camps: Those who supported the virtues of military training and service, individuals who became antiwar advocates, and, to a lesser degree, students that were against the war and black military training and service. As America became more entrenched in the war, black college campuses became the central point for political debate in the black community.

AFRICAN AMERICAN STUDENTS SPEAK OUT AGAINST THE WAR

On black college campuses such as Southern University, the antiwar movement was vastly different from the mass demonstrations and physical altercations at white colleges and universities. During this period, many faculty and students first denounced the U.S. presence in Vietnam and by the late 1960s moved to advocating the termination of compulsory ROTC programs, all without ever truly condemning those in ROTC uniform. In fact, antiwar supporters and individuals who believed in the merits of military training and service became engaged in a verbal standoff concerning America's escalation of the war in Vietnam and the virtues of military service. Antiwar and promilitary advocates were locked into a rhetorical battle debating such issues as "What Good Can Military Training Do You?" and "Is Military Training Necessary?" Moreover, African American administrators no longer possessed the influence they once enjoyed in prior decades and were challenged by many students and faculty who believed they represented obstacles to social progress and the struggle for civil rights. According to Donald Matthews and James Prothro, "as the Negro masses grew more militant and demanding, the established black leaders like college administrators were caught in a crossfire of conflicting demands. On the one hand, their position as leaders depended on their access to and acceptance by white community leaders and politicians. On the other hand, if the black leaders failed to reflect the growing militancy of their followers, they would lose their influence among the rank and file."[1] In addition, the generational divide between university officials and faculty and students became more acute during the period as the direction of the civil rights movement began to shift to embrace a militant style of activism that allowed little compromise on the part of youth. As international independence movements accelerated around the world in the late 1950s and early 1960s, young people viewed their personal plight as part of a worldwide struggle of colored nations to free themselves from the control and exploitation of totalitarian and imperialistic governments such as the United States.[2]

THE HISTORIC LINK BETWEEN MILITARY SERVICE AND THE CIVIL RIGHTS MOVEMENT

To truly understand the modern civil rights movement, one must appreciate the vital role of African American military veterans and the value of military service in the pursuit of equal citizenship and social justice. Many of black America's most courageous civil rights leaders were wartime veterans who organized and provided the leadership of formidable grassroots movements throughout the South in the post–World War II era. Christopher Parker asks us to "imagine the movement without Hosea Williams leading the 'Bloody Sunday' march over the Edmund Petus bridge between Selma and Montgomery, Alabama; without Aaron Henry's leadership of both the Mississippi Freedom Democratic Party and the NAACP of Mississippi; consider the Student Nonviolent Coordinating Committee without the leadership of James Forman; and how can we forget the bravery and selfless actions of James Meredith and other black military veterans?"[3] Though many students of the civil rights movement may be vaguely familiar with the exploits of the famous leaders previously mentioned, it is not well known that scores of student activists and leaders on black college campuses during the same period were ROTC cadets who felt it was their duty to spearhead local demonstrations, to protest, and to promote democratic rhetoric of self-determinism and autonomy to effect social change. That is why civil rights activism is important to understanding attitudes toward military service at Southern University and black colleges and universities in general.

In 1960, students at Southern University actively led protests for social and political change in Louisiana. Student leaders at Southern University organized sit-in demonstrations and marches demanding equal rights and justice. Following the efforts of four North Carolina Agricultural and Technical College students in Greensboro, North Carolina (including one in ROTC uniform), in February 1960 students at Southern decided to voice their dissatisfaction with racial inequality in Louisiana. The response of students and faculty at Southern was a well-coordinated effort that reflected the general reaction of African American youth at black colleges and universities throughout the South. Within six weeks of the initial demonstration at the Woolworth's store in Greensboro, student activists enrolled at Bennett College (Greensboro, North Carolina), Alabama State University (Montgomery, Alabama), Allen University (Columbia, South Carolina), Benedict College (Columbia, South Carolina), Fisk University (Nashville, Tennessee), Tennessee A&I State University (Nashville, Tennessee), Virginia State College (Petersburg, Virginia), Texas Southern University (Houston, Texas), and many other HBCUs started sit-down demonstrations in their respective communities.[4] In an act of solidarity, students at Tuskegee Institute (Tuskegee, Alabama) and Dillard University (New Orleans, Louisiana) held protests on their college campuses as well.[5] Weeks before the student protest at Southern, four hundred students at Tuskegee marched downtown to protest the deprivation of voting rights, to call for civil equality in general, and to express sympathy with other student demonstrations throughout the country.[6] While the president of Tuskegee, Dr. L. H. Foster, supported the students in principle, he attempted to discourage them from demonstrating in the city of Tuskegee.

STUDENT ACTIVIST IN BATON ROUGE
CHALLENGES JIM CROW

In late March, the movement in Baton Rouge began after the all-white State Board of Education issued a stern warning to all colleges and universities under its jurisdiction that disciplinary action would be taken if anyone engaged in student protests or actions that disgraced the institution. Joseph A. Davis, a member of the state board, also suggested that the statement "is in no way connected with the segregation issue or recent lunch counter demonstrations. The board had no specific instance or issue in mind when it drew up the statement."[7] According to Southern student leader Major Johns, "the sit-in movement had not yet spread to Baton Rouge but as one law student expressed it: When the Board spoke, it became a challenge to us and we could not ignore it."[8] As student activists at Southern contemplated how to respond to the state board's ultimatum, nearly fifteen hundred students from Hampton Institute initiated a mass demonstration at ten stores in Newport News, Virginia. Approximately four hundred white students from Harvard University, the Massachusetts Institute of Technology, Boston University, and Brandeis University staged similar demonstrations at twelve Woolworth stores in the city of Boston. National media outlets reported that parades, picketing, and rallies were organized by student leaders and sympathizers and had quickly spread throughout New England, the Midwest, and the far West.[9] In the meantime, a student committee met with Dr. Clark to inquire about the university's policy concerning similar behavior. Clark informed the students that the state board of education had mandated expulsion.[10] Despite this prior warning, seven well-dressed and well-behaved students entered the Kress drugstore in downtown Baton Rouge and respectfully asked for service at the lunch counter. A short time later, the students were arrested and escorted out of the drugstore.

Before the students were released on bond nearly six hours later, a mass rally was under way near the Southern University campus as thousands of students threatened to boycott classes if the arrested students were expelled.[11] Louisiana governor Earl K. Long characterized the students as foolish and recommended that they return to Africa if they were dissatisfied with American society. In condescending fashion he further remarked, "I don't think that colored people of this state have anything fundamentally to complain about. There is hardly a negro man over 65 in the state who fails to draw a public welfare old age payment." Governor Long affirmed his confidence in Dr. Clark's ability to lead Southern University and remarked that President Felton G. Clark "is a very reasonable, intelligent school man, I knew his father before him [the first Southern University president] and I know he would have thought these upstarts as foolish."[12]

The very next day, seven more students traveled from Scotlandville to downtown Baton Rouge and entered the Greyhound bus station and requested service at the lunch counter. They too were promptly arrested without incident and booked in the city-parish jail for disturbing the peace. When asked the purpose of the sit-in demonstration, a student spokesman answered, "Each of us at school knows we should have these things [equal rights] and we want them. We want some human dignity. We don't want to have to eat in any filthy place." Unidentified white supremacists hung a Southern University student in effigy at the Huey P. Long Field House at LSU and entered the black community of Southern Heights in Scotlandville in the early morning hours to burn a four-foot-high cross in the yard of a Southern employee, but students and supporters were undeterred by these acts of terrorism and intimidation.[13]

PRESIDENT CLARK IS THREATENED BY THE STATE BOARD OF EDUCATION

President Clark was quickly summoned to the governor's office after the second group of students was arrested. The governor and the state superintendent of education, Shelby Jackson, informed Clark that the future of Southern University was in jeopardy if a resolution was not reached soon.[14] E. C. Harrison, vice president of academic affairs, attended the meeting with Clark. Harrison vividly remembers that Clark left the meeting a torn man and in tears. Harrison reports that Clark was explicitly told that he would be fired if he did not discipline the student demonstrators.[15] For Clark, this dilemma represented the worst possible scenario for him. As Southern University's second president and executive leader since 1938, he had devoted nearly his entire life to the progress and success of the institution and its students. Clark believed that the ability to receive a higher education was not only a privilege for African Americans, but a necessity for personal and collective social progress. For the good of African Americans in the state of Louisiana and millions more throughout the nation, he determined that Southern University *must* remain open. Huel D. Perkins believes that very few individuals truly understand how difficult a decision this was for Clark. The decision went far beyond the fact that Clark could leave Baton Rouge as a civil rights hero and easily secure employment in another state. Perkins explains that:

> Felton G. Clark was born to be president of Southern University. He grew up on the campus of Southern University and nearly spent his entire life there. His father was the first president at the present site of Scott's Bluff. Felton's blood was mixed up with Southern University. It was hard for him to distance himself from Southern or make decisions to do that. Well, I knew him very well. I think in the end he took the position that would keep the institution alive and keep it solvent and supported. I expect that he felt that he would defy the board if he would have made any other decision other than expel the students and that would have been detrimental to Southern University

and its financial support. His fear was that Southern University would be irreparably damaged if he did not do what the governor and members of the board wanted him to do.[16]

Felton G. Clark had earned a well-deserved reputation as an international educator and African American intellectual during the 1940s and 1950s. Southern University benefitted a great deal from his steady rise to national prominence, in the form of an expanded physical plant, a new law school, enhanced academic programs, and a student body that ranked the school among the largest black institutions in the United States. Southern's success during this period can be attributed to Dr. Clark's tireless work ethic, leadership skills, unwavering commitment to the institution, and ability to successfully navigate the racial politics of the state. Unquestionably, Southern University was Louisiana's favored Negro institution of higher learning and Clark was considered the leading African American scholar among Louisiana politicians, local officials, and white higher education administrators. As a result, he was held in high regard among his peers at other black colleges and universities. Clark's prescription for success was simple and coincidently embraced by many black leaders of the period: African Americans' greatest hope for a brighter future, personally and collectively, was through educational pursuits and working with the white power structure.

The decision to expel eighteen student leaders and demonstrators for their ideological stand was heart-wrenching for Clark. On the one hand, he despised racial discrimination and segregation. And on a philosophical level, he agreed with the students morally and ethically. On the other hand, the future of Southern University and the employment and education of thousands of African Americans hung in the balance.[17] Louis E. Lomax believes that "Dr. Clark and Negro college presidents like him [were] faced with a choice between two goods: integration and education of the Negro. Their dilemma [was] that they must choose one over the other. If they support[ed] integration, they [were] in trouble with state officials; if they [didn't] they [were] in trouble with the students."[18]

While Clark struggled to find a solution that could give him a peace of mind, one thousand students marched from the campus in Scotlandville to the state capitol to demonstrate their determination and commitment to the movement and their displeasure with state officials.[19] Clark had no choice but to announce that disciplinary action would be taken against the eighteen student protesters and leaders. As a result, at an off-campus rally Major Johns encouraged the entire student body to withdraw from the institution. At the rally, one of the expelled students, Marvin Robinson, declared, "there are certain people in the United States today who are living in 'legalized slavery.' We cannot do this, we cannot do that, we cannot do the other. Negroes that claim to be satisfied with the present situation fall into one of three categories. These categories are, one they are either too scared or they haven't got enough sense; or two they're making more profit from segregation than they would from integration and they like living in a luscious jail; or three they're lying."[20] The next day, approximately three thousand students, nearly half of the entire student body, marched to the school registrar's office to fill out papers to permanently leave the institution. In an effort to save the university from certain closure, Clark quickly called a meeting with African American community leaders to solicit their support and asked to meet with Major Johns and another expelled student, Donald Moss, to negotiate an end to his nightmare. In the meeting, Clark stressed very clearly that if the demonstrations did not cease immediately, the institution and the black community would be irreparably damaged. In an emotional decision Major Johns and Donald Moss agreed that all eighteen students would leave the school if those that had attempted to withdraw would be allowed to stay at the institution.[21] Ultimately, less than two hundred students voluntarily left Southern University. In a matter of weeks, the campus appeared to be back to normal, with few visible scars.[22]

Though Southern University's worst days to date had come to an end, no one could truly claim victory at the institution. While the students found a powerful voice that was able to garner the attention of the school administration and state officials, they never achieved their goal of effecting real and permanent change. And whereas President Clark was able to save the university from closing and maintain his standing among state officials, he lost something even more valuable: the trust and admiration of the student body and many African Americans in the community. Many national and state African American leaders castigated Clark for not supporting the students. Even Thurgood Marshall stated that "Black college Presidents like Clark should stand up and be counted." Louisiana's most widely circulated

African American newspaper, the *Louisiana Weekly*, also suggested that Felton Clark should resign for honoring the request of the state board.[23]

FELTON G. CLARK'S LEGACY IS TARNISHED

There is little question that Clark deserves greater scrutiny for his role in Southern's most divisive moment. Although he was placed in high esteem among many faculty, staff, and students at the institution, he also had a well-deserved reputation for being "remote and dictatorial" and for treating the university "like his personal fiefdom, hiring and firing individuals at will."[24] So it is not surprising that several faculty members, such as Adolph Reed Sr., and student leaders were highly critical of Clark for his decisions and managerial style. From this dilemma, one may also ascertain that Clark and student leaders became engrossed in a test of wills that could only result in the mutual failure of both parties because Clark's success was predicated on the students and their achievements, while student accomplishments were highly influenced by Clark and his many talents.

Even to this day, many African Americans are still divided on the issue. Southern University ROTC graduate and retired Army lieutenant general Russel L. Honoré believes that many individuals did not truly understand Clark's purpose and mission. In a 2010 interview he stated, "People were mixed up. 'He [Clark] should be leading us to Kress,' they would say. 'No he shouldn't! He is leading us to the state capitol to try to get funds.'" He was "competing with other institutions at a time when individuals could overtly say, 'No, we are not going to give *you* funds for a building.' Much of the academic progress and funding for buildings and construction at Southern University to this day happened during Clark's tenure. So I do think that he was a powerful force in the space that he operated. He understood his place, in that peaceful protest was an end to a means, but you were still a student."[25]

If the cliché *misery loves company* is true, then Felton G. Clark and student activists at Southern University were in great company. Student activism and the corresponding conflict that ensued on Southern's campus between the administration and the student body was played out at nearly every HBCU throughout America in 1960. What happened in Baton Rouge was not unique. Joy Ann Williamson argues that "throughout the South, black students harshly judged their colleges and administrators for their timid approach in confronting white supremacy and pushed the movement forward on and off their campuses."[26] Young African Americans of the baby boom generation in post–World War II America were at the vanguard of the struggle for social change and racial progress, and despite the movement's coming to a temporary end at Southern University, it continued to flourish and even gain momentum at other HBCUs and throughout the South.

MILITARY TRAINING SURVIVES TURMOIL

While the civil rights movement received the attention and support of black students throughout the South, military training and related activities continued to be popular on black college campuses. Reminiscent of attitudes toward military training and service during the 1950s, the early 1960s saw little change at HBCUs. The Vietnam War had not begun in earnest at that point, and although black students became increasingly involved in student demonstrations, protests, and the goals of the civil rights movement, there were no visible signs of dissension among supporters of military training. At Southern University, student organizations such as the Association of the United States Army, the Pershing Rifles, and the Scabbard and Blade continued to garner the attention of many male students for a host of personal and collective reasons associated with leadership opportunities, the desire to belong to a drill team, to participate in military activities, and the occasion to belong to a popular organization.[27] In fact, many campus student leaders, such as Otis D. Jones, editor-in-chief of the student newspaper and freshman class president, and D'Army Bailey, *Digest* staff writer, were not only enrolled in ROTC, but worked to excel as cadet leaders. Jones was awarded the honor of Distinguished Military Student and received an appointment in the Adjutant General's Corps as a service branch as well as Infantry as a combat branch. D'Army Bailey served as the ROTC drill team announcer and often referred to the drill team's achievements in his popular column, "Campus Expose," in addition to encouraging student activism for African American social equality.[28] For many students like Jones and Bailey, civil rights activism and military training and service were not philosophically opposed. On the contrary, they supported and served the same purpose: African American civil and political legitimacy and social progress.

Even when predominately white colleges, such as Colorado State University, Oregon State College, and the University of California at Los Angeles openly debated the necessity of compulsory ROTC in 1961, the news made a scant impression on the students at Southern.[29] For much of the period, large portions of the campus newspaper were devoted to singing the praises of the Army ROTC staff, distinguished cadets and graduates, unit awards and honors, and branch assignments.

From time to time an article appeared on the front page with a picture of a young lady who had chosen to pursue a career in the military upon graduation and was receiving specialized training in an attractive occupational field. As a junior, Myrtle L. Flowers entered into the Student Army Dieticians' Program in the U.S. Army Reserve and received a monthly $200 stipend while completing her studies at Southern University. After graduation Flowers would receive a commission as a second lieutenant in the Medical Specialist Corps Reserve.[30] At Tuskegee, individuals interested in the Air Force ROTC program were encouraged by the news that many of its former cadets were employed as jet fighter pilots, navigators, and air police. Sixty percent of the school's former cadets were serving on active duty and enjoying the benefits of military service.[31] Young women also made personal gains while serving in the military. Former nursing students who received commissions as naval officers after completing eight weeks of training at the U.S. Naval Schools Command were praised by Tuskegee officials.[32] Though most female students chose not to join the armed forces, military service was a career option. The Women's Army Corps (WAC) regularly sought interested candidates at Tuskegee and offered young women the opportunity to become Army officers and career soldiers.

During the annual Armed Forces Day celebration at Southern, the campus and black community enjoyed the ability to attend numerous military activities and functions. In 1961 the celebration theme was "Power for Peace." The public was invited to an open house on the campus, the Pershing Rifles drill team performed, and the ROTC band and brigade marched in a downtown parade. The celebration ended with the well-anticipated social event of the year, the annual ROTC Ball, where Miss ROTC was crowned as campus guests, administrators, faculty, staff, and students looked on. The festivities were usually followed by extensive newspaper coverage in the *Baton Rouge News Leader*, the community newspaper, and the *Southern University Digest*.[33]

Much like Southern, Tuskegee celebrated Armed Forces Day during the early 1960s. The occasion marked an opportunity for university officials, faculty, students, and local citizens to commemorate the contributions of African American servicemen and the success of Tuskegee's military programs. The celebration included an impressive display of military weapons and aircraft and concluded with a parade. Colonel Vance H. Marchbanks, director of base medical services at George Air Force Base in California and "one of four selected to serve in Project Mercury—a project on America's first manned space flight, was offered the opportunity to serve as keynote speaker."[34]

Technical students at Tuskegee took advantage of military-related job recruitment when recruiters from the Lockheed Missiles and Space Company, the U.S. Army Engineer Division, and the Federal Aviation Agency visited the campus. Tuskegee placement director G. L Howell believed that "a sharp rise in job recruitment at the Institute [was] due to industry's discovery of an untapped source of talent in the predominately Negro colleges."[35]

ROTC OFFICIALS PROMOTE BENEFITS OF MILITARY SERVICE TO STUDENTS

In 1962, although student editorials that focused on social and political events in the broader society began to appear more frequently in the *Southern University Digest*, military training and service continued to receive the lion's share of attention. More noticeably, for the first time U.S. Army and Air Force advertisements began appearing on a regular basis in the student newspaper, highlighting service benefits, such as a $535 subsistence allowance, $300 uniform allowance, thirty days paid vacation, opportunities to pursue an advanced degree, and the ability to travel throughout the world.[36] The U.S. Army even attempted to make the ROTC curriculum more attractive to students by allowing cadets to use a larger number of electives to satisfy curriculum requirements. The military science program also publicized changes that would move the curriculum from a four-year to a two-year schedule and increase the pay for advanced cadets and offer the same monthly stipend to attend summer training camp as the service academies' cadets received.[37]

The effort to make military training and service more attractive to college students during the early 1960s reflects the desire to recruit a larger pool of military officers—in particular, African American officers. In addition, changes to the ROTC curriculum represented efforts of the Department of Defense and university officials to enhance the academic rigor and value of ROTC courses while improving cadet decision-making and analytical skills.[38]

THE WAR IN VIETNAM IMPACTS THE WAR ON POVERTY

Although military training and service remained widely esteemed at HBCUs in the early 1960s, America's growing commitment to contain communism and support democracy in Vietnam became a heated topic on college campuses. Many African American students began not only to question the legitimacy of military intervention in Southeast Asia, but to reason that the war undermined the federal government's commitment to fighting the war on poverty, as funding for social programs experienced drastic cuts. Between 1960 and 1964, President John F. Kennedy's and President Lyndon B. Johnson's administrations allocated hundreds of millions of dollars to special programs concerned with job training, health care, education, and urban development. In many cases, these programs were intended to reduce high unemployment and social unrest among African Americans. Before World War II, the vast majority of the economically underprivileged lived in rural areas throughout the United States. By 1960, over 55 percent of the poor lived in America's inner cities and another 30 percent lived in small towns. For the most part, the millions of poor individuals who populated the inner cities were invisible to middle-class Americans in suburbia.

Spurred on by the civil rights movement and Michael Harrington's *The Other America*, President Kennedy asked his economic advisors to study the problem of poverty and ways to address it.[39] While the Kennedy administration placed poverty and civil rights legislation at the top of its agenda, America's commitment to contain communism in Southeast Asia was challenged by the communist forces of North Vietnam. As early as 1950, according to George Herring, "American foreign policy makers had firmly embraced what would become known as the domino theory, the belief that the fall of Indochina would bring in rapid succession the collapse of the other nations of Southeast Asia"[40] "From the time of the Geneva conference of 1954 through the moment of the American decision to go to war," David Kaiser believes, "Indochina had figured as one of many battlegrounds in the Cold War. There as elsewhere, successive administrations tried to prevent the further spread of communism, first economically and politically, then through an advisory role, and finally with direct military intervention. All of these measures reflected the containment policy that the United States followed for more than four decades after the Second World War."[41] In 1962 the Kennedy administration developed a two-pronged plan to prevent North Vietnamese forces from occupying South Vietnam. The number of U.S. advisers had increased to over nine thousand and tons of military supplies were flown in daily. By the fall of 1963, Kennedy received reports that at least one-third of potential U.S. military draftees were judged unfit and ineligible for military service. To address this problem, the U.S. Office of Education and the President's Committee on Youth Employment, headed by Labor Secretary Willard Wirtz, was charged with exploring ways to address the deficiencies in America's military manpower pool.

Though America was not fully engaged in the war in Vietnam in 1963, it was, however, committed to victory in the War on Poverty. Historically, military training and service were used as mechanisms for social change after the Civil War and during World Wars I and II, and the early 1960s would be no different. The War on Poverty quickly became a way for President Kennedy to address numerous social and economic problems while moving his political agenda forward. The War on Poverty addressed the continued rise in youth unemployment, school dropout rates, and the number of individuals unfit for military service. President Kennedy established the Task Force on Manpower Conservation, which was directed to prepare a program for the guidance, testing, training, and rehabilitation of young men available to serve in the armed forces.[42] At the conclusion of the study, the task force compiled a report titled *One Third of a Nation: A Report on Young Men*

Found Unqualified for Military Service. Within the report the task force listed important findings:

> One-third of all young men in the nation turning 18 would be found unqualified if they were to be examined for induction into the Armed Forces. Of these, about one-half would be rejected for medical reasons. The remainder probably would fail through inability to qualify on the mental test.
>
> A nationwide survey carried out by the Task Force of persons who have recently failed the mental test clearly demonstrates that a major proportion of these young men are products of *poverty*. They have inherited their situation *from* their parents, and unless the cycle is broken, they will almost surely transmit it to their children.
>
> If all of the 1,400,000 young men turning 18 in 1964 were to be examined, about half a million, or one-third, would be found disqualified. The total of potential rejections would rise to more than 600,000 a year for the rest of the decade.[43]

During World Wars I and II, the average rate of rejection was approximately 30 percent. During the Korean War it rose to just over 37 percent. By 1961, the draft rejection rate was 49 percent and rising. In December 1962, the draft rejection rate reached an all-time high of 58 percent. Most of these men were physically over- or underweight and characterized as functionally illiterate. These findings were dismaying to military officials, to say the least. Initially, Selective Service officials believed that the alarming rate of rejection was due to the steady rise in draft standards. But after further review, they realized that draft requirements had remained fixed since 1951. America's youth were failing miserably and the military had few explanations.

The task force study ultimately suggested that the military lower its entrance requirements and provide special training to those individuals with medical and social handicaps. One of the main organizers of the presidential task force, Assistant Secretary of Labor Daniel Patrick Moynihan, believed that the military represented America's greatest socializing agent and institution. Given its ability to assemble diverse groups of people and transform their lives socially and economically, Moynihan contended that black Americans in particular would benefit from the organizational attributes of structure, order, discipline, and male authority that appeared to be lacking in the lives of a growing number of black youths.[44]

ROTC OFFICERS BATTLE PESSIMISM AND SHOCK OF FIRST CASUALTY OF THE WAR

While the Selective Service System experienced manpower difficulties and growing pessimism among the draft age population, ROTC officers and cadets at Southern labored to maintain the public image of the university military training program. In an editorial an anonymous author wrote:

> As a cadet, you are automatically looked upon as a representative of the Army, so that your conduct tends to be accepted as typical—whether it really is or not. The simple truth is, our uniform hasn't lost its prestige with our people. Civilians still like to see it. Veterans single out the man in uniform to brag to him of their old great outfit. Very likely many National Guardsmen and Reservists retain their citizen-soldier status only for the privilege of wearing the uniform as often as they can. If you affect public opinion, public opinion also affects you—For better or worse.[45]

In 1964 the war in Vietnam began to impact the lives of Americans as U.S. casualties increased. Southern University and its ROTC department mourned the loss of a former cadet. Captain Bryford G. Metoyer, class of 1959, was killed when his helicopter was shot down while flying over enemy territory. Captain Metoyer was described as "a symbol of a new spirit of daring, dedication and devotion that so typifies those who would desire to truly lead in today's world."[46] In a related article, ROTC instructor Captain Clarence J. Young wrote, "To understand the war in Vietnam is not easy for one who has never taken part. The Viet Cong have used guerrilla warfare to a degree that they are becoming the masters in this type of warfare. Americans as advisors can only advise and pilots who are ferrying troops can only fly. It is not our war but one of the many gaps in the wall of freedom that the Communists are trying to exploit. It is not our job to fight but to advise."[47]

AMERICA ENTERS THE VIETNAM WAR

By late 1964, after the Gulf of Tonkin incidents it became clear to most Americans that the Johnson administration intended to commit the U.S. armed forces in an all-out effort to defeat the communist-backed North Vietnamese. Antiwar demonstrations began to attract the attention of the national media, and many Americans were unsure of Vietnam's significance to national security and whether the war was a civil conflict between two groups for self-determination. To compound the level of uncertainty, the draft and the civil rights movement were issues of greater concern for many African Americans. To young black people in particular, it did not make much sense to go to another part of the world to fight for the freedom of others while blacks in the South were living in poverty as second-class citizens.[48] In an effort to improve morale on the campus, Southern University professor of military science Major Pervis M. Bates wrote an open letter to the ROTC cadets of Southern University in the form of a prayer to give them strength in the upcoming school year:

> Almighty God, we who soon will become leaders of men, come to you for guidance in this awesome responsibility. Keep ever before us our goal, which is not to perpetuate war, but to safeguard your greatest gift to man . . . freedom. Let us never forget our duty to the men whom we lead. May we instill in them the qualities of HONOR, INTEGRITY, and DUTY. Give us the courage, O Lord, in the face of hardship. Keep us pure in heart, clean of mind, and strong of purpose. We ask your blessings as we prepare for the great honor of serving our Country. AMEN.[49]

By 1965, South Vietnam appeared to be collapsing into communist hands. In response, Herring believes, "Johnson made the most important political decision of his career. He authorized a sustained air offensive against North Vietnam and dispatched American ground forces to stem the tide in the south. At that point, the United States was engaged in a major war on the Asian mainland."[50] The antiwar movement began to gain momentum, and on black college campuses throughout the South the war became a focal point among many faculty and students.

ANTIWAR MOVEMENT BEGINS ON BLACK COLLEGE CAMPUSES

In May 1965, students and faculty members at Tuskegee organized a forum to debate the pros and cons of American intervention in Vietnam and discuss reasons for continued support.[51] Months later, the Tuskegee student newspaper, the *Campus Digest*, conducted a poll on attitudes of students concerning the war. The poll implied that students were still overwhelmingly supportive of the armed forces and American presence. When respondents were asked, "Do you believe that the U.S. should withdraw its troops?" seventy-three percent of the males and 60 percent of the females answered, "No." When participants were asked, "Do you condone the tearing up of draft cards by draftees to prevent their induction in the armed forces?" seventy percent of males and 72 percent of females replied "No." When male participants were asked, "If called, would you fight in Vietnam?" almost 60 percent answered "Yes."[52]

At Southern University, though articles appeared in the student newspaper more frequently covering civil rights marches, demonstrations, and protests throughout the South, military training and service received as much attention or more. The main difference compared to past stories was that there was a clear effort by the ROTC department to justify America's presence in Southeast Asia and why it was important to defeat communism. On February 6, 1965, excerpts of an Army pamphlet titled "Our Stake in Vietnam—Freedom From Peril" were printed in the paper, addressing why American forces were in Vietnam and what was truly at stake:

> The Republic of Vietnam is trying to remain free from communist tyranny and has asked us to help them. It has long been a basic principle of American foreign policy that we will respond to any nation's call for help when its freedom is in peril from external aggression or subversion.
>
> By our unflinching support of the Republic of Vietnam, the United States is demonstrating, to the Communist and Free Worlds alike, that we do not intend to stand aside and let freedom die in South-east Asia or anywhere else.[53]

While the ROTC department attempted to convince students and cadets that Vietnamese freedom was worth African Americans fighting for, an article on the front page of the newspaper highlighting the struggle for social and political rights in Alabama was visibly more militant than past stories. In it, an aide of the Reverend Martin Luther King Jr. exclaimed, "We are no longer fighting for a seat at the lunch counter, the stakes are higher now. We are fighting for a seat in the Legislature. If we get out and work, Sheriff Jim Clark will be out picking cotton with my father in about two weeks."[54]

In one of the first student editorials written about the U.S. presence in Vietnam, political columnist Jacob Bouie Jr. suggested that the American press was purposely lying to the Western world about events in Vietnam. As a member of the U.S. Army Special Forces and one who recently spent a considerable amount of time in the country, Bouie felt compelled to enlighten the students, faculty, and staff at Southern University. Bouie remarked, "a fault of the war is that the Western World is grossly misled and ill informed concerning the crisis in southeast Asia. The lies and half-truths are spreading through the best and most widely read propaganda machine the world has ever known, the American Press." In one instance, "a demonstration was suppose to be held in Tuy Hoa, the American press published the results of the demonstration two days before the actual demonstration."[55] Approximately a month later, *SU Digest* writer Wade Hudson made a passionate plea for students to be more assertive when dealing with the university administration concerning student policies and liberties. Hudson stated, "Freedom must begin somewhere and it must start now. When I see the civil rights struggle in Selma, Alabama, it weakens my masculinity. Almost any hearted person will be affected by the harsh treatment given the peaceful civil rights demonstrators by the city of Selma and state of Alabama. Only Jews in Nazi Germany have been treated worse than the Negroes in their civil rights struggle in recent years."[56]

STUDENTS RESPOND TO MALCOLM X ASSASSINATION

A couple weeks after the assassination of Malcolm X, *SU Digest* staff reporter Eddie Sanderford wrote a full-page article paying tribute to black America's most politically charged leader. Sanderford highlighted Malcolm X's political and racial philosophy as well as why so many individuals feared him. But for many young African Americans, Malcolm X was embraced because he taught them to value who they were and where they came from. Sanderford wrote, "but his aim was not hate. The aim of his teachings was to create awareness. An awareness of what has been done to the Negro. This awareness, he hoped would produce an abundance of energy, both positive and negative that could then be channeled constructively."[57] If young black Americans were divided on Malcolm X's political or racial views, there is little question about his ability to promote black intellectualism, cultural pride, and a philosophy of self-determination.

ROTC CADETS CONTINUE TO LEAD STUDENTS IN QUEST FOR SOCIAL CHANGE

During the next twelve to eighteen months, despite the growing disaffection for the Vietnam War and the increasing popularity of the Black Power movement, military training at Southern University continued to resonate with many students. Newspaper articles, human interest stories, pictorials, and military advertisements highlighting the benefits and virtues of military service dominated the student newspaper. Much like during the early 1960s, student leadership on the Baton Rouge campus reflected the presence of ROTC cadet leaders and military veterans. Political columnist Jacob Bouie Jr. was honored for outstanding duty in Vietnam by the U.S. Army for his efforts against Viet Cong forces and while serving as an administrator at the Army Special Forces training school.[58] In the fall of 1966, Cadet Major Isaiah Leggett was elected president of the Student Government Association. Cadet Leggett was also selected as a Distinguished ROTC Student by the military science department and served as sports editor for the *Digest*.[59] Leggett's election is significant because as president of the Student Government Association he was invited to the Southern College Personnel Association's annual meeting in New Orleans, where he would participate in various panels with other student leaders to discuss student grievances and suggest ways to improve the student climate at Southern.[60]

PROJECT 100,000

By 1966, campus-based and antiwar resistance movements worked to expose inequalities in the Selective Service System. While full-time students were deferred, part-time students were marked as potential draftees. In addition, students with poor grades could lose their deferments, in contrast to students with high marks, who also had the opportunity to enter graduate school. The prejudicial nature of the Selective Service System prompted thousands of students to protest and voice their disapproval of the Johnson administration. For President Johnson, draft demonstrations attracted unwanted attention to America's military buildup in South Vietnam and made it difficult to attract congressional and popular support. Secretary of Defense Robert McNamara informed Johnson of the changes he was implementing regarding entrance qualifications for military enlistment. McNamara explained that "the purpose of the revision was to increase the number of men qualified for the draft, thereby permitting a broader sharing of the draft burden and increasing the intake of volunteers."[61]

In August 1966, during a speech at the Veterans of Foreign Wars national conference, McNamara disclosed his plans to rehabilitate America's disadvantaged youth in a program called Project 100,000. "The rehabilitation of young men who fail to pass the standard aptitude tests because of physical or education deficiencies, or both will be accomplished by special training programs," he explained.[62] McNamara's Project 100,000 was strictly promoted as an antipoverty program with social benefits in mind. McNamara believed that the Defense Department represented the world's largest educator of young men. Through advanced educational and medical techniques, the military could create the most favorable conditions to train and educate America's "subterranean poor."[63]

Project 100,000 was composed primarily of poor, working-class, and minority individuals. The average age was twenty. Almost 50 percent had failed or repeated a grade in high school, and nearly 15 percent read on or below a fourth grade reading level. Over half of these men could not or did not graduate from high school. Approximately 10 percent had prior court convictions for misdemeanor offenses. Forty percent of Project 100,000 inductees were African Americans. In comparison, African Americans made up 25 percent of all enlisted men.

The Defense Department had little trouble acquiring men to fill Project 100,000 rosters. Within major cities, hundreds of poverty stricken areas were target markets for military recruiters. "President Johnson wanted these guys off the street," recalled Colonel William Cole of the Army's Sixth Recruiting District, headquartered in San Francisco. "The Defense Department gave us an objective. We never had any problem. We got more than one hundred percent every time."[64] Army recruiters set up temporary offices in low-income neighborhoods and even worked out of mobile recruiting vans. Agencies such as the Boys and Girls Clubs, Youth Opportunity Centers, unemployment offices, and high schools were frequently visited by recruiters in search of potential volunteers or draftees. Special care was taken to send African American recruiters to black areas, which accepted their presence with little suspicion. Recruiters occasionally worked in teams as they roamed street corners, hamburger stands, public basketball courts, and recreation centers. "We use their language," established Sergeant Paul Conti, the noncommissioned officer who was in charge of the Marines' Oakland Station. "You know, we say 'man.' We even call the cops 'pigs.'" Staff Sergeant Pascal Thigpen, another white recruiter, added: "A really big selling point is that everybody starts out even at boot camp."[65] While Project 100,000 did not directly affect Southern University or other HBCUs in particular, it placed added pressure on individuals to stay in school if they wanted to avoid combat in Vietnam. Despite the "Great Society" rhetoric or stated intentions of the program, African Americans, poor whites, and Latinos were chosen to fill the roster of Project 100,000 inductees.

BLACK LEADERS QUESTION SENSIBILITY OF WAR

While black nationalists and traditional civil rights leaders differed on many issues concerning the social and political direction of the black community, many began to agree on their opposition to the war in Vietnam. In previous wars that were unpopular in the black community, black leaders still encouraged participation, in the hope that equality and full citizenship would result from their support. However, attitudes toward the Vietnam War were different. African Americans characterized the conflict as a war that robbed the community of much needed financial support and diverted attention from domestic issues and problems. The war was thus seen as an obstacle to improvements rather than as an opportunity for advancement. In addition, the civil rights movement was motivated by moral and ethical principles; by contrast, many individuals questioned whether the United States was supporting a corrupt, dictatorial regime in South Vietnam and intervening in a civil war for self-determination and independence from Western influence.[66] As Robert Mullens argues, many black leaders "agreed that the stated war aims of the United States were hypocritical, that a bond of color existed between Black Americans and the Yellow Vietnamese, that the United States was capable of committing genocide against a nonwhite people, and that the war spending, when contrasted with spending to improve conditions of America's Black and poor, illustrated the inhuman priorities of American society."[67]

When the Mississippi Freedom Democratic Party in 1965 publicly denounced the war in Vietnam and urged young blacks not to honor the draft, America paid little attention. It was not until Martin Luther King Jr. requested that the president call for immediate peace talks that most Americans connected civil rights protests with the antiwar movement. Randall Fisher argues:

> In the opinion of many Americans this placed black protest on the side of the doves in that war who advocated, vaguely, something less than an American military victory which made the black civil rights movement suspect in their eyes. Then, when just a few years later, [Stokely] Carmichael and other black power speakers openly urged blacks to avoid the draft with shouts of Hell no, we won't go! an even larger group of Americans found it easy to identify black protest with those who didn't really want to combat the spread of communism and who might, in fact, be in sympathy with communist goals.[68]

King continued to voice his opposition to the war, and in March 1965 he addressed Howard University students and reported, "The war in Vietnam is accomplishing nothing."[69] King and black leaders believed not only that the war was immoral, but that it seriously jeopardized the future and progress of poverty programs directed toward minorities. While the Johnson administration increased the defense budget, many individuals believed it decreased the amount of money and attention devoted to the Great Society welfare programs.[70] The military's involvement in Vietnam was now affecting how African Americans began to view military service. According to Herbert Shapiro, "The linking of the peace and civil rights movement was reinforced by the realities of the American military machine. For Blacks the armed services traditionally had often appeared to offer an avenue of advancement, but the statistics of Vietnam told a story that could not be ignored. In 1967 64% of eligible Blacks were drafted while the draft took only 31% of eligible Whites."[71] African Americans were starting to feel that they were being unfairly chosen to fight for a cause in which many did not believe.

STUDENTS EXPRESS INTEREST IN BLACK POWER

In October 1966, the political science department at Southern University sponsored an open forum on Black Power to allow students to express their beliefs and to better understand the most debated topic on campus. Students and faculty discussed African American history and the importance of black unity, and some suggested that the concept of "Black Power" was a regenerated philosophy that had its origins in the nineteenth century. But others pointedly reflected the views of Malcolm X, Stokely Carmichael, and others when they remarked: "Black Power is only a negro affair. This excludes any acceptance of whites in defining the political, social, or economic future of the Negro. The Afro-American should be led only by black leaders because only the black man can fully understand and interpret objectively the problems of black men. We should go back to the ghetto and black communities where much needed work should be done."[72] Though the forum did not accomplish more than allowing students to articulate their views on the state of black America, participants did agree that cultural pride and respect for one another was necessary for the advancement of the people.

The year of 1966 ended with much discussion and debate about the war in Vietnam. In a poem printed in the *Southern University Digest,* Private First Class Franklin D. Wells suggested that the "War Must Be Won." In addition, the "Roving Reporter" newspaper editorial queried students whether women should be drafted into the U.S. armed forces. Though the majority of students answered no and pointed to the need to fulfill traditional gender roles, two freshman students stated that women are needed to help fight in Vietnam and have a right to fight as equals with men.[73] In the same issue, a half-page article titled "What Good Can Military Training Do You?" expounded upon the virtues and benefits of military training. The manifesto reported that, "among the highest paid executives listed in 'Who's Who' earning between $100,000 and $330,000 a year, 28% are ROTC trained. These statistics indicate that the student who included military training in his civilian education was 6 times more likely to become a top executive than the young man who concentrated exclusively in other areas. We believe that Army ROTC makes a significant contribution to the chances of success."[74]

BLACK POWER LEADERS AND ORGANIZATIONS OPPOSE THE WAR

Over the next few years, civil rights organizations, many of which were student and youth based, voiced their opposition to the war. The Student

Nonviolent Coordinating Committee (SNCC) announced its opposition in 1966, and in October of the same year "the Black Panther Party issued its ten point program. Point six declared: We want all Black men to be exempt from military service. We believe that Black people should not be forced to fight in the military service to defend a racist government that does not protect us. We will not fight and kill other people of color in the world who, like Black people, are being victimized by the white racist government of America."[75] In fact, many African Americans not only recognized a common struggle with the Vietnamese people and colored members of the "Third World," but acknowledged that there were close physical similarities as well. In 1965, Robert S. Browne, a civil rights activist, economist, and U.S. Civil Service employee, wrote an essay titled "The Freedom Movement and the War in Vietnam," where he recalled his personal experiences in living in Vietnam with his native wife and children. Browne remarked, "although I could never escape the obvious truth that I was a foreigner, the fact that I was a non-white, Vietnamese-speaking member of a Vietnamese family frequently made me privy to conversations intended for only Vietnamese ears." Browne also recounts how shocked he was when he first met Tri Quang, leader of the Vietnamese Buddhists. To Browne's surprise, the Buddhist monk physically resembled the average African American male walking down 125th Street in Harlem, New York.[76]

As the number of American troops in Vietnam increased and public discontent with the war heightened, students at black colleges and universities began to voice their opinion more readily on the war and the political and social direction of the nation. The popularity and success that military programs enjoyed on black college campuses was now threatened by African American criticism of the war and the Johnson administration's efforts (such as Project 100,000) to commit additional troops. In addition, the Black Power movement and its antiwar rhetoric coincided with the demand for equality and a new militancy embraced by many young leaders and black students. For young popular leaders, such as Eldridge Cleaver, Stokley Carmichael, and H. Rap Brown, who quickly gained a growing audience of supporters on black college campuses, the war in Vietnam and the struggles for independence throughout the world were just additional indications of white imperialism and the desire to subjugate people of color.

Stokely Carmichael argued, "Black Power means that black people see themselves as part of a new force, sometimes called the 'Third World'; that we see our struggle as closely related to liberation struggles around the world. We must hook up with these struggles. We must ask ourselves: when black people in Africa begin to storm Johannesburg, what will be the role of this nation—and black people here?"[77] Eldridge Cleaver wrote, "The relationship between the genocide in Vietnam and the smiles of the white man toward black Americans is a direct relationship. Once the white man solves his problem in the East he will then turn his fury again on the black people of America, his longtime punching bag. It is no accident that the U.S. government is sending all those black troops to Vietnam. Some people think that America's point in sending 16 percent black troops to Vietnam is to kill off the cream of black youth. But it has another important result. By turning her black troops into butchers of the Vietnamese people, America is spreading hate against the black race throughout Asia."[78] Former Southern University student and SNCC chairman H. Rap Brown also highlighted the hypocrisy of fighting for the liberation of the Vietnamese people in Southeast Asia and being incarcerated for defending oneself and one's family in the South: "It's legitimate for a Black man to go over there and kill 30 Vietcong and get a medal, but you come back here and kill a racist, red-necked, honky, camel-breathed pecker-wood who's been misusing you and your people all your life and that's murder. That's homicide, because the white man has the power to define and legitimize his actions."[79]

Other black leaders, such as Robert S. Browne, agreed with the assessment of young Black Power leaders and stalwarts. Browne described the African American fight for self-determination as part of a worldwide struggle against white supremacist. He also believed that racism and the inability of white Americans to see people of color around the world as social equals enhanced the desire to work with political leaders of the Third World.[80]

THE PROS AND CONS OF MILITARY SERVICE ARE DEBATED

At Southern University and other HBCUs where military training and service had flourished, faculty and students squared off to debate the pros and cons of American involvement in the war. At Tuskegee Institute, several students were asked to express their views on the war. Many students were supportive of U.S. efforts in Asia:

> Edward Bell remarked, The U.S. should stay in Vietnam. We should adopt a new policy to put an end to the limited war there. Delanyard Robinson believed that, to insure the future of world wide democracy, we must win the war in Vietnam, or condition ourselves to living in communistic conditions. Benny Mayfield suggested that, . . . if the United States pulls out of Vietnam much of the faith which other Asiatic countries have in the United States would be lost. Gwen Patton countered with, I would desperately like to know what is actually going on in Vietnam. I can say however, that I think it is completely ironic that people are being killed, our American soldiers, and we don't even know why.[81]

Alton Hornsby Jr. defended American intervention by reporting, "Many are saying that the United States should not be there and that our purpose is not clear. The United States is in South Vietnam at the request of the Vietnamese government. This country is following a long-standing policy of containing communism. It is necessary to understand these things before one undertakes to praise or condemn our present involvement."[82]

CIVIL RIGHTS VIOLENCE INTENSIFIES CRITICISM OF THE WAR

Student activism at Tuskegee intensified when over three thousand students and faculty began a series of demonstrations to protest the shooting death of Tuskegee freshman Samuel L. Younge. Younge was killed for attempting to use a public restroom at a Standard Oil gas station in downtown Tuskegee.[83] Many believed that antiwar sentiment and student activism went hand-in-hand because students had a right to criticize and challenge failed government policies:

> Today's college student had little or no contact with developments which led to the present situation in Viet Nam. Precious few voices were raised in question when President Eisenhower first committed American troops in Southeast Asia as early as 1956. The adults who today criticize the student for inspecting his government's policies paid pitifully little attention to the warn-

ings sounded a decade ago about America fighting a land war in Asia. Today students would rather have a chance to finish school, find a job, and perhaps marry and raise a family, uninterrupted by nuclear inferno.[84]

When Tuskegee held its annual president's essay contest, Benjamin Rixson's essay on American intervention in the Vietnam War won first prize and the support of many faculty and students. Rixson argued: "I do not believe that my generation is less able or willing to fight in protection of this country than any other generation, but the fundamental reason for fighting eludes us. If it came to dying to sustain and perpetuate this expanding society for forthcoming generations few of us would shirk from combating a genuine threat to this country's well being. Our motivation to complete that effort is presently non-existent."[85] Rixon further exclaimed that for him military service was not an issue of contention; rather, he did not agree with the Johnson administration's motives for escalating the war in Vietnam.[86] Other students who wrote the student newspaper at Tuskegee questioned the sensibility in investing millions of dollars in the war in Vietnam while racial minorities were suffering in the inner cities and America was losing the War on Poverty.[87] During the period, young black leaders such as Stokley Carmichael toured black college campuses and also championed this cause.[88]

COMPULSORY MILITARY TRAINING IS QUESTIONED AT BLACK COLLEGES

Between 1965 and 1967, students and faculty at black colleges and universities that were involved in the civil rights movement were beginning not only to question U.S. motives for the war, but to call for the termination of compulsory ROTC at their respective campuses. At Morgan State College in Baltimore, Maryland, where the ROTC department had earned a well-deserved reputation for producing some of black America's finest soldiers, students who were members of a civil rights group called DISSENT opposed the faculty's decision to maintain compulsory ROTC. The organization sponsored a public forum on "Vietnam and the American Conscience," where they voiced their disapproval of mandatory military training.[89] In Hampton, Virginia, 416 students at Hampton Institute signed a petition calling for the termination of compulsory ROTC because military training and service did not coincide with their career goals and future plans. Weeks later, faculty committee members voted to implement a new policy of nonmandatory military training at the institution.[90] In 1967, Tennessee A&I State University also switched from a compulsory military training to a voluntary program. School officials suggested that political tensions were relieved almost immediately in relation to the war in Vietnam.[91] Howard University in Washington, D.C., is another black college that found itself at the center of the debate concerning the war. Faculty and students were divided on the issue of mandatory military training. In 1967, student protesters demanded action on a list of grievances that included the elimination of compulsory ROTC.[92]

While students and public figures continued to speak out against American involvement in Asia, students at Tuskegee began to also question the function of compulsory ROTC. In the school newspaper's Letters to the Editor section, John Stanford defended the practicality of military training:

> Recently, in the compulsory chapel crisis, the Army ROTC program has been the object of numerous attacks by outsiders and Tuskegee Institute students. The cry has been the 'Why make something mandatory that is training us (the cadets) to KILL.' As a member of the Association of the United States Army and as a responsible citizen, I feel that it is my duty to somewhat clarify the false picture projected of the ROTC program. One need not be trained to kill in order to take a person's life, but, one must be trained to defend that which he calls his or that which he wishes and must prepare to take it by force. KILLING IS TOO OFTEN WASTEFUL, BUT, OFTEN TIMES IT IS A "NECESSITY" IN THE CAUSE OF MANKIND.[93]

Students and faculty displayed outrage when the man accused of killing Samuel Younge was released after his trial. Over fifteen hundred students assembled in the town square to hold a demonstration. When many individuals were asked their reaction to the verdict, several used the opportunity to criticize American involvement in Vietnam. Walter Gross, a physics instructor, exclaimed, "It is the criticism of 300 years of racism in this country. I am not surprised that this murdering of oppressed Non-white people is typical of American policy both at home and abroad. Both Governor George

Wallace, who has instigated this sort of action and President Johnson have done nothing to prevent it and are equally responsible for this travesty of justice. Johnson is more interested in killing people in Viet Nam."[94] "I would rather be in Viet Nam if this is justice," declared Eugene Johnson. "Why send Negroes to Viet Nam when they can get killed here? I know that there are a lot of advanced ROTC cadets who are scared to express their candid opinions on the Viet Nam issue—well that's too bad."[95]

Discontent with the Vietnam War was also demonstrated in a full-page announcement in the student newspaper at Tuskegee Institute. The federal government was accused of fighting an immoral war while failing to address the needs of the poor and the political rights of African Americans:

> On April 15 there will be a massive mobilization in New York and San Francisco against the war in Vietnam. We at Tuskegee Institute who support the mobilization but are not able to travel to participate in it wish to express here our opposition to the war. We believe that our government is fighting an oppressive war 10,000 miles from home while failing to defend the rights of blacks here. We cannot carry out domestic programs such as the War on Poverty while sacrificing thousands of lives and wasting billions of dollars in Vietnam.[96]

Over 150 names of students and faculty members appeared in the announcement as supporters of a ten-minute silent vigil to be held on the campus. Students and faculty were also urged to "initiate protest activities on their own."[97] As another form of protest, many students refused to pay federal income taxes because the money would be used toward military expenditures. In an editorial, seven Tuskegee students described why they supported such a position:

> This year a number of us have decided to join the tax refusers because of the increasing barbarism on the part of the United States in its conduct of the war in Vietnam and of the failure of normal political channels to bring about changes in the Administration's Vietnam policy.
>
> If refusal remains on a small scale the tactic may still serve the purpose of distracting a certain amount of the Great Society's bureaucratic energy from total involvement in the exercise of its warfare activities.[98]

Letters to the editor critical of U.S. military intervention continued to appear in campus newspapers in the late 1960s. Kenneth D. Tomkinson offered ten reasons why military intervention in Vietnam was wrong. Tomkinson suggested America violated international law, moral codes, the United Nations Charter, and the American Constitution. He wrote, "military intervention violates article I of the U.S. Constitution: Wars are declared by Congress, representing all the people; or are we forgetting that our nation is a republic?"[99]

AFRICAN AMERICANS CONTINUE TO SUPPORT MILITARY SERVICE

Despite a decrease in enthusiasm for military training at black colleges and universities, many individuals believed that the majority of African Americans and black soldiers in Vietnam remained supportive of American efforts overseas. *Newsweek* magazine conducted another major survey in 1966 on African American politics, social issues, and support for the war. Several African American servicemen were asked to comment on military service and racial discrimination in the military. Captain Randolph Sturrup replied, "You might say I'm military all the way. I hope to make it for 30 years. It's a chance to improve yourself professionally."[100] Staff Sergeant Seman Jenkins exclaimed, "In the service, I have felt more a real part of the Great Society. I have been recognized as a man in every sense of the word."[101] When Lieutenant Holmes was asked why he reenlisted in the armed forces, Holmes declared, "I'd call for an appointment about a job I knew was open, and when I'd get there they'd say, 'I sorry, sir, this job is no longer open. But we have something in the janitorial field.' At 25, I saw no reason why I should accept a job as a garbage man."[102] The *Newsweek* survey suggested that in 1965, while only 17 percent of whites reenlisted, over 45 percent of African Americans decided to remain in the military. Military training and service continued to attract a consistent percentage of young African Americans at black colleges and universities because of the economic and social benefits military service offered. Between 1964 and 1967, Army commissions remained relatively stable, with only a few institutions experiencing a noticeable reduction.

TABLE 5.1. African American ROTC Army commissions, 1964–1967

	1964	1965	1966	1967
North Carolina A&T	24	22	10	17
Central State	29	14	26	25
Florida A&M	29	15	23	15
Hampton	29	34	20	19
Lincoln	19	14	16	19
Morgan State	21	27	12	16
Prairie View	20	27	31	38
South Carolina State	16	23	24	24
Southern	23	37	19	21
Tuskegee	14	14	20	26
Virginia State	21	14	18	21
West Virginia State	22	19	15	14
Howard	19	37	30	23
Total	**286**	**297**	**264**	**278**

Source: Johnson, 191.

While the war in Vietnam and America's working-class military became the object of increased criticism in the mid-1960s, African American support for the armed forces and American efforts overseas persisted. The U.S. military was still considered to be the most integrated institution—where black men and women, despite obstacles, could achieve success. This attitude was also reflected in the 1966 *Newsweek* poll, which reported, "civilian Negroes agree by a margin of 47 to 26 percent that a young Negro stands a better chance in a military uniform than civilian clothes."[103] The survey also suggested that nearly 60 percent of rank-and-file African Americans did not consider the draft to be unfair to minorities and 87 percent considered America worth fighting for.[104]

In part, the black press was responsible for these attitudes. Like in the Korean War, during the early 1960s the mainstream black press encouraged African American support for the U.S. presence in Vietnam and for the U.S. military. *Ebony* magazine, as early as 1965, highlighted the accomplishments and contributions of African American servicemen and women in a regular feature called "Armed Forces." African American military nurses, Air Force pilots, tank commanders, and military doctors were honored for exemplary service. In November 1965, *Ebony*'s main story was "Negroes in Vietnam: 'We, Too, Are Americans.'" In addition to interviewing black soldiers, Simeon Booker emphasized how military integration had produced a "new" army: "brother Joe [an African American soldier] courageously supports the overall effort in Vietnam. He faithfully backs his white counterpart—obviously in trouble in a part the world where a white face sticks out like a Negro's on Capital Hill. As one soldier put it: 'Out here, we, too, are Americans.'"[105] Another soldier announced, "We tell Vietnamese we're not white, but we make the counterpoint that we're brothers to whites in America and that's what democracy is—brotherhood."[106] Though Booker clearly made the effort to write a story that demonstrated how military integration produced a strong sense of equality and "brotherhood" among the troops in Vietnam, he did admit:

> Vietnam is no racial utopia. For all the field camaraderie, for example, social segregation between whites and Negroes is not unknown in Saigon. But the conflict is notably free of the more obnoxious racial inequities that have characterized America's past wars. There has been no instance of a white officer hurling racial epithets at his Negro troops, such as was often the case in World War I. There have not been the appalling brawls between white and Negro Americans on the streets of foreign cities, so often characteristic of World War II. There is even a distinct improvement on Korea, where certain units still were segregated, seriously damaging the morale of Negro fighting men.[107]

In the process of acknowledging the success of integration in the armed forces, the black press was especially critical of the second-class status of African Americans evident in reports that black soldiers were killed in disproportionate numbers in Vietnam. The *Pittsburgh Courier* wrote, "With so much opposition to Negroes seeking an end to second-class citizenship in this country, it might be a good time to remind Negrophobes of the roles being played by Negro servicemen in far-off Vietnam. The most recent statistics show that the Negro death ratio there exceeds that of whites."[108] Many African Americans and Black Power leaders used the news to highlight American hypocrisy "that Negroes were being compelled to fight in a war overseas to assure democratic rights abroad that were denied to Negroes in the United States."[109] But other leaders voiced the classic appeal "that Negroes are serving their country with distinction, some having made the supreme sacrifice. Therefore, Negrophobes should think twice about denying Negroes the full rights of American citizenship guaranteed under the Constitution."[110]

STUDENT ACTIVISM INTENSIFIES ON THE BLUFF

While the Southern University ROTC department attempted to remind cadets and students of the virtues and benefits of military training and service on the Bluff, many believed that the 1967–1968 school year reflected a new era on the campus. Like at dozens of black college campuses throughout the South, the period reflected a new urgency on the part of students who demanded real change at their institutions and in their communities. Students at Southern asked the administration to amend its policies on housing, student recreation, discipline, student organizations, campus security, and the dining hall. More specifically, there was an urgent call to publicize information concerning summer jobs, internships, and scholarships and the need to build a bridge or overpass near the railroad tracks at the school entrance on Harding Boulevard.[111] Among student leaders, one of the most popular and determined was Samuel Mims, the student body president. Not surprisingly, Mims was also a cadet major in the Army ROTC program and honored among four cadet seniors selected as Distinguished Military Student.[112] In an open letter to the university administration, Mims wrote, "The Southern Student Senate feels that the conditions on Southern University's campus that led to the demonstration of April 1967 have again reached the same dangerous proportions this year. Too much negligence on the part of the faculty, staff, and especially administrators has caused discontent and unhappiness among students. Yes, the students want to demonstrate and the Senate has been a pacifying agent. If the administration does not wish to aid us in solving problems, then this school is going to have one whale of a demonstration, nor the police will be able to control."[113]

Unfortunately for Dr. Clark and the school administration, Cadet Mims's threat of a massive demonstration was something to take seriously. During the same period, another black college in north Louisiana, Grambling State College, made national and state news headlines when twenty-five students, including the student body president and the editor of the student newspaper, led demonstrations which included a student walk-out of classes. Louisiana governor John McKeithen decided to call in five hundred National Guard soldiers to discourage student involvement and to present a show of force. Nearly three thousand of the four thousand students at Grambling met and decided to continue a boycott of classes until their demands were met. Student demands included:

- Dismissal of seven Grambling administrators.
- Improve conditions in the realm of academic policy
- The President perform his duties without prejudice and paternalistic views of the students.
- See that student funds are handled honestly.
- Stress political awareness among faculty members and thus provide a check on the white power structure.[114]

Though student leaders acknowledged that most of the demands would take some time to implement, their immediate goal was to encourage a dialogue between students and the college administration. Ultimately, all twenty-five student leaders, twenty-two males and three females, were expelled from the north Louisiana campus.

Fortunately for President Clark and the Southern University campus, social unrest there was avoided when the majority of the administration and the Student Senate were able to meet and discuss many of the issues in the proposed amendments to policies concerning student life on campus. Vice President G. Leon Netterville suggested that regular discussions take place with student representatives in order to find solutions to campus problems. The meeting was described as beneficial for both parties.[115] In an editorial describing the tone and significance of the meeting, the author remarked, "The student leaders are to be commended for such a rarity on Southern's campus scene. However, the significance of these conferences with the administrators is not in the success or failure in gaining these university reforms—at least not yet. Nor does the significance lie in the intellectual 'competence' or 'maturity' of the students involved—as some people will allege. The significance is in the fact that we as students of this university will no longer remain apathetic toward our college life or remain alienated from the rest of society."[116]

Four months after student leaders and the school administration met to discuss student grievances in order to avert the demonstrations that plagued other college campuses throughout the nation, Louisiana governor John McKeithen made a surprise visit to Southern to assess the facilities first-hand and to discuss ways to improve conditions. Student body president Cadet Major Mims escorted the governor from building to building as campus leaders suggested improvements. During the visit the governor promised students that plans to build a new overpass at the entrance of the campus would begin immediately. The governor also suggested that university appropriations would be increased in order to pay for construction of a new gymnasium and student union building. During the meeting, Mims publically reminded the governor that students had mailed several hundred letters to his office highlighting some the same problems that the governor now acknowledged needed to be addressed.[117]

In December 1967, Mims and the student senators composed an open letter to Dr. Clark asking for permission to organize and host a national conference on the Black Power movement at Southern. Earlier in the year, at the National Student Association meeting attended by student representatives from HBCUs, Southern University had been selected as the most desirable site to host the conference. In a direct plea to Dr. Clark, the letter exclaimed:

> We believe that you, by virtue of your being able to pass "a yes or no" on our proposals, have the power to end this era of uprisings, demonstrations and general discontent on Negro college campuses by granting us the right to meet at the conference table to discuss issues. Southern can be the place to change the face of the Negro college campus from the image of anarchy that it is swiftly heading for. Let Southern be the place that the world will refer to as the site where the Black colleges "got together."
>
> If our schools are ever to realize their potentials, we are going to have to alleviate the animosities that restrict our thinking and act collectively. We can do it now! It makes no sense to pass the buck any longer. Let Southern accept the challenge of the times; indeed someone must. Let us not take too lightly the urgency of this matter. Let us never again, as far into the future as we can see, witness another Central State closing or another college president—just as black as we are—put on the spot because he and the students could not communicate.[118]

President Clark quickly responded to the Student Senate's request in a manner that did not jeopardize his reputation or standing with the Louisiana State Board of Education but also did not reflect his personal opinion or desire on the matter. Knowing that a national conference on the Black Power movement at Southern University would invite the criticisms and disdain of Louisiana legislators and state officials, Clark stressed that it was not under his personal authority to authorize the use of campus facilities for nonacademic purposes. Only the State Board of Education could do so, and as president of Southern University he would submit the request to the governor's office and board officials. The request Clark submitted was understandably denied.[119]

STUDENTS CRITICIZE THE WAR

Students continued to criticize the administration for a lack of effectiveness and positive change on campus, all while the Vietnam War was making headlines throughout the nation. Recent setbacks on the battlefield encouraged national demonstrations, antiwar protests, and pessimism among students at Southern University. In the *Southern University Digest*, letters to the editor and editorials that highlighted negative opinions concerning the war and even compulsory ROTC appeared more frequently. Student Jesse Bryant listed ten reasons why he believed the war in Vietnam was wrong.[120] *Digest* sports editor Timothy E. Pratt even suggested that ROTC departments at black colleges distributed new uniforms to discourage African American cadets from protesting compulsory ROTC. Pratt sarcastically referred to the theory that "all men are basically egotistic. In particular, all minority groups have a severe case because of lack of recognition given them." The point was driven home when Pratt remarked, "Two days before Xmas, I noticed an ROTC cadet sporting his new uniform in his home town. Many wore them home."[121] Even as young African Americans began to view the military uniform as a tool of white manipulation and control, many individuals continued to embrace it with the same zeal as African Americans had done throughout history. For many students, the uniform continued to represent the virtues of discipline, sacrifice, and civic duty in a manly way that indicated a sense of entitlement.[122] Retired four-star general Colin Powell experienced a physical transformation when he wore his ROTC uniform for the first time:

> When I returned to school in the fall of 1954, I inquired about the Reserve Officer Training Corps, and I enrolled in ROTC. There came a day when I stood in line in drill hall to be issued olive-drab pants and jacket, brown shirt, brown tie, brown shoes, a belt with a brass buckle, and an overseas cap. As soon as I got home, I put the uniform on and looked in the mirror. I liked what I saw. The uniform gave me a sense of belonging, and something I had never experienced all the while I was growing up; I felt distinctive.[123]

CONCLUSION

The 1960s began with an invigorated civil rights thrust along with the new hope and bright promises of the Kennedy administration, but by the mid-1960s economic and social programs designed to address the needs of minorities and the poor were overshadowed or neglected because of America's commitment to the war in Vietnam. Between 1965 and 1967, although Black Power leaders such as Stokley Carmichael "toured black colleges of the South to urge students to 'fight for liberation by any means necessary,'" many students on black college campuses continued to embrace the benefits of military service and the opportunity to serve their country.[124]

However, by the end of the decade, as Americans became more ambivalent about the war and the U.S. military, so did African Americans and numerous black students. Racial and urban violence, riots, and political assassinations of black leaders increased African American resentment of American society. By 1969 it became apparent that many African Americans were unwilling to participate in an unpopular war. Despite this fact and the challenges to compulsory ROTC on black college campuses, military training at Southern was able to survive and attract highly motivated young men who sought the social and economic advantages of military service.

6

KEEP OUR BLACK WARRIORS OUT OF THE DRAFT

THE ANTIWAR MOVEMENT AT SOUTHERN UNIVERSITY,

1968-1973

During the late 1960s and early 1970s, the antiwar movement gained momentum and introduced a new wave of protests and demonstrations throughout the nation. Antiwar demonstrators clashed with law enforcement officials, university administrators, and working-class hawks. At many colleges and universities, military training programs were discontinued or in jeopardy of losing their appeal. Many individuals associated with the antiwar movement used the opportunity to denounce numerous social and economic inequities that existed in American society.[1]

Although antiwar protests occurred at black colleges and universities, they were quite different from the front-page confrontations at the University of California, Berkeley, and Ivy League institutions. In large part, there were no sit-in demonstrations, marches, or clashes with state police or the National Guard. Most of the protests were rhetorical, in the form of a speaker addressing small gatherings or newspaper debates. Much of the violence that did involve students on black campuses directly related to civil rights protests or demonstrations involving administrative policies, not military training. Compulsory ROTC was only mentioned in addition to other civil rights issues and university complaints. Black institutions with a history of military training, such as Southern, Tuskegee, Prairie View, Hampton, Virginia State, and Howard, did not witness any violence as a direct result of the antiwar movement.[2]

THE CALL TO ABOLISH COMPULSORY ROTC AND
THE ANTIWAR MOVEMENT INTENSIFY

In 1968, the antiwar movement at Southern University and other black college campuses was generally subdued in comparison to their white counterparts throughout the nation. Russell L. Honoré remembered being confronted on only a few occasions by student demonstrators as his ROTC unit marched through the campus. Honoré remarked, "When we marched across the campus, people [students] who were active in the movement would on occasion line-up across the bridge as we walked in formation. They would have signs or yell out, 'Why are [you] going into the Army?' I think that it was an extension of the protest that was happening across the country on university campuses. As cadets we were trained to ignore it and focus on what we were doing. I don't believe it was personal. That was a normal part of campus life at that time."[3]

The contradiction of fighting for democracy abroad while African Americans continued to experience racism and discrimination at home buttressed the antiwar rhetoric of Black Power leaders. Many African Americans criticized the federal government for sending hundreds of thousands of soldiers to fight for South Vietnamese freedom while only a few hundred law enforcement officers were assigned to protect black American citizens in the South from brutal attacks and murders when attempting to vote.[4] Numerous African American soldiers questioned why they were serving in the military and became less tolerant of racism and discrimination within the ranks. Wallace Terry believes that in 1968 and 1969 a new black soldier emerged in Vietnam: "The war [had] used up the professionals who found in military service fuller and fairer employment opportunities than blacks could find in civilian society, who found in uniform a supreme test of their black manhood. Replacing the careerist were black draftees, many just steps removed from marching in the Civil Rights Movement or rioting in the rebellions that swept the urban ghettos from Harlem to Watts. All were filled with a new sense of black pride and purpose. They spoke loudest against the discrimination they encountered on the battlefield in decorations, promotion and duty assignments."[5]

Attitudes of African American soldiers were also reflected in the black community and on college campuses during this period. According to a

Newsweek poll of African American attitudes on the war in 1969, blacks considered the war to be a source of many of their social ills. Unlike previous military conflicts, in which African Americans benefited from their participation and support, the war in Vietnam redirected black youth from addressing problems in their communities and siphoned away billions of dollars originally allocated for national social uplift programs.[6]

The late 1960s also witnessed an increase in campus antiwar organizing. In 1968, antiwar demonstrations occurred at over one hundred college campuses and high schools. At many Ivy League universities, including Columbia University, black nationalists and Students for a Democratic Society (SDS) combined their efforts to protest the war in Vietnam and to disrupt recruiting activities of Columbia University's ROTC program and of defense contractor Dow Chemical. Student activists also protested the university's plans to eliminate area public housing to expand campus facilities. Student demonstrations lasted approximately eight weeks, with nearly one thousand arrests.[7]

MARTIN LUTHER KING JR. IS ASSASSINATED

In the spring of 1968 Martin Luther King Jr. was assassinated, and the tragedy was devastating news on black college campuses. In addition to being America's most recognized civil rights leader, King had become a staunch critic of the war. On numerous occasions King had repeatedly spoken out against the war in Vietnam and warned that if America did not find a way out of the immoral conflict, it may be necessary to initiate mass demonstrations and protests. King also suggested that African Americans, poor whites, and the Vietnamese were being exploited by America.[8]

While black college campuses throughout the South reacted to King's assassination, in Baton Rouge over two thousand students and community residents marched to the state capitol to protest racism and discrimination in Louisiana. Once the demonstrators reached the capitol, under the watchful eye of armed city and state police, the first speaker, Southern University student leader Jodie Bibbens, vented his frustration to the crowd. "Today we'll be what they call responsible Negroes, good and humble, but at night we're gonna play like the KKK. We are moving from non-violence and civil disobedience to guerilla warfare and civil rebellion."[9] Bibbens announced that white racism had caused the death of Martin Luther King and that "contrary to what President Clark said, there is a great deal of unrest at Southern. We are not happy and we're going to show it in the future."[10] Another student leader, Temon Hawkins, tore up his draft card and voiced his unwillingness to serve in the armed forces of a racist society.[11] After the death of Martin Luther King Jr., the antiwar movement on black college campuses appeared to take on new urgency. Many African Americans began to feel that the civil rights thrust had stalled and the war in Vietnam was another cynical attempt to further American imperialism against people of color. Shortly after the student demonstration at the state capitol, a call to abolish compulsory ROTC appeared in the student newspaper at Southern:

> I am opposed to the compulsory ROTC program on our campus because I feel that it is of questionable academic value to most students' education; its courses are as academic as physical ed. It is often an unnecessary drain of students' time and federal funds. In bringing it closer to home—Nowhere, perhaps is the military image of the U.S. lower than it is among the black male students especially those of Southern U. The reason is compulsory ROTC which finds its 'right to be' in the draft. Our black male students are forced to participate in the program and because of that, most of them hate it.[12]

FELTON G. CLARK RETIRES FROM SOUTHERN UNIVERSITY

While many students began to question the value and benefits of military training on the Bluff, the professional career of the ROTC program's biggest supporter was coming to an end. By the fall of 1968, Felton G. Clark had reached the age of sixty-five and was forced to retire by the Louisiana State Board of Education. Though Clark had several health related problems, it was clear that he was not ready to step down as president. In preparation for his departure, Clark took an official leave of absence to bring G. Leon Netterville, the former vice president of business affairs and new president, up to speed and make a smooth transition to retirement. After thirty years as president, Clark left Southern University physically and spiritually broken by the thought of severing official ties with the institution his father founded on the bluffs of the Mississippi River and to which he devoted an immeasurable amount of time and energy to advance. Within twelve months of leaving the university, Clark passed away with little fanfare and acknowledgment from the surrounding community.[13]

As Southern's strongest supporter of military training and the individual most responsible for the institutional success of the ROTC department, even in his final year as president Clark was busy writing letters to the Department of the Navy for the establishment of a Naval Reserve Officers Training Corps unit.[14] Despite his efforts to promote the virtues of military training, students representing various organizations at a campus student leadership conference decided to push harder for the abolition of compulsory ROTC, noting that "land-grant colleges [were] no longer obligated to force it upon its students."[15]

COMPULSORY ROTC IS FUNDAMENTAL TO LEADERSHIP SKILLS

Throughout the fall semester, compulsory ROTC continued to be a hot topic on Southern's campus. Critics of compulsory military training proudly announced that colleges and universities throughout the nation were changing from mandatory training programs to voluntary programs:

> Should compulsory ROTC be eliminated as a degree requirement at Southern? Campus-wide sentiments indicate that abolition of compulsory ROTC courses would be more beneficial to the University. The latest trend by colleges and universities to shift from compulsory to voluntary ROTC programs has been rapid since 1963. In eleven Southern States, there are 40 schools with voluntary programs and 33 with compulsory. Now less than 19 out of 68 land grant schools of which Southern University is one, have compulsory ROTC.[16]

Southern University Digest staff writer Frank Williams reported that most students on campus did not support compulsory ROTC. By contrast, Colonel Warren B. Rhodes, the professor of military science, "[felt] that ROTC should be compulsory at some phase of a young black man's life in college. Military science teaches the basic fundamentals of being a man, especially how to stand on one's own two feet, and how to accept responsibility for himself and others. It is in this respect that ROTC strives to establish leadership. It teaches a student to accept what he really believes in and tends to enable him to speak out."[17]

U.S. MILITARY ESTABLISHES NEW ROTC PROGRAMS

Though many land-grant institutions in the South moved from compulsory to a voluntary ROTC obligation, it is worth noting that between 1968 and 1974 the southern region of the United States was where the largest growth occurred in relation to the establishment of new ROTC programs. The U.S. military shifted its focus from the East, where a predominate number of Ivy League and private institutions phased out military training, to concentrate on "military friendly" communities that had a long-standing relationship with the armed forces, such as Fayetteville State, near Fort Bragg, North Carolina, Benedict College, near Fort Jackson, South Carolina, and Alabama State, near Maxwell Air Force Base in Montgomery, Alabama.[18] In comparison, the military obligation at land-grant institutions continued to be more resilient than at private institutions, liberal arts colleges, and non-land-grant institutions. Because of a lack of interest in military training and the low number of officer commissions, ROTC units were deactivated by the Department of Defense at schools such as the University of Michigan, the University of Illinois, Stanford, Harvard, Yale, Grinnell College, and Franklin and Marshall.[19]

While numerous student organizations and activists throughout the nation lobbied for the abolition of compulsory ROTC, the U.S. Army and college administrators met to discuss how to increase ROTC enrollment. During this period, the number of students who identified with the antiwar movement increased from 35 percent in 1967 to nearly 70 percent in 1970.[20] Dr. Martin L. Harvey, dean of student affairs, represented Southern University at the Educators Conference held by the Fourth Army at Fort Bliss. Upon returning to Baton Rouge, Harvey presented the new president, G. Leon Netterville, with a detailed report of the conference. Harvey announced, "Many colleges have changed the ROTC curriculum to non-military subjects. Special attention should be given to increasing the number of Negro students in the advanced course. There is only 1 Negro officer to every 30 enlisted men."[21] Surprisingly, Harvey also reported that institutions that dropped the mandatory requirement for military training experienced a reduction in enrollments but noticed an increase in the number of highly motivated cadets. Harvey's memo also listed student dissident organizations located throughout Louisiana that the U.S. military was concerned about. Two of those organizations were the Student Nonviolent Coordinating Committee and W.E.B. Du Bois Clubs. Although Black Power activists were intensely antagonistic toward white faculty at HBCUs, Harvey further reported, "I raised the question about racial integration of the ROTC Staff, since the former President [Clark] had made it clear in writing that Southern University was interested."[22]

THE SILENT MAJORITY SPEAK OUT

The *Southern University Digest* increasingly printed militant editorials and articles supporting the Black Power movement, but many students and faculty believed that those publications did not accurately reflect their convictions or opinions:

> There can be little doubt that the *S.U. Digest* is fast becoming the mouthpiece of the Black Student Union and is, therefore, no longer representative of most students of S.U. I make this charge with full knowledge of the facts. As a test of this charge I challenge the editors of the *Digest* to publish this article which flies in the face of their expressed views on blackness, or on what I have called elsewhere the black mystique. I also challenge them to publish my letter, "The Black Militant Fad," submitted for publication in the March 7th issue of the *Digest*.[23]

In fact, the debate that persisted between antiwar supporters and promilitary advocates in student newspapers or student unions at black colleges and universities was simply a reflection of the tension that existed in the black community concerning the war and the political direction of African Americans. While many African Americans became more militant and less tolerant of social inequities in American society, others acknowledged those problems but continued to search for ways to advance themselves socially and economically.

STUDENT ACTIVIST AT SOUTHERN UNIVERSITY DEMAND CHANGE

While the war in Vietnam continued and America grappled with the moral issues the conflict raised, students at Southern University in Baton Rouge and the branch campus in New Orleans began a series of demonstrations and boycotts to protest their dissatisfaction with university facilities, curriculums, health insurance, rules and regulations, conditions of streets and roads, and the administrations. Those demonstrations and boycotts ultimately led to the end of compulsory ROTC. Student strikes and demonstrations reached an all-time peak in 1969. "According to *Student Protests 1969*, a study by the Urban Research Corporation, there were 292 major student protests on 232 college and university campuses in the first six months of 1969."[24] While only 5 percent of the nation's college students were African American, more than 50 percent of the protests involved African American students and were overwhelmingly nonviolent. Contrary to student protests on white college campuses, only 2 percent of African American demonstrations directly related to the war in Vietnam.[25]

In April 1969, student activists at Southern University-New Orleans (SUNO) delivered a list of demands to the university administration. In addition to a black studies department and a course on black liberation that was to be taught by Student Nonviolent Coordinating Committee (SNCC) chapter director Jimmie "Scrooge" Lagare, demand #5 insisted that "there be a Black Draft Counseling Center established immediately on campus. This center is to be headed by Brother Walter Collins," the demand read, "who is unofficially one of the foremost authorities on the draft. Countless numbers of Black males are taken out of school and forced to serve in the system of legal slavery every year. This is because of the inefficiency of the Registrar's Office and the lack of student knowledge concerning the draft."[26] Even though full-time students at Southern could receive a draft exemption, they were still vulnerable to the threat of conscription. Campus-based and antiwar resistance organizations, such as SNCC, worked to expose inequalities in the Selective Service System. According to Christian Appy, "the Selective Service System's class-biased channeling, the military's wartime slashing of admission standards, student deferments, and medical exemptions, favored the well-informed and economically privileged."[27]

In an effort to avert trouble, President G. Leon Netterville quickly responded and made preparations to meet with SUNO department heads and student leaders. As president of the Southern University system, Netterville made every effort to reduce tension among students as well as to keep lines of communication open between student leaders and the governing body of the Southern University system. A faculty committee was organized to discuss each demand and to begin work on development of a black studies curriculum. Netterville attended each faculty meeting with the intention of presenting recommendations at the next meeting of the State Board of Education.[28]

On the day the State Board of Education was to meet in Baton Rouge, more than 250 students from SUNO arrived at the State Department of Education building to show support for their agenda. The state police were immediately informed, and once they arrived students left the building and reassembled at the Baton Rouge campus administration building. University officials assured them that their demands would be addressed. However, when students learned that the board had quickly moved through its agenda and left the building without addressing their concerns, they returned and attempted to enter the office of William J. Dodd, the state superintendent of education. Sheriff's deputies and state police were called out once again, and after a brief standoff students returned to the Baton Rouge campus. Again, Netterville assured students that their demands would be addressed in the coming months.[29]

A few days later, two hundred student demonstrators at SUNO entered the administration building and refused to leave. The state police and National Guard were notified. It was reported that students were upset that nothing was done about the demands they had presented to university officials a month earlier during boycotts and demonstrations that lasted for twelve days. Members of the Student Afro-American Society demanded that Southern University-New Orleans's Dean Emmitt Bashful be immediately fired or removed from the New Orleans campus because many believed that he was apathetic to student concerns.[30]

In a similar incident on the Baton Rouge campus, students placed barricades throughout the university to prevent traffic flow onto the campus. Rumors that an African American female was assaulted by a white male and that a black male was unlawfully arrested prompted students to act. President Netterville reported that both incidents were untrue. He went on to say, "These are times when all young people feel frustrated—what with the Vietnam War and all. And obviously black young people feel the most frustrated of all, because of the race situation."[31] Despite the actions of many students and the position of the State Board of Education, Netterville believed that an understanding could be reached between the two parties.

On May 14, 1969, student leaders at Southern University met with Governor John McKeithen to discuss their grievances. Both parties characterized the meeting as productive. The governor agreed to several demands, including a major legislative bill for $100,000 for campus security. Of the fifty-three demands, many individuals believed that the most popular was that students should have a stronger voice in campus affairs. Other demands ranged from better cafeteria facilities to more library books to better street lighting. Coincidently, while the student leaders and Governor McKiethen worked on solving many of Southern's problems, the Louisiana legislature sent a strong message to student protesters around the state when they voted unanimously for a bill that provided harsh penalties for anyone involved in occupying campus buildings or demonstrators that disrupted campus life at Louisiana institutions.[32]

WHITE HIGHER EDUCATION INSTITUTIONS IN LOUISIANA PROTEST COMPULSORY ROTC

While Southern University did not experience any protests or demonstrations solely aimed at removing ROTC programs from the campus, other Louisiana colleges did. The antiwar movement that found its base of support at colleges and universities throughout the nation caught the attention of many interested individuals who believed in the merits of military training. In the Baton Rouge city newspaper, anti-ROTC agitators were described as a minority of "militants" who promoted revolution. Many of these sentiments were articulated in an editorial in which the author remarked, "To the pleasant surprise of ROTC supporters and the dismay of its enemies, ROTC appears to be doing quite well."[33] At Southern, E. C. Harrison also described anti-ROTC students as a minority. "As I remember, the vast majority of students supported ROTC. You will always have a nucleus of people who disagree with the majority, but they were a minority."[34] Frank Ransburg described anti-ROTC sentiment at Southern as "talk." "The only thing you heard was *talk*. On a college campus there will always be different opinions circulating on everything. People didn't pay attention to such talk."[35]

Although Ransburg's characterization of anti-ROTC reaction maybe oversimplified, one clearly gets the impression that at Southern the majority of individuals did not share the views of anti-ROTC advocates.

THE GOVERNOR OF LOUISIANA VISITS SOUTHERN UNIVERSITY

In an effort to show concern, Governor McKiethen toured the Baton Rouge campus with students to get a first-hand account of some of the problems. Student body president William Jefferson expressed the desire of many students to have an overpass constructed connecting the campus to the surrounding community, which had been previously requested several years earlier. In addition, the governor inspected several dorms, the cafeteria facilities, and was asked to address the problem of mosquitoes at a nearby lake. Hours before the governor arrived on campus, student leaders met with State Board officials to discuss their concerns. The meeting was described as productive, but no immediate action was taken by the governor.[36]

ROTC BECOMES VOLUNTARY THROUGHOUT LOUISIANA

While tensions subsided between Southern students and State Board officials, another Louisiana college experienced student unrest. Twenty-one students and a faculty member from Tulane University disrupted ROTC instruction in an effort to express their frustration with the program. The incident was one of many in recent weeks designed to interfere with military training on campus. Campus police immediately arrested the demonstrators and charged them with willful disruption of university activities.[37]

As students at Southern concentrated on making physical improvements and better funding opportunities a reality on both campuses, several predominately white institutions moved to abolish compulsory ROTC on their campuses. On April 20, 1969, the McNeese State College president announced that the ROTC evaluation committee agreed to implement a voluntary program.[38] A few weeks later, Louisiana State University's decision made front-page news when it reported, "Members of the LSU Board of Supervisors killed compulsory ROTC by a vote of 9–4."[39] A couple of months later, Northeast Louisiana State College made the decision to abolish compulsory ROTC in an effort "to become a stronger corps."[40] Southern's decision to move to a voluntary ROTC program came on the heels of other Louisiana institutions. With little publicity president Netterville announced his plans to abolish compulsory ROTC in conjunction with other concessions made to students. "Dissent and demonstrations will be tolerated but forced cessation of class activities will not be at Southern. The right of persons will be protected if they desire to attend classes."[41] Following this statement Netterville revealed his decision to have voluntary ROTC at Southern University.

Unlike other Louisiana institutions that witnessed social unrest as a result of ROTC activities, student-led protests and demonstrations at Southern were concerned with giving students a stronger voice in administrative issues, physical improvements to the campus, and more social freedom at the university. Military training did not receive the type of negative attention that it did at white institutions because either individuals supported its presence on campus or they were more concerned with other issues. Frank Ransburg suggested that a major part of the decision to abolish compulsory ROTC at Southern was convenience of scheduling:

> Students asked for fifty-three changes at Southern University, one of which was that they no longer wanted Saturday classes. If you were taking ROTC certain classes were scheduled during the week. So you were forced to schedule classes on Saturday. I don't think that the abolishment of compulsory ROTC was anti-military, I think that it was a scheduling concern when most colleges in Louisiana had already abolished Saturday classes except Southern University. By 1969 you [African Americans] could go to any school in the state. Why would you want to go to a school that had Saturday classes when every other institution did not? So the movement to abolish compulsory ROTC was not anti-military as much as it was a convenience in scheduling courses.[42]

Ransburg further remarked, "I think that recommendation came from the Committee on Student Affairs and he [Netterville] approved it. Knowing Netterville as I did, he probably cleared it with the State Board of Education. But as I said before, at that time, unless it was something outlandish, the president of the university could do pretty much what he wanted to do. The decision to abolish compulsory ROTC was sort-of routine because all of the other state colleges were eliminating compulsory ROTC on their campuses."[43]

ROTC OFFICIALS SEE SILVER LINING IN VOLUNTARY PROGRAM

At Southern, the fall semester began with the news that compulsory ROTC was officially abolished and that for the first time male students could choose whether they wanted to participate. The majority of faculty members at Southern had voted to discontinue compulsory military training, and student participation in ROTC dropped by more than 50 percent.[44] Although the number of ROTC cadets decreased, Lieutenant Colonel Warren Rhodes, professor of military science, believed that "because ROTC [was] voluntary, the cadets should be dedicated to the program; and the corps should be 'as good as or better than' the past years."[45]

Despite a reduction in ROTC enrollment, the Army ROTC program continued to actively recruit male students and present itself as an organization with vast growth potential and much to offer young African Americans:

> The fact that a considerable percentage of the student population has voluntarily registered for the program is offered by the staff as evidence that the ROTC does have a future in the S.U. Curriculum. The university, a predominantly black institution, is the leading single producer of qualified Negro officers for service in the United States Army. This year forty-nine (49) students entered the Advanced Program, which is the highest number in the history of this university. This particular point is significant because the program presently is under a voluntary system which would suggest a decrease in participation in the advanced program; however, statistically the opposite is true.[46]

The ROTC department proudly reported that in addition to many social events, an ROTC flight program would be offered at Southern. The program was designed to "stimulate college students' interest in Army aviation and expose selected ROTC cadets to an actual flight environment."[47]

KENT STATE AND JACKSON STATE STUDENTS ARE MURDERED DURING ANTIWAR DEMONSTRATION

In May 1970, when President Nixon announced U.S. plans to invade Cambodia, antiwar activism intensified at college campuses across the nation. Demonstrations were held at Temple University, Villanova University, State University of New York, and the University of Arizona. Violence erupted when student protesters at the University of Maryland in College Park stormed the ROTC building and attempted to burn uniforms, files, and classroom furniture. The governor of Maryland immediately sent the National Guard and state police to restore order to the campus. A day later, the ROTC departments at Michigan State and Princeton were both attacked by student protesters.[48] Throughout the Northeast, students at thirteen colleges and universities reacted by organizing sit-ins, demonstrations, and student strikes. On May 4, on the campus of Kent State University, after student protesters attempted to burn down the ROTC barracks a couple of days earlier, the National Guard and demonstrators began tossing tear gas canisters at one another while students threw rocks and verbally assaulted the troops. In a heated exchange, guardsmen fired on the crowd and four students were killed. Once news of the Kent State killings spread across the country, student demonstrators protested the atrocity at private and state institutions, women's colleges, and parochial schools.

While student antiwar protests at black colleges such as Albany State College and Paine College in Georgia, Miles College in Alabama, and Lincoln University in Pennsylvania were ordinarily nonviolent and uneventful, Jackson State College proved to be the exception. Located approximately 150 miles northeast of Baton Rouge in Jackson, Mississippi, Jackson State College, with a student enrollment of approximately thirty-five hundred, was never considered to be a trailblazer in civil rights activism. Nevertheless, the escalation of the war, the killings at Kent State University, the report that African Americans were being killed in disproportionate numbers in Vietnam, and the idea that Mississippi draft boards were making it all possible provided the right combination to inspire students to action.[49]

Generally, students at Jackson State voiced their disdain for issues involving race discrimination and social injustice. Days after the tragic event at Kent State University, students were prompted to assemble by a sign that read:

JSC Students
Be Concerned
Meet in Front
of the Dining Hall
at 2 p.m. Today
To Discuss Cambodia[50]

At the appointed hour, a crowd of five hundred students assembled at the dining hall to discuss the draft, the war in Vietnam, and the African American struggle for social justice and equal opportunity in Mississippi. Warner Buxton, the student government president, addressed the enthusiastic gathering and suggested that "the students weren't too pleased about the Cambodia situation. They thought it was outrageous and it was probably going to cause a lot more people to go into service and it might cause the war to get bigger and more prolonged."[51] Though the "hot topic" on campus was Kent State and the escalation of the war, surprisingly only a handful of students bothered to participate in a downtown antiwar rally a couple days later. What appeared to worry students the most was, Why didn't Jackson State College close in the aftermath of the Kent State slayings, like many institutions throughout the country? As a result, a rumor quickly spread among the student body that the ROTC barracks would be set afire that night.[52]

On May 14, 1970, at 10:00 P.M., a group of individuals referred to as *corner boys*, local school dropouts, began throwing rocks at cars carrying white passengers traveling through the campus. The day before, Jackson City's mayor, Russell Davis, had requested that five hundred National Guard troops be placed on alert in addition to eighty state troopers and 125 city police in order to discourage student unrest and social disturbances that plagued many college campuses throughout the nation.[53] Campus security immediately responded to the rock throwing, but was also repelled by the youths. By 10:30 P.M., 150 students had gathered near the student union and began shouting antiwar slogans and voicing their disgust with ROTC training. It was not long before the crowd began to shout, "Let's burn down 'Rotsy!' 'Burn it down! Burn it down!'" By the time several ROTC cadets and officers who were in the building approached the students and tried to defuse the situation, the crowd had swelled to two to three hundred students. A witness to the incident, Vernon Weakley, confirmed, "It looked as if the kids had surrounded the ROTC building. They were screaming and hollering, 'Burn it down! Burn it down!' They were rushing the building, as if trying to get in or tear it down or something like that. The security guards would pull their guns and make a run, and then the kids would go back aways."[54] Once the students became tired of the standoff, they quickly left the area. However, hours later three individuals returned carrying bottles filled with gasoline and tossed them on the roof and porch of the ROTC building. Although the building ignited, the fire was quickly doused by ROTC officers and cadets.

The next morning, Jackson State College president John Peoples began to investigate the sequence of events. Much like Felton Clark and G. Leon Netterville, Peoples was a strong supporter of military training. In fact, Peoples was a former Marine Corps drill instructor who believed that the armed forces afforded African Americans dignity and honor in a racist society.[55] He was especially proud of the fact that while other institutions were removing ROTC from their campuses, Jackson State had recently received approval for its unit. Peoples also felt, like many of his contemporaries, that the value of education had never been more important to the collective progress of African Americans and that he must do everything necessary to maintain that opportunity. He remarked, "We're in a fight, and we're going to win it. But we can't win it with guns. We exist in the milieu of Mississippi, and blacks still have no power here. I personally must go before the legislature each year and present our program and our needs."[56]

The next evening the *corner boys* once again began pelting campus traffic, while one hundred students cheered the vagrants on. Windows were shattered and white passengers were assaulted. "At 10:30 p.m. police, highway patrolmen and National Guard troops began to materialize out of the night, marking off their perimeter four blocks from campus with a line of sawhorses."[57] Approximately an hour later, the police reported the sound of gunfire in the direction of Alexander Hall and proceeded in that direction. Once a skirmish line was formed by the police on campus, students began to shout obscenities and several officers called students "Nigger" and other racial epithets. The loud exchange even drowned out the officer on the bullhorn addressing the students. After a student leader and the police unsuccessfully attempted to disburse the crowd, someone lobbed a bottle at the police. When it burst on to the ground it sounded like gunfire. "And as if on cue, the police let loose at the crowd with machine guns, shotguns, pistols, and rifles. They raked the building and the squirming students on the ground. One student said that those in front of the dormitory were trying to get inside. Blood was everywhere."[58] In the wake of a barrage of bullets that shattered windows and left over two hundred bullets holes in Alexander Hall, two individuals lay dead: Phillip Lafayette Gibbs, a twenty-one-year-old pre-law student, and seventeen-year-old Earl Green, who happened to be walking home from his job through the campus. Nine male and female students were wounded.⁵⁹

JACKSON STATE COLLEGE: AN ANOMALY

The Jackson State slayings were the only violence at a black college or university associated with the antiwar movement and ROTC training. Surprisingly, although the terrible events began with students attempting to burn down the ROTC building the night before, military training at the institution did not suffer from a lack of interest or student support thereafter. In fact, a year later, according to *Newsweek*, "less understood [was] the remarkable diffidence of the students. Perhaps their most militant act has been the formation of the first campus chapter of the NAACP. But of real activism there was virtually none; when an attempt was made to organize a march on City Hall to protest a proposed relocation of the Jackson State campus, less than ten students showed up."⁶⁰

The tragic events at Kent State and Jackson State were atypical incidents that reflect how quickly a series of actions could escalate into the unnecessary deaths of innocent bystanders. Furthermore, they also represent how the war in Vietnam became a springboard to student activism and the need to vent youth frustration with perceived societal injustices and the hypocrisy of fighting for South Vietnamese freedom. While the killings at Kent State elicited an emotional response from young white Americans that disrupted university operations at 20 percent of the nation's colleges and universities, the reaction of students at Jackson State was an anomaly. The origin of the tragedy embodied a combination of aggravation and mischief by three determined individuals with a minority of students who linked civil rights activism and the war in Vietnam.⁶¹

SUPPORT FOR ROTC CONTINUES TO GROW IN THE BLACK COMMUNITY

The social and economic benefits of military service and training programs at HBCUs like Prairie View, Tuskegee, Morgan State, and Southern had a far greater impact on those schools' students than did the war. At those HBCUs many students were able to differentiate between the moral and ethical issues concerning the war in Vietnam and the advantages of military training and service. Actually, the appeal of the benefits of military training and service continued to grow among African American students at several HBCUs that received approval for new ROTC detachments, such as Alabama A&M in Normal, Alabama, Alcorn A&M in Lorman, Mississippi, and Grambling State College in north Louisiana.[62]

On the campus of Southern, while the antiwar movement across the nation made headlines, many students continued to voice their displeasure with the draft even as administrators persisted with their commitment to military training. President Netterville received the good news from the Department of the Navy that the school's application for a Naval Reserve Officers Training Corps (NROTC) unit had been approved.[63] Chief of Naval Personnel Vice Admiral D. H. Guinn wrote, "We believe that the environment and facilities at your Institution are such that a Naval ROTC Unit there would contribute appreciably to the education and training of officer candidates with a view toward increasing the percentage of minority group officers in the Naval Service. It is desired to establish a Unit of the Naval ROTC at a predominantly Negro university with a target date of September 1971."[64] Though military training programs continued to be criticized in the student press and at student gatherings, Netterville believed that the military tradition at Southern could successfully support another ROTC program and attract a sufficient number of cadets.

STUDENT ACTIVIST HIGHLIGHTS CONTRADICTION OF AFRICAN AMERICAN MILITARY SERVICE

Southern University Digest staff writer Wilbur Robinson continued to criticize individuals who participated in ROTC and suggested that ROTC departments were part of a federal conspiracy by the U.S. military to control and oppress minorities:

> For those of you who aren't aware of it, your friends in ROTC may, one day, have to kill you in order to "protect and preserve your freedom." But in order to really understand this we must first know what the military is doing to us and how ROTC fits into this. The Army's domestic intelligence plan that you have been hearing and reading about was devised amid the city riots of

1967 and 1968 so as to enable the Army to move as rapidly as possible to deploy sufficient troops to "control an outbreak" with the so-called minimum amount of force. If you still aren't convinced about what is being done to you, notice where the National Guard Armory in Baton Rouge is located! It is located at a point where the Black area of Scotlandville and white Baton Rouge is separated.[65]

Robinson added, "You [ROTC cadets] can go all over the world to defend another country's freedom but when you come back home your black brothers and sisters will be waiting for you to do some fighting for their freedom too. This is before and after you leave!"[66] Though Robinson's attitude toward military training and ROTC cadets was fairly common in the late 1960s, once compulsory ROTC was abolished most students were not as passionate concerning military training.

During the fall semester of 1971 the commission date for the NROTC program was established in addition to plans for a ceremony. The university asked Rear Admiral Samuel Gravely, the first African American to attain the rank of admiral, to be the keynote speaker. The first commander of Southern's NROTC program was Commander D. A. Griffin. In an interview Griffin explained the purpose of the program and what students should expect: "NROTC was introduced to predominately Black schools in an effort to increase the number of Black officers in the Navy and Marines. A study was done in 1962 to determine the number of Black officers in the navy and the figures showed only 0.3 of one percent were Black. The study was up-dated in 1970 and the findings revealed that the number has risen only 0.4 and as a result of this the programs were instituted in an effort to raise the figures."[67]

According to *Digest* reporter Larry St. Amant, Griffin believed that NROTC held special rewards for African Americans in particular and he understood the reluctance to join and the opposition to the war, but, St. Amant added, "though he doesn't agree with the War in Viet Nam he still feels that young Blacks should join the Armed Forces if they wish because the war will not go on forever and that they could be receiving invaluable training. You can serve without being a flag waver, he said."[68] During the dedication ceremony, Admiral Gravely declared that the Navy could improve the life of young African Americans and provide well-deserved social opportunities. "I know that there are problems of discrimination, but I believe, however, that the Navy of today is one of the most integrated structures in

American Society. It surpasses many of our churches, most of our schools and certainly the majority of our neighborhoods. The Navy's aim is simply this—we want one Navy—NO Black Navy: NO White Navy," Gravely said.[69]

U.S. MILITARY REPORTS GOOD NEWS

The end of 1971 held good news for military training programs throughout the nation, but for African American institutions in particular. The deputy assistant secretary of defense for education, Dr. George C. S. Benson, reported that ROTC programs were multiplying around the country despite recent setbacks. Benson proclaimed, "According to a recent *U.S. News and World Report,* there are more Reserve Officers' Training Corps Units on college campuses this fall than ever before despite 400 anti-ROTC actions in 1969–70 and 110 in 1970–71. Only 11 universities have voted to end ROTC and 15 new units have formed—seven at predominately black colleges."[70] While private white institutions were removing their ROTC programs, African American colleges and universities continued to request the establishment of military training programs at their institutions. Benson believed that not only did black institutions help boost the number of ROTC programs, but they provided a source of much needed African American officers to the armed forces. "We have several new units," observed Benson, "in what are predominately black colleges and I would really rather have them than Harvard and the others. In the first place we need black officers. Predominately black colleges realize that the Negro still has to fight his way forward and the armed forces have been the fairest arena in U.S. life."[71] The Department of Defense planned to increase the number of cadets by offering financial incentives and raising the number of scholarships available to students. Students who enrolled in ROTC programs would receive $100 per month instead of the previous amount of $50. Over the next five years the Department of Defense planned to add $50 million dollars to the ROTC budget.

In preparation for the all-volunteer armed forces and America's withdrawal from Vietnam, the Selective Service System made policy changes that reduced the number of draftees inducted. The news received front-page attention at Southern because for the first time it afforded enlistees the opportunity to determine whether they would serve on active duty, in the National Guard, or in the Reserves. "The only option to men who had received induction orders in past months was to join one of the Regular branches of the service for at least three years active duty. No Guard or Reserve enlistments or appointments were authorized after the mailing of induction orders."[72] But under the new policy, "Men who receive induction orders and desired to enter in the Guard or Reserve must locate unit vacancies on their own. They should request that their enlistments or appointments in the Guard or Reserves require at least 4 months active duty for training and the balance of six years participating in the Ready Reserve."[73]

TRAGIC EVENTS AT SOUTHERN UNIVERSITY

Before the end of the 1972 fall semester at Southern University, support for military training and service would once again be questioned by a large number of students. A series of unfortunate events would lead to the saddest days the university ever experienced. In late October, Students United (a student organization) delivered a list of grievances and demands to President Netterville that would give students a greater voice in campus affairs and policies that included student members on the University Senate, the creation of a student and faculty advisory council, improvements in campus facilities and equipment, student input on the university Food Service Committee, and the resignation of Netterville. The following day university officials suggested that the students follow normal protocols to present complaints and in the future not present them to the president. Students United promptly organized a boycott of classes until the university decided to address their concerns. A few days later, representatives of the school administration and the State Board of Education met with student leaders to begin a dialogue. During the meeting, student leaders reiterated their demands and suggested that student demonstrations would end once students were given a greater stake in the operation and direction of the institution. State officials agreed to study the grievances, but stated unequivocally that institution officials would not be removed.[74]

Over the next several weeks, the university made token gestures at satisfying student demands in an attempt to prevent a confrontation with law enforcement officials. While the boycott continued, the majority of students attended class, but they were periodically harassed and confronted by dissident students. For example, an English professor filed a complaint with Dr. E. C. Harrison, vice president of academic affairs, charging that:

> My class meeting today, the class met at 9:30 a.m., with about three students present on time, and discussion started. At 9:40 a group of about eighty persons bearing several "Boycott" placards entered the classroom, filled the seats and occupied standing room. They tried to persuade my few students to leave the classroom, and blocked the door so that any students who arrived late could not enter the classroom. My students, however, remained in their seats and refused to leave. At 9:50, after I had talked with the demonstrators, they left the classroom. I then led my students to my office, and continued the discussion there; and dismissed them at 10:30. P.S./ There were no security officers or law enforcement officers of any kind in the building.[75]

On the 7th of November 1972, while Louisiana's governor, Edwin Edwards, was meeting with State Board officials to discuss how to address student unrest at Southern and avoid any violence, he was informed that two buildings on campus exploded and that Molotov cocktails were discovered at the horticulture barn. As a result, arrest warrants were issued for eight students. A week later, Netterville decided to end the stalemate with student activists and offered amnesty to all students in exchange for their returning the campus to normalcy. Black Power student leaders rejected his offer and continued the boycott. On November 11, students protested at a football game and three days later interrupted several classes on campus. While student protest continued, on November 15 Netterville withdrew his amnesty offer and asked university officials to notify the sheriff's office that students were breaking the law by disrupting classes throughout the campus.[76]

The campus police asked Al Amiss, the East Baton Rouge Parish sheriff, to place his deputies on alert. On November 16, at approximately 4:00 in the morning, four students were arrested by sheriff's deputies. The students were charged with "obstruction or interference of educational institutions." In an act of solidarity, a large group of students approached the administration building hours later, demanded to see President Netterville, and insisted that the students be released. Initially Netterville agreed to meet with five students, but after a brief exchange he informed them that he had a meeting to attend downtown with the State Board of Education but that upon his return he would meet the students in the men's gym because of the large number of students present. At that point his secretary notified him that he had a phone call and Netterville excused himself but never returned. At approximately 9:15 A.M., Netterville asked the chief of campus police to contact James L. Hunt, the director of administrative services, to inquire if the sheriff's deputies were en route to campus.[77]

Shortly thereafter, over fifty sheriff's deputies and a thirty-man tactical unit from the state police arrived on campus, according to the attorney general's report, "the Sheriff's personnel understood that President Netterville was being held in his office by students; then that the President had been released; and finally, that the students had occupied the Administration Building and were holding a campus security guard hostage. The fact was: No university personnel were held hostage or forcibly detained in the Administration Building at any time on the morning of November 16th."[78] The sheriff's deputies and the state police, equipped with shotguns, automatic weapons, handguns, and tear gas, therefore surrounded the administration building. Surprisingly, there was very little communication between university officials and law enforcement personnel in order to properly assess the threat. After a brief conference between the officers in charge, it was agreed that if the students did not comply with their command to disperse, tear gas would be used to clear the area. When Sheriff Amiss ordered the students to leave the area, more than half began to vacate the premises. Unfortunately many did not, and several students responded, "Come and get us!" Without an order to engage the students, one deputy preemptively launched three tear gas canisters toward the students. Two of the canisters were tossed back at the deputies, and confusion quickly caused law enforcement officials to break their lines to search for their gas masks. In a matter of minutes deputies were firing gas canisters from shotguns and students were tossing the projectiles once again at the police. As students began to run in the opposite direction for safety, Leonard Douglas Brown and Denver Allen Smith were mortally wounded by shotgun fire from an unidentified sheriff's deputy.[79] Once notified, President Netterville returned to campus and immediately closed the university.

KENT STATE, JACKSON STATE, NOW SOUTHERN UNIVERSITY

On the same day, before these tragic events at Southern, a prophetic editorial appeared in the *Morning Advocate* newspaper written by Stanley Morris, an assistant professor of physics at Southern University and a 1951 graduate of the institution. Morris was deeply disturbed by recent student unrest and President Netterville's refusal to negotiate with student leaders, and he suggested that the university was headed down a path of "self-destruction." Morris also compared Southern University's quagmire with a very familiar worst-case scenario, the massacres at Kent State University and Jackson State College. Morris further exclaimed, "Those who would support the administration say they are loyal to the university. Those who would support Students United also say they are loyal to the university. I say this to both groups, you are wrong. If you are loyal to the concept of Southern University, then support meaningful negotiation between persons of reason and good will."[80]

Though President Netterville never publically blamed the recent turmoil on the students, he did search for someone to blame. A few days after the death of Brown and Smith, two university professors were fired for encouraging the ordeal and advising student leaders: Dr. Joseph Johnson, chairman of the department of physics, and Professor George W. Baker from the engineering department. The dismissal letters read: "By serving as adviser to the dissident students, you have been instrumental in promoting activities which disrupted the normal educational process of the university." It is believed that Netterville also dismissed six other faculty members for the same reasons. Though several calls were made throughout Louisiana and the nation for Netterville to resign, Netterville reported that he would remain president of Southern University.[81]

SOUTHERN UNIVERSITY BEGINS THE PROCESS OF HEALING

Even though the university remained closed during the month of December, university officials, student leaders, faculty, and staff met frequently to discuss student grievances and how to improve student-administration relations.[82] From those meetings, an extensive progress report was issued highlighting such issues as food service, housing, academic changes, fine arts, and improvements to the music building. The report suggested that university officials planned to improve the cleanliness of the dining halls throughout campus as well as the quality of the food. In addition, students were appointed to the university Food Service Committee (a demand previously made by Students United) and given a greater voice in the operation of the Student Union Cafeteria. Housing improvements was another concern that occupied much of the negotiation. Students asked for new draperies in three dormitories, new fire hoses and extinguishers, new water coolers, improved exterminator service and pest control, new paint in the stairwells of Jones and Boley Halls and the dorm rooms of Grandison Hall, purchase orders for new beds, box springs, and mattresses for Fisher and Smith halls, and general maintenance on all locks, water faucets, and doors.[83]

On December 27, a one-day symposium was held by 120 students and twenty members of the administration, faculty, and staff that focused on student grievances, the impact of past events, and how to move forward as a university community. From that meeting six resolutions were adopted from student views and recommendations. Three of those resolutions gave students a greater voice in university governance and more control over their lives as students at Southern University:

1. Be it resolved that the student participants of this group serve as liaison persons in departmental meetings to relate events of this meeting to other students.
2. Be it resolved that students become an active part of any contingency plans for campus security. There were seven student volunteers to serve on the committee which is planning campus security.
3. Be it resolved that University's administration immediately develop, communicate, and implement ways of receiving and giving immediate attention to student grievances. The presence of such a mechanism could conceivably prevent the recurrence of the tragic events of November 26, 1972.[84]

Surprisingly, the report also suggested that students and university officials were able to agree on many issues during the symposium with relative ease and virtually no tension or animosity between the two sides. Student participants truly reflected the student body in that they represented all academic departments and included male and female students from all geographic regions of the state.

UNIVERSITY REOPENS WITH FEW DISRUPTIONS

On January 3, 1973, Southern University reopened and attempted to complete the semester. University officials and the community were apprehensive because it was not entirely clear how the students would respond or whether the boycott would continue. Over the weeks following the killings, many students believed that the murders of Brown and Smith were part of a premeditated plan by the sheriff's deputies and that President Netterville, Governor Edwin Edwards, and Sheriff Al Amiss were solely to blame for the unfortunate events.[85] But to the pleasant surprise of university officials, students returned to the campus with few incidents or residual effects. There were, however, a few occasions where a small number of students disrupted classes in an attempt revive the boycott. The day after classes resumed, an education instructor reported that several students entered her classroom and began to harass her students for attending class. She remarked:

> On Thursday, January 4, 1973, I was in the process of teaching 202 Elementary Shorthand at 2:00 p.m. in the T.T. Allain building, Room 223.
>
> Several students were walking the hall (one at a time). They would stop by the door and look into the classroom. I thought they might have been out-of-towners looking for a relative. Then one young man stood in the doorway and asked if he could say something to the class. I agreed.
>
> He asked the class how did they feel attending classes after two persons had died—Did they die in vain? Is it right for you to continue going to class? He waited for an answer—and everyone was very quiet. Then one of my students attempted to answer him. I told her she did not have to answer him. He said he wanted to *speak* to the class. I told him that he had said what he wanted, now please leave. Then a lot of students started crowding around the door.
>
> I went to close the door and the other students were pushing the students into the door. But I managed to close the door and it locked. While at the door, they mumbled antagonisms toward me a few minutes, then left.[86]

MURDERS AT UNIVERSITIES AND COLLEGE REPRESENT MISTRUST FOR AUTHORITY

Although no one was ever arrested for the murders of Denver Smith and Leonard Brown, the incident left a lasting impression on the university, the black community, and Netterville. Less than a year after the incident, Netterville resigned as president of Southern University.[87] While the killings on Southern's campus had nothing directly to do with military training or the ROTC department, the incident only magnified the mistrust that many students felt for symbols of authority and government officials. The tragic events at Southern were very similar to those at Kent State and Jackson State College. Young people were discouraged by the state of American society and saw themselves as victims of oppressive authority. Coincidently, Students United distributed a flyer titled "Murder at SU" throughout the campus the very next day. They compared themselves with the students and victims of Kent State University and Jackson State College and appealed to the surrounding community to support the impeachment of Governor Edwin Edwards and the criminal indictment of Sheriff Al Amiss and President G. Leon Netterville. The flyer also stated, "Kent State, Jackson State—now Southern University. How many more senseless brutal murderings must your sons and daughters endure before the concerned elements in our community speak out in one forceful, effective voice to remove the racist elements which inflict GENOCIDE on the helpless Black people."[88]

U.S. MILITARY BEGINS TO WITHDRAW FROM VIETNAM

By 1973, Nixon's plans for the American withdrawal in Vietnam were well under way and Congress had already approved the termination of the draft. Protest against the war or the armed forces did not hold the same urgency or attention that it once did. According to Michael Lanning, "One of the most crucial factors in racial unrest and negative attitudes toward the military during the Vietnam era was the Selective Service System. Blacks believed that boards drafted them in disproportionate numbers and that liberal deferments were more readily available to whites."[89] With the end of the draft, the U.S. military attempted to make military service more attractive by improving the pay, benefits, and housing conditions.[90] A decade of antiwar protest appeared to enter a cooling off period and to have little influence over the thousands of African Americans who filled recruiting stations to enlist in the all-volunteer force or participated in ROTC.

ROTC AT SOUTHERN AND JACKSON STATE CONTINUES TO PROSPER

Though unarmed students at Jackson State College and Southern University were murdered by overzealous National Guard soldiers and local police during student demonstrations, Army ROTC continued to attract a faction of motivated and enthusiastic students that eagerly embraced life in the armed forces and the virtues of military training and service. In fact, ROTC programs at both institutions reached another milestone when they began admitting women into their ranks. As early as the spring of 1972, the Naval ROTC department at Southern became one of four higher education institutions and the first African American university to admit female cadets.[91] During the fall of 1973, Southern's Army ROTC department proudly announced that female students were eligible for military training. Army captain Robert C. Meager, director of instruction, confirmed that "this is the first year that this has been authorized. The program has expanded throughout every university in the country. Presently, the ROTC program does not offer a major or minor but nonetheless, fifteen freshman women have responded to the benefits of this program."[92] During the same period, the Army ROTC detachment at Jackson State College also admitted its first group of female cadets under the command of Dorothy Fortune, a U.S. Army veteran. In 1976, ten Southern University women were commissioned as second lieutenants in the U.S. Army, making it the largest class of female ROTC graduates at an HBCU in the nation.[93] That the armed forces had incorporated an aggressive affirmative-action program and that women were now being recruited by the U.S. military had a tremendous impact on the number of female students interested in military service. In addition, there was a greater number of occupational specialties available to women, and female students took full advantage of those enhanced opportunities.

CONCLUSION

Between 1968 and 1973, the war in Vietnam caused many social and political problems in American society. The war unleashed political tensions between "hawks" and "doves," generational divisions between young adults and middle-aged Americans, and political struggles between pacifists and cold warriors. In particular, African Americans and poor Americans witnessed Great Society reform efforts stall, while the underclass became marked for combat in Southeast Asia.[94] The student antiwar movement developed from these struggles and polarized America even more.

On the campuses of black colleges and universities, the antiwar movement divided the students and faculty on many issues. Antiwar supporters focused on political and ideological reasons not to support the war or military training, while promilitary advocates concentrated on the social and economic advantages of military service. Although military training programs at Southern University and other black colleges and universities would never again reach the height of popularity they had in the 1950s, the fact that they continued to attract interested men and women as draft calls shrank and ended altogether demonstrated that the long-standing appeal of military service at those institutions had survived its most turbulent days and continued to impact the black community as well as the U.S. armed forces.[95]

7

CONCLUSION

African American attitudes toward military service at historically black colleges and universities during the post–World War II era were reflective of attitudes in the black community. Military training and service were at the height of their popularity in the 1950s and early 1960s, but by the start of Nixon's administration the civil rights movement, the Black Power movement, the war in Vietnam, and the antiwar movement influenced many individuals to resist serving in the armed forces or to view compulsory military training as an oppressive form of control. Nonetheless, although a shift in attitudes toward military training and service occurred during this period, it was met by a faction of military supporters who continued to eagerly embrace the merits of military service for young African Americans. Tuskegee graduate, L. F. Koons explains: "There was considerable debate concerning whether or not the ROTC program should be abolished. For the most part, activists on both sides were talking past one another. Proponents emphasized the benefits of military service to those who took advantage of it and, to a lesser extent, such abstract concepts as patriotism. Opponents argued that the military was an instrument of oppression abroad, and in certain circumstances at home, and was an evil to be combated. These seem to have been the main issues, although there were others."[1]

While the number of ROTC cadets at HBCUs sharply fell between 1968 and 1973, enthusiasm for military training programs at black colleges did not. New ROTC units representing each armed service branch appeared on black college campuses. "The Navy added units at Florida A&M (Florida), Prairie View A&M (Texas), Savannah State (Georgia), and Southern University (Louisiana). The Air Force established units at Grambling (Louisiana),

Mississippi Valley State (Mississippi), Fayetteville State (North Carolina), and Tennessee State (Tennessee). The Army added units at Alabama A&M (Alabama), Fort Valley State (Georgia), Alcorn State (Mississippi), Jackson State (Mississippi), St. Augustine's College (North Carolina), Benedict College (South Carolina), Bishop College (Texas), and Norfolk State (Virginia)."[2] The number of new ROTC programs at black colleges and universities represented not only an attempt by the U.S. military to increase the number of African American officers in the armed forces, but also an effort to expand the program where there existed a relative degree of support.

ROTC IS A GOOD CHOICE

Military service continued to attract many individuals who wanted to take advantage of the social and economic benefits the armed forces had to offer. In addition to a shift in attitudes toward military training and service, there was also a change in African American motivations to serve in the armed forces. According to Michael S. Neiberg, "African American leaders had traditionally seen the military as a means for African Americans to demonstrate loyalty, reliability, patriotism, and courage, as well as a place to gain valuable training and access to good jobs. The student bodies of black colleges and universities supported the establishment of ROTC units, indicating that they shared the view of the military as a means of advancement for the African American community, for themselves personally, or both."[3]

While the U.S. military had a major impact on the further development of the black middle-class during the post–World War II era, by the early 1970s many individuals interested in military service focused on personal advancement rather than motivations of "uplift" for the race.[4] Lieutenant General Russel Honoré supported this argument. Honoré reported, "When you had an opportunity to serve—you served. To me it was an opportunity to lift myself where I came from to a higher social economic class and put myself in the status of having a degree and being an officer in the U.S. Army. For me, that overshadowed the dichotomy of serving a nation that did not always appreciate your presence. I decided to be a part of the solution and not to disengage society but to rather engage."[5] This development occurred for at least two reasons. First, the creation of the all-volunteer force (AVF) was designed in part to attract a greater number of African Americans to a new system of benefits available to recruits. The U.S. military offered a more competitive pay scale in addition to an elaborate array of benefits and educational opportunities that were directed toward minorities in hopes of increasing their representation in the armed forces. The monetary incentives, it was believed, would at least gain the attention of minorities and poor whites, who had few economic opportunities in civilian society. According to Nalty, the Gates Commission (established to study the feasibility of the AVF) reported that while "Some blacks are compelled to serve in the armed forces at earnings below what they would earn in the civilian economy, under the new system, the black volunteer should see military service as an opportunity rather than a burden, exchanging his services for remuneration in terms of pay, training, and travel."[6]

ALL-VOLUNTARY FORCE CHANGES FUTURE OF MILITARY TRAINING PROGRAMS

The establishment of the AVF during the 1970s is described by Charles Moskos and Frank Wood as the U.S. military "moving away from an institutional format to one that increasingly resemble[d] that of an occupation."[7] The occupational format was market driven, and although a competitive pay scale and benefits package were central to the recruitment process, the AVF continued to incorporate such institutional values and norms as duty, honor, and country.[8] For African Americans, both the institutional and occupational formats had always been present in relation to serving in the armed forces. African Americans enjoyed better economic opportunities while serving in the U.S. military as well as a chance to prove themselves worthy of citizenship and equal rights. However, once the U.S. military increased the financial incentives and adjusted the pay scale to compete with civil society, African American men and women were further motivated to volunteer for military service.

Second, with the establishment of the AVF, African Americans no longer viewed military service as a requirement to obtain citizenship rights. By the 1970s, many believed that the civil rights movement had lost its momentum and that without the charismatic leadership and national support present during the 1950s and 1960s the fight for racial equality had stalled. The historic relationship between military service and African Americans began to lose its basis as a collective link to a social struggle. Though many African American leaders would continue to recite the history of African American military service and patriotism when discussing civil rights or racial discrimination, most African Americans began to primarily view military service as a way to improve their individual lives socially and economically. The military quickly became a mechanism of "personal uplift," where a black man or woman could enlist for a short period to learn a trade, travel, or obtain financial support for a college or advanced degree without a long-term commitment. This attitude was also reflected in many ROTC units at black colleges and universities. ROTC cadets enjoyed a larger monetary stipend and the guarantee of an officer's pay once commissioned. Neiberg believes that "these efforts paid dividends almost immediately. In 1973, 12.9 percent of those attending ROTC summer camp were African Americans, up from 9.1 percent in 1972 and 4.9 percent in 1971. Within ten years African American students accounted for 25 percent of AROTC cadets."[9]

While many African Americans were attracted to the benefits and competitive salary that the armed forces offered, others decided to forego service in the military for the greater civilian opportunities of the 1970s and 1980s. The civil rights struggles of the 1960s had achieved a great deal in terms of dismantling Jim Crow laws and establishing state and federal laws that made institutional discrimination illegal. Though racism still existed, many African Americans were able to apply for jobs and seek social and economic opportunities that were not available two decades earlier. Many African Americans perceived that their chances for individual advancement in civil society were much better than before.

MILITARY TRAINING AND SERVICE EXPANDS BLACK MIDDLE CLASS

African American military service during the height of the Cold War made a significant contribution to the social, political, and economic progress of African Americans. Black men and women improved their lives with greater opportunities for education, travel, and gaining dependable employment with the federal government. Many individuals, such as my grandfather and uncles, were able to move from the underclass of the rural South to black middle-class status and enjoy a better lifestyle. While African American attitudes toward military service have never been monolithic, there is no question that hundreds of thousands of blacks who served in the armed forces during the 1950s and 1960s were able to improve their lives in some way. Former Southern University professor Henry L. Essex proclaimed that, "I feel individuals have a responsibility to decide if military service will provide a [means] for their goals. I have no doubt that individual abilities and personalities will lead to military accomplishments and economic and or political success."[10] Many African Americans in the military may have experienced racism or discrimination during this period, but that was always a possibility in civilian society as well.

Black colleges and universities received financial support from the federal government for the establishment of ROTC units, and many black leaders believed that military training exposed young African American men to many character-building attributes that were essential to their success. Individuals such as four-star general Daniel Chappie James of Tuskegee Institute embraced the benefits of ROTC programs for young African Americans, and Brigadier General Charles E. Honore of Southern University credited his experience as an ROTC cadet as a major influence in his military career.[11]

ROTC PROGRAMS OFFER LIFE LESSONS

Decades after the Vietnam era, young African Americans were still attracted to the benefits and economic opportunities of military training and service. Thirty percent of the U.S. Army was composed of African Americans, and even though many individuals may have believed that they represented a disproportionate number of combat soldiers during the Persian Gulf War, the truth is that they reflected less than 10 percent of new recruits for infantry units. In fact, in many ROTC units African American women composed over 30 percent of the cadets.[12] One of the major attractions of military training and service for minorities is the ability to serve in leadership roles and the valuable life lessons that leadership affords. It is no coincidence that the first African American appointed as Chairman of the Joint Chiefs of Staff, General Colin Powell, was a former ROTC cadet. As a cadet, Powell learned many important lessons that served him well throughout his military career. He later remarked, "I learned that being in charge means making decisions, no matter how unpleasant. If it's broke, fix it. When you do, you win the gratitude of the people who have been suffering under the bad situation. I learned in a college drill competition that you cannot let the mission suffer, or make the majority pay to spare the feelings of an individual. Long years afterward, I kept a saying under the glass on my desk at the Pentagon that made the point succinctly if inelegantly: Being responsible sometimes means pissing people off."[13]

Though the number of African Americans serving in the U.S. Army is still disproportionately higher than their percentage of the general population, the number of African Americans seeking a commission is steadily falling. In 2005 and 2006, African American officers that were commissioned through ROTC programs represented 11 percent and 10 percent of the entire Army Officer Corps. Several years later, between 2007 and 2009, that figure reached only 9 percent of the Army Officer Corps.[14] This is due to several factors relating to the enrollment and retention of African Americans at colleges and universities. While the number of African Americans enrolled in HBCUs increased in the decades following the Vietnam War, today graduation and retention rates are steadily declining as students attempt to overcome financial problems, academic deficiencies, personal challenges, and the need to immediately enter the job market after high school to support their families.[15] In order for the U.S. Army to reverse this disturbing trend, higher education leaders and military officials will need to make a collaborative effort to improve the learning environment, provide financial assistance, and enhance academic support programs to ensure that young African Americans are counted among the leaders of tomorrow.

SOUTHERN UNIVERSITY ROTC: A MODEL OF SUCCESS

Between 1948 and 1960, the Jaguar ROTC Battalion at Southern University produced over two hundred Army lieutenants.[16] By 2010, ten former students from the Baton Rouge campus had reached the rank of flag officer, arguably making Southern University's ROTC program one of the most successful African American military training programs and further highlighting the influence of the military tradition at Southern University and black colleges throughout the nation.

SOUTHERN UNIVERSITY FLAG OFFICERS

- Lieutenant General Edward Honor (Class of 1954)—U.S. Army
- Major General Isaac D. Smith (Class of 1954)—U.S. Army
- Major General Charles Honore (Class of 1956)—U.S. Army
- Brigadier General Donald Delandro (Class of 1956)—U.S. Army
- Brigadier General Sherian Cadoria (Class of 1961)—U.S. Army
- Brigadier General Jude W. P. Patin (Class of 1962)—U.S. Army
- Lieutenant General Joe N. Ballard (Class of 1965)—U.S. Army
- Major General Gregory Rountree (Class of 1970)—U.S. Army
- Lieutenant General Russel L. Honoré (Class of 1971)—U.S. Army
- Brigadier General Craig C. Crenshaw (Class of 1984)—U.S. Marine Corps[17]

SURVEY AND RESEARCH RESULTS

During my research I developed a two-page questionnaire to provide me with quantitative data on African American attitudes toward military service in addition to giving me a sense of how people viewed certain issues and events. Approximately 150 questionnaires were mailed, and I received 72—a 48 percent response rate. The contact list included former Southern and Tuskegee University students, faculty, and administrators. The respondents were divided into four categories: Individuals affiliated with Southern or Tuskegee and military veterans and nonveterans. The Southern participants made up 64 percent of the respondents, and Tuskegee 36 percent. Veterans represented 73 percent and nonveterans were 27 percent. Each individual was associated with Southern or Tuskegee between 1934 and 1972, with ages ranging from sixteen to fifty. Military veterans represented every rank from private to major general.

If there were any defects in the questionnaire results, it would be the high percentage of neutral or missing responses. On several statements, such as "I did not want to participate in ROTC," twenty-three individuals did not answer. Also, fifteen persons (20.8 percent) did not respond to the statement "While attending college, I was never encouraged to avoid military service." For other statements, I received neutral responses 15 to 25 percent of the time. This was a little disheartening because I was hoping to get a better indication of opinions. I believe the high percentage of neutral or missing responses is due in large part to the way the statements were worded and the fact that I could not clarify the content of the statements to survey participants. Once the questionnaires were returned, I quickly noticed that many individuals read the first question in a section and skipped the subsequent questions. However, I feel comfortable that the information received from the questionnaires is accurate enough to generalize about African American attitudes toward military training and service.

The survey suggests several interesting findings. Over 65 percent of the participants agreed that African Americans who served in the military from rural areas in the South had better opportunities for personal advancement. Many of the individuals interviewed, such as Huel Perkins, agreed: "The military as a profession was appealing to many individuals, especially young blacks who came from small towns like Sunset or Bogalusa, Louisiana. They saw the military service as a way not to go into the classroom. You see, teaching was a popular profession. But the military was another way to make a living."[18] Military service was commonly recognized as a way to obtain better social and economic opportunities. John Sibley Butler contends that "black soldiers perceived the military as being more equalitarian than the civilian sector. Although the organization was not without racial problems, they saw better opportunities for advancement and economic stability than in the civilian sector."[19] Despite nearly 50 percent of the respondents indicating that African Americans were critical of the draft during the Vietnam era, 82 percent reported that they were never encouraged to avoid the military. This can be explained by the fact that many African Americans during this period were critical of American intervention in Vietnam but continued to believe in the merits of military training and service. Tuskegee graduate James Lund explains: "For us that worked in civil rights, we were often critical of the military, but we also could see that it was an organization that at times made more progress in civil rights than the rest of society. I had a number of friends at Tuskegee and other schools that became officers and were killed. I hated the war more than the U.S. military."[20] The belief that military training and service was attractive to young African Americans was also affirmed when 69 percent of former ROTC cadets disagreed that they did not want to participate in military training.

The most obvious indication that a shift occurred concerning attitudes toward the military was revealed in questionnaire results and personal interviews. When respondents were asked, "During the Korean War black Americans resented being asked to support the war while being treated as second-class citizens," 44 percent agreed or strongly agreed. By contrast, when the same individuals were asked, "During the Vietnam War black Americans resented being asked to support the war while being treated as second-class citizens," nearly 60 percent agreed or strongly agreed. Nearly the same percentage, 56 percent, agreed that after 1965 black college students became more reluctant to participate in the military. These statistics were supported by interviews. The interviewees were asked if they could remember a shift in attitudes toward the military (ROTC) at HBCUs, and nearly all of them answered yes. They were also asked if they could recall when military training and service was at the height of popularity in the black community. Tuskegee alumnus Dr. William O. Jones declared, "Yes, I believe a shift in attitudes toward military ROTC occurred during the Vietnam era."[21] Jones also reported that during the 1950s and early 1960s military training was most popular at Tuskegee. Major General Charles Honore (Ret.) from Southern agreed with Jones: "I attended SU from 1952–1956. I went back to SU as an instructor in ROTC from 1964–1967. During my second tour there students exhibited less pride in ROTC than we did as students."[22] General Honore also believed that military training was most popular at Southern University between 1952 and 1958. Former student L. F. Koons remembers a more complex assortment of attitudes concerning the military at Tuskegee:

> As I think back on the attitudes of the students concerning military service, there seems to have been several sets of attitudes. 1) It was wrong to force people to serve in the military against their will, especially so in the case of blacks, whose rights were restricted. 2) All citizens, including blacks, have a duty to support the government. 3) Military service offers the opportunity for a comfortable career, of the learning of skills that will lead to lucrative employment. Of course each of the categories may be further divided. For example, there were those in the first group who actively opposed conscription, as well as those who acquiesced to it. There were also those who were inclined not to express any opinion on the matter. I knew students who fell in each of the categories.[23]

Koons's characterization of the attitudes concerning military training and service best describes how profound those attitudes were. There was no single dominant opinion on military training and service on black college campuses. But it is also safe to say that there was very little antiwar or anti-ROTC agitation on campus, or in the community. Huel Perkins believes that the popularity of military training and service suffered because the war in Vietnam was unpopular. "I think that the shift in attitudes toward military training came in connection with the Vietnam War. It wasn't military service, it was the nature of the war and American participation in it. It was a national issue, and of course at Southern, it was just a bad time for military service in general."[24] Although Americans never fully supported the U.S. intervention in Vietnam, there was no full measure of support for the war in Korea either.

While it is clear that a shift occurred concerning attitudes toward military training and service during the late 1960s and early 1970s, it is also evident that a great number of African Americans continued to support the military and seek the social and economic benefits military service offered. Black colleges and universities searched for ways to strengthen their military programs and continued to solicit the federal government for additional units. The Department of Defense (DoD) supported those efforts because black institutions allowed the DoD the ability to increase the number of officers while promoting itself as an institution of equal opportunity. After 1970 the officer corps at black colleges and universities was responsible for producing a great number of African American military officers. Even as late as 1996, HBCUs located in the South were responsible for 45 percent of the 436 commissions awarded to African Americans.[25] Moskos and Butler believe that "ROTC units at HBCUs enjoy a prestige that would be the envy of units at most predominately white campuses. Professors of military science at HBCUs are often revered names in the black officers' world."[26] Statistical data demonstrates that current attitudes toward military training and service among African Americans is mostly positive. When survey participants were asked, "As long as blacks are treated as second-class citizens, we should not fight for the United States," 73.6 percent disagreed. Also, 61 percent agreed that African Americans should always support the armed forces.

African American attitudes toward military service that were mostly positive during the 1950s and early 1960s shifted during the decade to demonstrate African American discontent with the war in Vietnam and the state of American race relations. Many African Americans continued to support military training and service despite the turmoil and turbulence of the 1960s. But after 1973, once the all-volunteer force was enacted and the civil rights movement lost momentum, many African Americans moved away from a philosophy of racial uplift to self-interest and personal advancement. For many African Americans, military training and service were a way to achieve that personal success.

NOTES

PREFACE

1. Certificate of Achievement, Headquarters, 13th Quartermaster Battalion, March 8, 1965.

INTRODUCTION

1. Charles Johnson Jr., *African Americans and ROTC: Military, Naval and Aeroscience Programs at Historically Black Colleges, 1916–1973* (Jefferson, N.C., 2002).

2. Rod Andrew Jr., *Long Gray Lines: The Southern Military School Tradition, 1839–1915* (Chapel Hill, N.C., 2001); Michael S. Neiberg, *Making Citizen Soldiers: ROTC and the Ideology of American Military Service* (Cambridge, Mass., 2000), 165–169.

3. See Charles Vincent, *A Centennial History of Southern University and A&M College, 1880–1980* (Baton Rouge, La, 1981); Martha E. Dawson, *Hampton University: A National Treasure* (Silver Springs, Md., 1996); Lelia Gaston Rhodes, *Jackson State University: The First Hundred Years, 1877–1977* (Jackson, Miss., 1979); Benjamin Brawley, *History of Morehouse College* (Manchester, N.H., 2009); Rodney T. Cohen, *Fisk University* (Mt. Pleasant, S.C., 2001); Rayford W. Logan, *Howard University: The First Hundred Years, 1867–1967* (New York, 2004); Henry N. Drewry and Humphrey Doermann, *Stand and Prosper: Private Black Colleges and Their Students* (Princeton, N.J., 2001).

4. Andrew, 2.

5. Mary Frances Berry, *Military Necessity and Civil Rights Policy: Black Citizenship and the Constitution, 1861–1868* (Port Washington, N.Y., 1977), 1; also see Andrew, 3; Cynthia Enloe, *Maneuvers: The International Politics of Militarizing Women's Lives* (Berkeley, Calif., 2000), 247.

6. George O. Flynn, *The Draft, 1940–1973* (Lawrence, Kans., 1993), 102.

7. Herbert Shapiro, "The Vietnam War and the American Civil Rights Movement," *Journal of Ethnic Studies* 16, no. 4 (winter 1989): 118–119.

CHAPTER 1

1. Johnson, 5–7.

2. Christian G. Samito, *Becoming American Under Fire: Irish Americans, African Americans, and the Politics of Citizenship during the Civil War Era* (Ithaca, N.Y., 2009), 4.

3. Ibid., 5–7.

4. James Marten, "The Ambiguous Legacy of Blacks in Wartime America," *USA Today*, January 9, 1991, 80–84; David W. Blight, *Frederick Douglass' Civil War: Keeping Faith in Jubilee* (Baton Rouge, La., 1989), 161.

5. Bernard Nalty, *Strength for the Fight: A History of Black Americans in the Military* (New York, 1996), 43–46; Harry A. Ploski and Ernest Kaiser, *The Negro Almanac* (New York, 1971), 556–568; Gail Buckley, *American Patriots: The Story of Blacks in the Military from the Revolution to Desert Storm* (New York, 2001), 109.

6. Edward G. Longacre, *A Regiment of Slaves: The 4th United States Colored Infantry, 1863–1866* (Mechanicsburg, Pa., 2003), 16–17.

7. Blight, 155–156.

8. Ibid., 160.

9. Scott Nelson and Carol Sheriff, *A People at War: Civilians and Soldiers in America's Civil War* (New York, 2007), 249.

10. Ibid., 284; Bruce Levine, *Confederate Emancipation: Southern Plans to Free and Arm Slaves during the Civil War* (New York, 2006), 2–4.

11. Nelson and Sheriff, 249.

12. Ibid., 118–119.

13. Levine, 125–126.

14. Dudley Taylor Cornish, "The Union Army as a School for Negroes," *Journal of Negro History* 37, no. 4 (October 1952): 368.

15. Ibid., 370

16. Ibid., 371.

17. John W. Blassingame, "The Union Army as an Educational Institution for Negroes, 1862–1865," *Journal of Negro Education* 34, no. 2 (spring 1965): 155.

18. Ibid.,156; Antonio F. Holland, *Nathan B. Young and the Struggle over Black Higher Education* (Columbia, Mo., 2006), 116–117.

19. Margaret Humphreys, *Intensely Human: The Health of the Black Soldier in the American Civil War* (Baltimore, Md., 2008), 14.

20. Heather Andrea Williams, *Self-Taught: African American Education in Slavery and Freedom* (Chapel Hill, N.C., 2005), 47.

21. Ibid., 52.

22. Harry S. Laver, "Refuge of Manhood: Masculinity and the Militia Experience in Kentucky," in *Southern Manhood: Perspectives on Masculinity in the Old South*, ed. Craig Thompson Friend and Lorri Glover, 4–5 (Athens, Ga., 2004).

23. Humphreys, 20.

24. Ibid., 27.

25. Heather Andrea Williams, "Commenced to Think Like a Man: Literacy and Manhood in African American Civil War Regiments," in *Southern Manhood: Perspectives on Masculinity in the Old South*, ed. Craig Thompson Friend and Lorri Glover, 196–201 (Athens, Ga., 2004).

26. Ibid., 202.

27. Ibid., 196–213; James Henry Gooding and Virginia M. Adams, *On the Altar of Freedom: A Black Soldier's Civil War Letters from the Front* (Amherst, Mass., 1999)

28. Otis A. Singletary, "The Negro Militia during Radical Reconstruction," *Military Affairs* 19, no. 4 (winter 1955): 177–179.

29. Stephen Budiansky, *The Bloody Shirt: Terror after Appomattox* (New York, 2008), 122.

30. Thomas P. Lowry, *The Story the Soldiers Wouldn't Tell: Sex in the Civil War* (Mechanicsburg, Pa., 1994), 130.

31. Thomas P. Lowry, *Sexual Misbehavior in the Civil War: A Compendium* (Bloomington, Ind., 2006), 133.

32. J. Michael Martinez, *Carpetbaggers, Cavalry, and the Ku Klux Klan: Exposing the Invisible Empire during Reconstruction* (Lanham, Md., 2007), 121.

33. Budiansky, 5.

34. Serbrenia J. Sims, *Diversifying Historically Black Colleges and Universities: A New Higher Education Paradigm* (Westport, Conn., 1994), 6–9.

35. Marybeth Gasman and Christopher L. Tudico, eds., *Historically Black Colleges and Universities: Triumphs, Troubles, and Taboos* (New York, 2008), 1.

36. Julian B. Roebuck and Komanduri S. Murty, *Historically Black Colleges and Universities: Their Place in American Higher Education* (Westport, Conn., 1993), 25.

37. J. John Harris III, Cleopatra Figgures, and David G. Carter, "A Historical Perspective of the Emergence of Higher Education in Black Colleges," *Journal of Black Studies* 6, no. 1, The Black University: Assimilation or Survival? (September 1975): 55–68; John W. Davis, "The Participation of Negro Land-Grant Colleges in Permanent Federal Education," *Journal of Negro Education* 7, no. 3, The Purpose and Scope of the Seventh Yearbook (July 1938): 284.

38. Ronald R. Krebs, *Fighting For Rights: Military Service and the Politics of Citizenship* (Ithaca, N.Y., 2006), 116.

39. Ibid., 90–91; Johnson, 6.

40. William H. Watkins, *The White Architects of Black Education: Ideology and Power in America, 1865–1954* (New York, 2001), 57.

41. Andrew, 91–96; Johnson, 6–8.

42. Watkins, 59.

43. Albert L. Scipio II, *Pre-War Days at Tuskegee* (Sliver Springs, Md., 1987), 367.

44. Ibid., 377–378.

45. Ibid., 389.

46. Ibid.

47. Ibid., 397.

48. Vincent, 9–10.

49. Ulysses Simpson Lane, "The History of Southern University, 1879–1960" (Ph.D. diss., Utah State University, 1969), 58.

50. Vincent, 9–10.

51. Lane, 53–54.

52. Andrew, 93.

53. Felton G. Clark, "Administrative Control of Public Negro Colleges," *Journal of Negro Education* 3, no. 2 (April 1934): 246.

54. Lane, 90.

55. Ibid., 104–108.

56. Vincent, 140.

57. Ibid., 141–142.

58. Clark, "Administrative Control of Public Negro Colleges," 255–256.

59. Mary Jacqueline Hebert, "Beyond Black and White: The Civil Rights Movement in Baton Rouge, Louisiana, 1945–1972" (Ph.D. diss., Louisiana State University, 1999), 38–39.

60. Robert Jakeman, *The Divided Skies: Establishing Segregated Flight Training at Tuskegee, Alabama, 1934–1942* (Tuscaloosa, Ala., 1992), 83.

CHAPTER 2

1. Charles Chamberlain, *Victory at Home: Manpower and Race in the American South during World War II* (Athens, Ga., 2003), 4–5.

2. Jerry Purvis Sanson, *Louisiana during World War II: Politics and Society, 1939–1945* (Baton Rouge, La, 1999), 264; Harvard Sitkoff, "Racial Militancy and Interracial Violence in the Second World War," *Journal of American History* 3 (1971): 662; Chamberlain, 62–63.

3. Chamberlain, 62–63.

4. Herman Branson, "The Training of Negroes for War Industries in World War II," *Journal of Negro Education* 12 (summer 1943): 379.

5. Letter, J. W. Studebaker, Commissioner of the U.S. Department of Education, to F. D. Patterson, President, Tuskegee Institute, September 9, 1940, File: National Defense, Box Marked: Patterson 1940: Arthur W. Mitchell to National Urban League, F. D. Patterson Papers, Tuskegee University Archives, Tuskegee University, Tuskegee, Ala.

6. Daniel Kryder, *Divided Arsenal: Race and the American State during World War II* (Cambridge, Mass., 2000), 26–30.

7. John W. Davis, "Current Changes in Negro Higher Education to Meet the Immediate War Emergency," *Journal of Negro Education* 11 (July 1942): 294.

8. Branson, 380; E. Franklin Frazier, "Ethnic and Minority Groups in Wartime, with Special Reference to the Negro," *American Journal of Sociology* 48 (1942): 375.

9. Office of War Information, Records of Natalie Davisen, Program Manager for Homefront Campaigns, 1943–1945, File: Negro, Correspondence—April 1945 to Recruitment and Manpower, Record Group 208, Entry 84, Box 8, National Archives Building, College Park, Md.; Secretary of War Office, Asst. Secretary of War Civilian Aide to the Secretary, 1940–1947, File: Colleges, Army Training Courses, Colbert, Lt. Lowell, to Committee on Fair Employment Practices Departmental, Record Group 107, Entry 91, Box 190, National Archives Building, College Park, Md.

10. John Hope Franklin and Alfred A. Moss Jr., *From Slavery to Freedom: A History of African Americans* (New York, 1994), 449; Greta de Jong, *A Different Day: African American Struggles for Justice in Rural Louisiana* (Chapel Hill, N.C., 2002), 130.

11. Chamberlain, 63.

12. de Jong, 130.

13. David M. Kennedy, *Freedom from Fear: The American People in Depression and War, 1929–1945* (New York, 1999), 771.

14. Memorandum, Committee on Participation of Negroes in the National Defense Program to F. G. Clark, President, Southern University and A&M College, n.d., File: National Defense Program, F. G. Clark Papers, Southern University Archives, Southern University and A&M College, Baton Rouge, La.

15. Kryder, 47.

16. John Morton Blum, *V Was for Victory: Politics and the American Culture during World War II* (New York, 1976), 197. For additional information on the role of African Americans in defense training, see Neil A. Wynn, *The Afro-American and the Second World War* (New York, 1975), 77; James C. Evans, "The Contribution of Negro Higher Education to the War Effort," *Journal of Negro Education* 11, no. 3 (July 1942): 308.

17. National Defense, Cabinet N, F. G. Clark Papers, Southern University Archives, Southern University and A&M College, Baton Rouge, La.

18. Memorandum, The Subcommittee on Relationships with the Army and Navy of the Committee on Relationships on Higher Education to the Federal Government to F. G. Clark, President, Southern University and A&M College, October 27, 1942, File: Army Special Training Program, 1942, Cabinet A, F. G. Clark Papers, Southern University Archives, Southern University and A&M College, Baton Rouge, La.

19. Memorandum, Defense Conference to be held at Hampton Institute, to F. D. Patterson, President, Tuskegee Institute, November 8, 1940, File: Hampton Institute, Box Marked: Patterson 1943; Copernican National Committee to Hampton Institute, F. D. Patterson Papers, Tuskegee University Archives, Tuskegee University, Tuskegee, Ala.

20. See Chamberlain.

21. "S.U. Gets $4,000 for National Defense Work," *Southern University Digest* (October 21, 1941), 1; Vincent, 148–149; "Home Ec. Department to Knit Sweaters for Southern Soldiers," *Southern University Digest* 26 (November 4, 1942), 1.

22. Letter, Jesse O. Thomas, Defense Savings Staff, U.S. Treasury Department, to F. G. Clark, President, Southern University and A&M College, November 13, 1941, File: Defense Savings Bonds, 1941–1942, Cabinet D, F. G. Clark Papers, Southern University Archives, Southern University and A&M College, Baton Rouge, La.

23. Letter, F. G. Clark, President, Southern University and A&M College, to Jesse O. Thomas, Defense Savings Staff, U.S. Treasury Department, January 12, 1942, File: Defense Savings Bonds, 1941–1942, Cabinet D, F. G. Clark Papers, Southern University Archives, Southern University and A&M College, Baton Rouge, La.

24. Ibid.

25. Ibid.

26. Memorandum, F. G. Clark, President, Southern University and A&M College, to Faculty and Staff members of Southern University, n.d., File: Defense Savings Bonds, 1941–1942,

Cabinet D, F. G. Clark Papers, Southern University Archives, Southern University and A&M College, Baton Rouge, La.

27. V. R. Cardozier, *Colleges and Universities in World War II* (Westport, Conn., 1993), ix.

28. Truman K. Gibson Jr., *Knocking Down Barriers: My Fight for Black America* (Evanston, Ill., 2005), 94.

29. Walter G. Daniel and Marion T. Wright, "The Role of Educational Agencies in Maintaining Morale among Negroes," *Journal of Negro Education* 12, no. 3 (1943): 491–493.

30. Letter, F. G. Clark, President, Southern University and A&M College, to Louisiana Governor, Sam H. Jones, December 9, 1941, File: Civilian Defense Council, 1941, Cabinet C, F. G. Clark Papers, Southern University Archives, Southern University and A&M College, Baton Rouge, La.

31. Letter, F. G. Clark, President, Southern University and A&M College, to the Coordinator of Louisiana Civilian Defense, Roland Cocreham, December 17, 1941, File: Civilian Defense Council, 1941, Cabinet C, F. G. Clark Papers, Southern University Archives, Southern University and A&M College, Baton Rouge, La.

32. Minutes of Southern University Defense Council Meeting, February 24, 1942, File: Civilian Defense Council (Campus), 1941–1942, Cabinet D, F. G. Clark Papers, Southern University Archives, Southern University and A&M College, Baton Rouge, La.

33. Brochure: Civilian Defense Training School for Negroes, September 9, 1942, File: Civilian Defense School, 1941–1942, Cabinet C, F. G. Clark Papers, Southern University Archives, Southern University and A&M College, Baton Rouge, La.

34. "Negroes Urged to Join Defense," *Times-Picayune*, March 30, 1942.

35. Letter, Hugo Weidmann, Director, St. Tammany Parish Louisiana Civilian Defense Commission, to Franklin D. Roosevelt, President of the United States of America, April 8, 1942, File: Civilian Defense (General Matters), 1941–1942, Cabinet C, F. G. Clark Papers, Southern University Archives, Southern University and A&M College, Baton Rouge, La.

36. "Three Hundred Soldiers Join Parade of N.F.A. Members and Representatives of Fraternities and Sororities," *Southern University Digest* 15, no. 8 (March 31, 1942), 1.

37. Memorandum, Office of the Adjutant General, United States War Department, to F. G. Clark, President, Southern University and A&M College, May 18, 1942, File: War Department, 1941–1942, Cabinet U, F. G. Clark Papers, Southern University Archives, Southern University and A&M College, Baton Rouge, La. .

38. Memorandum, Headquarters, Eighth Service Command, Office of the Commanding General, August 20, 1942, File: War Department, 1942–1943, Cabinet U, F. G. Clark Papers, Southern University Archives, Southern University and A&M College, Baton Rouge, La.

39. Secretary of War Office, Asst. Secretary of War Civilian Aide to the Secretary, 1940–1947, File: Colleges, Army Training Courses, Colbert, Lt. Lowell, to Committee on Fair Employment Practices Departmental, Record Group 107, Entry 91, Box 190, National Archives Building, College Park, Md.

40. Letter, J. B. Cade, Dean, Southern University and A&M College, to John W. Davis, President, West Virginia State College, August 29, 1942, File: War Department, 1942–1943, Cabinet U, F. G. Clark Papers, Southern University Archives, Southern University and A&M College, Baton Rouge, La.

41. Letter, J. B. Cade, Dean, Southern University and A&M College, to F. G. Clark, President, Southern University and A&M College, September 5, 1942, File: War Department 1942–1943, Cabinet U, F. G. Clark Papers, Southern University Archives, Southern University and A&M College, Baton Rouge, La.

42. Cornelius A. King, "National Defense and the Negro," *Louisiana Colored Teachers Journal* 15, no. 4 (June 1942): 18; C. W. Rice, "Blunt Speaking on Negro Attitudes," *Louisiana Colored Teachers Journal* 15, no. 5 (October 1942): 16; Ruth Taylor, "What Are We Fighting For?" *Louisiana Colored Teachers Journal* 15, no. 5 (October 1942): 16.

43. Barbara Dianne Savage, *Broadcasting Freedom: Radio, War, and the Politics of Race* (Chapel Hill, N.C., 1999), 72–83.

44. Marguerite Smith Ampey, "'Freedom's People' Radio Programs," *Louisiana Colored Teachers Journal* 15, no. 4 (June 1942): 14.

45. S. U. Press Service, "Dean J. B. Cade Lists Southern Reserves," *Southern University Digest* 16, no. 1 (October 10, 1942), 1.

46. Letter, E. H. Miller, Division of Liberal Arts, Southern University, to F. G. Clark, President, Southern University and A&M College, October 28, 1942, File: War Efforts (Faculty), 1942, Cabinet U, F. G. Clark Papers, Southern University Archives, Southern University and A&M College, Baton Rouge, La.

47. Letter, A. P. Pertee, Dean of Men, Southern University and A&M College, to F. G. Clark, President, Southern University and A&M College, November 3, 1942, File: War Efforts (Faculty), 1942, Cabinet U, F. G. Clark Papers, Southern University Archives, Southern University and A&M College, Baton Rouge, La.

48. Gibson, 98.

49. Huel D. Perkins, former student and dean of Arts and Humanities, Southern University and A &M College, interview by author, tape recording, Baton Rouge, La., October 21, 1999.

50. Otis Hicks, "Student Morale in Wartime," *Southern University Digest* (April 2, 1943), 2.

51. Memorandum, Military Policy Implications of Report by Research Branch, Special Service Division, ASF, on "Attitudes of the Negro Soldier," July 31, 1943, File: Attitudes Toward Negro Soldiers, 1942–43, Entry 188, Box 224, Record Group 107, National Archives Building, College Park, Md.

52. Maggie M. Morehouse, *Fighting in the Jim Crow Army: Black Men and Women Remember World War II* (Lanham, Md., 2000), 23.

53. Frazier, 372.

54. Morehouse, 18.

55. Flora Bryant Brown, "NAACP Sponsored Sit-Ins by Howard University Students in Washington, D.C., 1943–1944," *Journal of Negro History* 85, no. 4 (2000): 277.

56. Sherie Mershon and Steven Schlossman, *Foxholes and Color Lines: Desegregating the U.S. Armed Forces* (Baltimore, Md., 1998), 8.

57. Joseph Schiffman, "The Education of Negro Soldiers in World War II," *Journal of Negro Education* 18 (winter 1949): 25.

58. Jordana Y. Shakoor, *Civil Rights Childhood* (Jackson, Miss., 1999), 51–57.

59. Morehouse, 6–7.

60. Gibson, 111–112.

61. Letter, F. G. Clark, President, Southern University and A&M College, to Southern University Staff Members, November 30, 1942, File: War Efforts (Faculty), 1942, Cabinet U, F. G. Clark Papers, Southern University Archives, Southern University and A&M College, Baton Rouge, La.

62. Felton G. Clark, "Negro Higher Education and Some Fundamental Issues Raised by World War II," *Journal of Negro Education* 11, no. 3 (July 1942): 283–284.

63. Ibid., 290; Also see Daniel and Wright, 492.

64. Clark, "Administrative Control of Public Negro Colleges," 255. Also see Felton G. Clark, "The Control of State Supported Teacher Training Programs for Negroes," *Teachers College Record*, no. 605 (Bureau of Publications, Teachers College, Columbia University, 1934): 1–4.

65. James Anderson, *The Education of Blacks in the South, 1860–1935* (Chapel Hill, N.C., 1988), 243.

66. Clark, "Negro Higher Education and Some Fundamental Issues Raised by World War II," 288.

67. Christopher Jencks and David Riesman, *The Academic Revolution* (New York, 1968), 424–425.

68. "Dr. Felton G. Clark Pleads for Return to Christian Idealism," *Southern University Digest* 15 (October 15, 1943), 1.

69. Letter, Colonel Herman Beukema, Director, Army Specialized Training Division, to F. G. Clark, President, Southern University and A&M College, February 25, 1943, File: War Department, 1942–1943, Cabinet U, F. G. Clark Papers, Southern University Archives, Southern University and A&M College, Baton Rouge, La.

70. Memorandum, Subcommittee on Relationships with the Army and Navy of the Committee on Relationships of Higher Education to the Federal Government to the American Council on Education, October 27, 1942, File: Army Special Training Program, 1942, Cabinet A, F. G. Clark Papers, Southern University Archives, Southern University and A&M College, Baton Rouge, La.

71. Letter, F. G. Clark, President, Southern University and A&M College, to Ambrose Caliver, United States Office of Education, March 4, 1943, File: United States Office of Education, 1943, Cabinet U, F. G. Clark Papers, Southern University Archives, Southern University and A&M College, Baton Rouge, La.

72. Letter, F. G. Clark, President, Southern University and A&M College, to J. W. Studebaker, U.S. Commissioner of Education, March 6, 1943, File: United States Office of Education, 1943, Cabinet U, F. G. Clark Papers, Southern University Archives, Southern University and A&M College, Baton Rouge, La.

73. Letter, Fred J. Kelly, Professional and Technical Service of the Office for Emergency Management War Manpower Commission, to F .G. Clark, President, Southern University and A&M College, April 3, 1943, File: United States Office of Education, 1943, Cabinet U, F. G. Clark Papers, Southern University Archives, Southern University and A&M College, Baton Rouge, La.

74. Letter, F. G. Clark, President, Southern University and A&M College, to Fred J. Kelly, Chief, Division of Higher Education, United States Office of Education, June 28, 1943, Cabinet

U, F. G. Clark Papers, Southern University Archives, Southern University and A&M College, Baton Rouge, La.

75. Letter, F. G. Clark, President, Southern University and A&M College, to Fred J. Kelly, Chief, Division of Higher Education, March 22, 1943, File: United States Office of Education, 1943, Cabinet U, F. G. Clark Papers, Southern University Archives, Southern University and A&M College, Baton Rouge, La.

76. Letter, F. G. Clark, President, Southern University and A&M College, to Paul V. McNutt, Chairman, War Manpower Commission, November 11, 1943, File: War, Box Marked: General 1943: Office of War Information-Z, F. D. Patterson Papers, Tuskegee University Archives, Tuskegee University, Tuskegee, Ala.

77. Clara Deamer, "A.S.T.P. Unit at Southern Unlikely," *Southern University Digest* 16, no. 11 (August 5, 1943), 1.

78. Pamphlet, "Essential Facts about the Army Specialized Training Program, August 30, 1943," File: Evans-ASTP (Army Specialized Training Program), Description: ASTP Pamphlet, Entry 188, Box 203, Record Group 107, National Archives Building, College Park, Md.

79. Letter, F. G. Clark, President, Southern University and A&M College, to John W. Studebaker, U.S. Commissioner of Education, March 6, 1943, File: United States Office of Education, 1943, Cabinet U, F. G. Clark Papers, Southern University Archives, Southern University and A&M College, Baton Rouge, La.; Vincent, 159.

80. "Campus 'Cuts' to Pay for War Bonds," *Southern University Digest* 16 (March 22, 1943), 3.

81. Letter, F. G. Clark, President, Southern University and A&M College, to Faculty and Staff at Southern University and A&M College, n.d., File: Community War Chest Fund, 1943, Cabinet C, F. G. Clark Papers, Southern University Archives, Southern University and A&M College, Baton Rouge, La.

82. Lee Finkle, *Forum for Protest: The Black Press during World War II* (Cranbury, N.J., 1975), 102.

83. Leroy Davis, *A Clashing of the Soul: John Hope and the Dilemma of African American Leadership and Black Higher Education in the Early Twentieth Century* (Athens, Ga., 1998), 229–230.

84. Vincent, 151–152.

85. "S.U. Assigned as Veteran Guidance Center," *Southern University Digest* (March 29, 1945), 1.

86. Ronald Roach, "From Combat to Campus: GI Bill Gave a Generation of African Americans an Opportunity to Pursue the American Dream," *Black Issues in Higher Education* 14, no. 13 (August 21, 1997): 27.

87. Brenda Gayle Plummer, ed., *Window on Freedom: Race, Civil Rights, and Foreign Affairs, 1945–1988* (Chapel Hill, N. C., 2003), 4. Also see Morehouse, 207.

CHAPTER 3

1. Morris J. MacGregor Jr., *Integration of the Armed Forces, 1940–1965* (Washington, D.C., 1981), 291. See also Richard J. Stillman II, *Integration of the Negro in the U.S. Armed Forces* (New York, 1968), 34.

2. Mary L. Dudziak, *Cold War Civil Rights: Race and the Image of American Democracy* (Princeton, N.J., 2000), 9–12.

3. Telegram, F. G. Clark, President, Southern University and A&M College, to Carl Murphy, President, Afro-American Newspaper, n.d., File: ROTC Unit Request, 1946–1948, Cabinet R, F. G. Clark Papers, Southern University Archives, Southern University and A&M College, Baton Rouge, La.

4. Letter, F. G. Clark, President, Southern University and A&M College, to James C. Evans, Assistant Civilian Aide to the Secretary of War, May 7, 1946, File: ROTC, 1941–1946, Record Group 107, Entry 188, Box 244, National Archives Building, College Park, Md.

5. Letter, Major General Terrell C. Holliday, Assistant Adjunct General, to F. G. Clark, President, Southern University and A&M College, August 3, 1946, File: ROTC Unit Request, 1946–1948, Cabinet R, F. G. Clark Papers, Southern University Archives, Southern University and A&M College, Baton Rouge, La.

6. Letter, F. G. Clark, President, Southern University and A&M College, to Howard C. Petersen, Assistant Secretary of the War Department, July 22, 1947, File: ROTC Unit Request, 1946–1948, Cabinet R, Southern University Archives, Southern University and A&M College, Baton Rouge, La.

7. Perkins interview, October 21, 1999.

8. E. C. Harrison, former student and vice president of academic affairs, Southern University and A &M College, interview by author, tape recording, Baton Rouge, La., September 9, 1998.

9. E. C. Harrison, former student and vice president of academic affairs, Southern University and A &M College, interview by author, tape recording, Baton Rouge, La., March 29, 2010.

10. Anonymous, former Tuskegee student, interview by author, transcript, Baton Rouge, La., April 15, 2000.

11. James C. Evans and Albert Parker, "ROTC Programs and Negro Youth," *Journal of Negro Education* (spring 1956): 130–131.

12. Memorandum, The Executive Committee of the Conference of Presidents of Land-Grant Colleges for Negroes to the U.S. Office of Education, April 2, 1948, File: Committee on Universal Military Training, 1947–48, Records of the Office of Education, Office File of Ambrose Caliver, Entry 17, Box 3; Record Group 12, National Archives Building, College Park, Md.

13. Ibid.

14. Charles C. Moskos and John Sibley Butler, *All That We Can Be: Black Leadership and Racial Integration the Army Way* (New York, 1996), 95–103.

15. Sanson, 264; Sitkoff, "Racial Militancy and Interracial Violence in the Second World War," 662; Chamberlain, 62–63.

16. William C. Berman, *The Politics of Civil Rights in the Truman Administration* (Columbus, Ohio, 1970), 77–78. For further treatment of the Truman Doctrine, see Edwin C. Rozwenc and Kenneth Lindfors, *Containment and the Origins of the Cold War* (Boston: Mass., 1967), 13–14. See also Mershon and Schlossman, *Foxholes and Color Lines: Desegregating the U.S. Armed Forces,* for how the Cold War and African American political aspirations intersected.

17. Richard M. Dalfiume, *Desegregation of the U.S. Armed Forces: Fighting on Two Fronts, 1939–1953* (Columbia, Mo., 1969), 3–4.

18. Brenda Gayle Plummer, *Rising Wind: Black Americans and Foreign Affairs, 1935–1960* (Chapel Hill, N.C., 1996), 183.

19. Letter, F. G. Clark, President, Southern University and A&M College, to Howard C. Petersen, Assistant Secretary of War, June 24, 1947, file: ROTC Unit Request, 1946–1948, Cabinet R, F. G. Clark Papers, Southern University Archives, Southern University and A&M College, Baton Rouge, La.

20. Letter, F. G. Clark, President, Southern University and A&M College, to M. F. Whittaker, President, South Carolina State College, July 16, 1947, File: ROTC Unit Request, 1946–1948, Cabinet R, Southern University Archives, Southern University and A&M College, Baton Rouge, La.

21. Letter, F. G. Clark, President, Southern University and A&M College, to General Edward S. Bres, Chief of Staff for Reserve and ROTC Affairs, July 30, 1947, File: ROTC Unit Request, 1946–1948, Cabinet R, F. G. Clark Papers, Southern University Archives, Southern University and A&M College, Baton Rouge, La.

22. Letter, Major General Edward S. Bres, Executive for Reserve and ROTC Affairs, to F. G. Clark, President, Southern University and A&M College, August 4, 1947, File: ROTC Unit Request, 1946–1948, Cabinet R, Southern University Archives, Southern University and A&M College, Baton Rouge, La.

23. Letter, F. G. Clark, President, Southern University and A&M College, to Major General Edward S. Bres, Executive for Reserve and ROTC Affairs, August 8, 1947, File: ROTC Unit Request, 1946–1948, Cabinet R, F. G. Clark Papers, Southern University Archives, Southern University and A&M College, Baton Rouge, La.

24. Letter, Grant Reynolds and A. Philip Randolph, Committee Against Jimcrow in Military Service and Training, to F. G. Clark, President, Southern University and A&M College, November 6, 1947, File: ROTC Unit Request, 1946–1948, Cabinet R, Southern University Archives, Southern University and A&M College, Baton Rouge, La.

25. Letter, F. G. Clark, President, Southern University and A&M College, to Brigadier General Wendell Westover, Executive for Reserve and ROTC Affairs, February 17, 1948, File: ROTC Unit Request, 1946–1948, Cabinet R, F. G. Clark Papers, Southern University Archives, Southern University and A&M College, Baton Rouge, La.

26. Letter, Brigadier General Wendell Westover, Executive for Reserve and ROTC Affairs, to F. G. Clark, President, Southern University and A&M College, March 8, 1948, File: Unit Request, 1946–1948, Cabinet R, Southern University Archives, Southern University and A&M College, Baton Rouge, La.

27. Newspaper clipping, *Afro-American*, March 2, 1948, File: ROTC, 1967–1948, Record Group 107, Entry 188, Box 244, National Archives Building, College Park, Md.

28. Letter, Carl Murphy, President, Afro-American Newspapers, to F. G. Clark, President, Southern University and A&M College, March 11, 1948, File: ROTC Unit Request, 1946–1948, Cabinet R, F. G. Clark Papers, Southern University Archives, Southern University and A&M College, Baton Rouge, La.

29. Memorandum, L. Eugene Hedberg, Special Consultant to the Deputy Director of Public Relations, File: ROTC, 1947–1948, Record Group 107, Entry 188, Box 244, National Archives Building, College Park, Md.

30. Paul T. Murray, "Blacks and the Draft: A History of Institutional Racism," *Journal of Black Studies* (September 1971): 67.

31. "Crisis in the Making: U.S. Negroes Tussle with Issue . . . ," *Newsweek*, June 7, 1948, 29; Paula F. Pfeffer, *A. Philip Randolph, Pioneer of the Civil Rights Movement* (Baton Rouge, La., 1990), 141–142.

32. Nalty, 242.

33. Letter, James C. Evans, Advisor to the Secretary of Defense, to F. G. Clark, President, Southern University and A&M College, May 19, 1948, File: ROTC Unit Request, 1946–1948, Cabinet R, F. G. Clark Papers, Southern University Archives, Southern University and A&M College, Baton Rouge, La.

34. Telegram, F. G. Clark, President, Southern University and A&M College, to James C. Evans, Civilian Aide to the Secretary of Defense, June 22, 1948, File: ROTC Unit Request, 1946–1948, Cabinet R, F. G. Clark Papers, Southern University Archives, Southern University and A&M College, Baton Rouge, La.

35. Vincent, 159; "Southern Gets R.O.T.C. Unit," *Southern University Digest* (November 1, 1948), 1.

36. "Major Taylor Heads R.O.T.C. Unit," *Southern University Digest* (December 9, 1948), 1.

37. Richard G. Axt, *The Federal Government and Financing Higher Education* (New York, 1952), 270.

38. Elaine Tyler May, *Homeward Bound: American Families in the Cold War Era* (New York, 1988), 117.

39. Vincent, 181.

40. Lionel S. Lewis, *The Cold War and Academic Governance: The Lattimore Case at John Hopkins* (New York, 1993), 223.

41. Anderson, 283–285.

42. Iris Johnson Perkins, "Felton Grandison Clark, Louisiana Educator" (Ph.D. diss., Louisiana State University, 1976), 38–39.

43. Memorandum, Southern University Discipline Committee to F. G. Clark, President, Southern University and A&M College, n.d., File: Department of State, Cabinet D, F. G. Clark Papers, Southern University Archives, Southern University and A&M College, Baton Rouge, La.

44. See File: Personal Letters—Confidential, Cabinet L, F. G. Clark Papers, Southern University Archives, Southern University and A&M College, Baton Rouge, La.

45. Memorandum, Southern University Discipline Committee to F. G. Clark, President, Southern University and A&M College, n.d., File: Department of State, Cabinet D, F. G. Clark Papers, Southern University Archives, Southern University and A&M College, Baton Rouge, La.

46. "Eisenhower Honors Dr. Clark," *Southern University Digest* 27, no. 13 (April 23, 1956), 1.

47. Speech delivered by J. Thomas Schneider, Chairman, Department of Defense, Personnel Policy Board, to the Conference of American Council on Education, October 6, 1950, File: Selective Service, 1950–1952, Cabinet S, F. G. Clark Papers, Southern University Archives, Southern University and A&M College, Baton Rouge, La.

48. See Plummer, *Rising Wind*, 198.

49. David Levering Lewis, *W.E.B. Du Bois: The Fight for Equality and the American Century, 1919–1963* (New York, 2000), 466.

50. R. Grann Lloyd, "Loyalty Oaths and Communistic Influences in Negro Colleges and Universities," *School and Society* 75 (January–June 1952): 8.

51. Ibid.

52. Harrison interview, September 9, 1998. Harrison indicated that Southern never required its employees to take loyalty oaths as a condition of employment.

53. "Why Fight Communism? Forums at Va. Union Seek to Give Answer," *Afro-American*, May 6, 1950, 6-A.

54. Ibid.

55. A speech from the Secretary of the U.S. Department of Agriculture, Charles Brannan, to College Presidents of the Association of Land-Grant Colleges and Universities at the annual meeting on November 16, 1950, File: Land Grant Colleges, Box Marked: General—1950 Box 2 of 2—Dr. Patterson, F. D. Patterson Papers, Tuskegee University Archives, Tuskegee University, Tuskegee, Ala.

56. "Southern University Man Returns from Washington Conference," *Morning Advocate*, February 14, 1953, 5-B.

57. Michael Sherry, *In the Shadow of War: The United States since the 1930s* (New Haven, Conn., 1995), 124. See also Martin Walker, *The Cold War: A History* (New York, 1993), 2–5; Christian G. Appy, ed., *Cold War Constructions: The Political Culture of United States Imperialism, 1945–1966* (Amherst, Mass., 2000).

58. Neiberg, 51.

59. Andrew, 1–7.

60. Letter, Dudley D. Brodie, Adjutant General, U.S. Department of the Army, to Commanding General, Fourth Army, Fort Sam Houston, Texas, September 7, 1950, File: Educational Institutions, Civil (May thru August 1950), General Correspondence, 1948–54, Entry 149, Box 5, Record Group 319, National Archives Building, College Park, Md.

61. Letter, G. Earl Guinn, President, Louisiana College, to Commanding General, Headquarters, Fourth Army, Fort Sam Houston, Texas, June 25, 1952, File: Educational Institutions, Civil (January through December 1952), Iowa, Kansas, Kentucky, Louisiana, Maine, General Correspondence, 1948–54, Entry 149, Box 6, Group 319, National Archives Building, College Park, Md.

62. Ibid.

63. Memorandum, Reserve Officers' Training Corps Units, October 3, 1947, File: ROTC, 1947–1948, Record Group 107, Entry 188, Box 244, National Archives Building, College Park, Md.

64. Memorandum, Office of the Assistant Secretary of Defense to Major General Hugh M. Milton, Executive for Reserve and ROTC Affairs, December 22, 1952, File: Educational Institutions, Civil—General, General Correspondence, 1948–54, Entry 149, Box 6, Record Group 319, National Archives Building, College Park, Md.

65. Memorandum, The National Urban League Southern Field Division to Southern University and A&M College, December 13, 1948, File: Reserve Officers Training Corps, 1948–

1952, Cabinet R, F. G. Clark Papers, Southern University Archives, Southern University and A&M College, Baton Rouge, La.

66. Letter, Major B. W. Johnson, Southern University PMS&T, to F. G. Clark, President, Southern University and A&M College, July 27, 1949, File: ROTC General Information, Box Marked: 1949—General Information, F. G. Clark Papers, Southern University Archives, Southern University and A&M College, Baton Rouge, La.

67. Letter, F. G. Clark, President, Southern University and A&M College, to Major B. W. Johnson, Southern University PMS&T, August 2, 1949, File: ROTC General Information, Box Marked: 1949—General Information, F. G. Clark Papers, Southern University Archives, Southern University and A&M College, Baton Rouge, La.

68. Memorandum, J.B. Cade, Dean, Southern University and A&M College, to All Freshman and Sophomore Men, September 27, 1949, File: Reserve Officers Training Corps, 1948–1952, Cabinet R, F. G. Clark Papers, Southern University Archives, Southern University and A&M College, Baton Rouge, La.

69. Perkins interview, October 21, 1998.

70. Harrison interview, September 9, 1999.

71. Frank S. Ransburg, former student, professor, and administrator, Southern University and A &M College, interview by author, tape recording, Baton Rouge, La., February 12, 1998.

72. For results of the questionnaire, see chapter 7.

73. Letter, Colonel F. T. Dodd, Acting Chief of Staff, Headquarters, Fourth Army, to F. G. Clark, President, Southern University and A&M College, October 10, 1949, File: ROTC General Information, Box Marked: 1949—General Information, F. G. Clark Papers, Southern University Archives, Southern University and A&M College, Baton Rouge, La.

74. Letter, F. G. Clark, President, Southern University and A&M College, to Brigadier General Hugh Hoffman, Chief of Staff, Headquarters, Fourth Army, October 27, 1949, File: ROTC General Information, Box Marked: 1949—General Information, F. G. Clark Papers, Southern University Archives, Southern University and A&M College, Baton Rouge, La.

75. Letter, Major Thomas B. Taylor, PMS&T, Southern University and A&M College, to James C. Evans, Civilian Assistant to the Secretary of Defense, November 30, 1949, File: ROTC General Information, Box Marked: 1949—General Information, F. G. Clark Papers, Southern University Archives, Southern University and A&M College, Baton Rouge, La.

76. Letter, F. G. Clark, President, Southern University and A&M College, to Mr. W. V. Reed Sr., American Legion Post 505, November 19, 1949, File: ROTC General Information, Box Marked: 1949—General Information, F. G. Clark Papers, Southern University Archives, Southern University and A&M College, Baton Rouge, La.

77. Letter, Raymond P. Scott, Commander, American Legion Post 502, to F. G. Clark, President, Southern University and A&M College, December 1, 1949, File: ROTC General Information, Box Marked: 1949-General Information, F. G. Clark Papers, Southern University Archives, Southern University and A&M College, Baton Rouge, La.

78. Buckley, 347–370; Gerald Astor, *The Right to Fight: A History of African Americans in the Military* (Novato, Calif., 1998), 345–399.

79. Memorandum, F. G. Clark, President, Southern University and A&M College, to Administrators and Faculty, April 11, 1951, File: Selective Service, 1950–1952, Cabinet S, F. G. Clark Papers, Southern University Archives, Southern University and A&M College, Baton Rouge, La.

80. Letter, F. G. Clark, President, Southern University and A&M College, to James C. Evans, Civilian Assistant to the Secretary of Defense, July 5, 1951, File: ROTC Matters, Cabinet R, F. G. Clark Papers, Southern University Archives, Southern University and A&M College, Baton Rouge, La.

81. Ibid.

82. Ibid.

83. Letter, Major General Hobart R. Gay, Deputy Commanding General, Fourth Army District, to F. G. Clark, President, Southern University and A&M College, December 14, 1951, File: ROTC Matters, Cabinet R, F. G. Clark Papers, Southern University Archives, Southern University and A&M College, Baton Rouge, La.

84. Nalty, 270.

85. "Thirty-five Cadets to Receive Commissions Today; Eighty-nine Prepare for Camp," *Southern University Digest* 24, no. 16 (June 3, 1953), 1.

86. "ROTC Unit Receives High Praise for Rescue Work in Flooded Areas of Louisiana Recently," *Southern University Digest* 24, no. 16 (June 3, 1953), 3.

87. Ibid.

88. "Gen. Weckerling Lauds ROTC," *Southern University Digest* 25, no. 10 (May 15, 1954), 1.

89. "Eighty-five ROTC Cadets to Be Commissioned at Commencement," *Southern University Digest* 25, no 11 (May 31, 1954), 1.

90. "Marching Cavalettes Give Homecoming Performance for Alumni and Friends," *Southern University Digest* 29, no. 3 (November 20, 1957), 4.

91. "Military Department Gets Girls Drill Team," *Southern University Digest* 28, no. 13 (May 13, 1957), 1.

92. Ibid.; "Military Day Set for May 25th," *Southern University Digest* 28, no. 13 (May 13, 1957), 1; "ROTC Military Day Held Here," *Southern University Digest* 28, no. 14 (June 1, 1957), 3.

93. "Team Becomes Pershing Rifles," *Southern University Digest* 29, no. 1 (October 11, 1957), 5.

94. "1957 ROTC Program Underway," *Southern University Digest* 29, no. 1 (October 11, 1957), 5.

95. Memorandum, Major General Charles L. Bolte, Assistant Chief of Staff, to Frank Pace, Secretary of the Army, July 26, 1950, File: Re establishment of an Antiaircraft Arty ROTC unit at Southern University, Baton Rouge, La, Record Group 407, AG Decimal File 1949–1950, Stack: 270/45/24/4, Box 1066, Description: Southern University and A&M College, National Archives Building, College Park, Md.

96. Vincent, 159.

CHAPTER 4

Note to epigraph: Alex Wilson, "Lt. Col. Lofton: Florida Officer Commands Thousands of Troops and Controls the lives of 3,000,000 persons in the land of the Rising Sun," *Chicago Defender* November 18, 1950, 14.

1. Alex Wilson, "Lt. Col. Lofton: Florida Officer Commands Thousands of Troops and Controls the lives of 3,000,000 persons in the land of the Rising Sun," *Chicago Defender* November 18, 1950, 14.

2. Jennifer E. Brooks, *Defining the Peace: World War II Veterans, Race, and the Remaking of Southern Political Tradition* (Chapel Hill, N.C., 2004), 11.

3. William G. Jordan, *Black Newspapers and America's War for Democracy, 1914–1920* (Chapel Hill, N.C., 2001), 3.

4. Finkle, 9–10.

5. "Race GIS Taking Advantage of Armed Forces Training," *Pittsburgh Courier*, January 5, 1952, 12.

6. "A Break for Korea Vets: A New GI Bill Now in Effect," *Pittsburgh Courier*, October 26, 1952, 1-A.

7. "M./Sgt. Branch Example of Progress in U.S. Army," *Pittsburgh Courier*, March 8, 1952, 11.

8. "In the Heart of Mississippi: Integration Complete at Keesler Air Base," *Afro-American*, March 18, 1950, 13-A.

9. "Report Reviews Progress Made in Race Relations in Armed Forces," *Chicago Defender*, May 27, 1950, 1-A.

10. Jimmy Oliver, "Uncle Sam's Southernites," *Southern University Digest* 23, no. 17 (May 23, 1952), 4.

11. *Southern University Digest* (March 8, 1952), 2

12. Ibid.

13. "Cadets Hold Annual Award Ceremonies," *Southern University Digest* 23, no. 17 (May 23, 1952), 3.

14. "Army's Trying," *Chicago Defender*, January 21, 1950, 6.

15. Ralph Matthews, "Korea Headquarters Speeding Integration: Tan Officers Hold Many Key Positions in 25th Infantry Division," *Afro-American*, November 10, 1951, 9.

16. "24th Infantry Takes Yechon in 16 Hours: Tan Yanks Push Back 'Reds' in Furious Battle," *Afro-American*, July 29, 1950, 1.

17. L. Alex Wilson, "See Citation for 503rd Artillery," *Chicago Defender*, October 28, 1950, 4.

18. James Hicks, "Integration in Korea," *Afro-American*, October 28, 1950, 19.

19. Louis Lautier, "Mixed Schools Should Follow Army Integration," *Afro-American*, August 11, 1951, 9.

20. Lee Nichols, *Breakthrough on the Color Front* (New York, 1954), 223.

21. John Modell and Timothy Haggerty, "The Social Impact of War," *Annual Review of Sociology* 17 (1991): 217.

22. "WAF Applicants Needed," *Campus Digest*, March 24, 1956, 8.

23. "Honor Grad," *Pittsburgh Courier*, November 1, 1952, 2.

24. "Nurse Earns Bronze Star!" *Pittsburgh Courier*, March 28, 1953, 3.

25. *Patty-Jo 'n' Ginger*, *Pittsburgh Courier*, November 4, 1950, 11.

26. Maureen Honey, ed., *Bitter Fruit: African American Women in World War II* (Columbia, Mo., 1999), 28

27. May, 103.

28. Cynthia Enloe, *Does Khaki Become You?* (London, England, 1993).

29. "Geraldine Jones Resigns as Miss ROTC," *Southern University Digest* 25, no. 5 (February 20, 1954), 1.

30. Arnold de Mille, "Air Base Integration Spotlights Abuses in West Point Mess Unit," *Chicago Defender*, September 15, 1951, 2.

31. "Fort Leonard Woods Bias Lowers GIs Morale," *Pittsburgh Courier*, February 9, 1952, 11.

32. "GI's Arrests Challenged: NAACP Set to Defend Fighters in Korea," *Afro-American*, November 18, 1950, 13.

33. "Two Officers Fight Ouster from Army," *Pittsburgh Courier*, January 5, 1952, 12-A.

34. "What New Army?" *Chicago Defender*, October 6, 1950, 6.

35. Gerald Horne, *Communist Front: The Civil Rights Congress, 1946–1956* (Rutherford, N.J., 1988), 176.

36. John E. Rousseau, "War with Korea Not Cure—Patterson Tells La. Negroes," *Pittsburgh Courier*, March 3, 1951, 1-A.

37. Ibid.

38. Ibid.

39. "The Loyalty of the Negro," *Ebony*, November 1950, 94.

40. James C. Smith, "The Marching Pershing Rifle Men of Southern University," *Southern University Digest* 30, no. 11 (April 17, 1959), 4.

41. "Pershing Rifles Make Two Appearances," *Southern University Digest* 30, no. 11 (April 17, 1959), 5.

42. "Southern's Cadets Make Fine Showing at Summer Camp in Fort Hood," *Southern University Digest* 31, no. 2 (October 31, 1959), 10.

43. Ibid.

44. Plummer, *Rising Wind*, 206.

45. "Anti-Segregation Policy Being Pursued—Ike," *Morning Advocate*, June 11, 1953, 10-A.

46. "Segregation Ended in D.C. Restaurants," *Morning Advocate*, June 10, 1953, 1-A.

47. "Races: The Unbunching," *Time*, February 22, 1954, 30.

48. Steve Estes, *I Am a Man!: Race, Manhood, and the Civil Rights Movement* (Chapel Hill, N.C., 2005). 11.

49. John Modell and Timothy Haggerty, "The Social Impact of War," *Annual Review of Sociology* 17 (1991): 219.

50. Christopher B. Strain, *Pure Fire: Self-Defense as Activism in the Civil Rights Era* (Athens, Ga., 2005), 55–56.

51. Krebs, 8.

52. Christopher S. Parker, *Fighting for Democracy: Black Veterans and the Struggle Against White Supremacy in the Postwar South* (Princeton, N.J., 2009), 61–74.

53. Ibid., 52; Felice F. Knight, "Portrait of a Community Activist: William 'Bill' Saunders and the Black Freedom Struggle in Charleston, SC, 1951–2004" (Master's thesis, College of Charleston, 2006), 45–46.

54. Robert F. Jefferson, *Fighting for Hope: African American Troops of the 93rd Infantry Division in World War II and Postwar America* (Baltimore, Md., 2008), 2.

55. Timothy B. Tyson, *Radio Free Dixie: Robert F. Williams and the Roots of Black Power* (Chapel Hill, N.C., 1999), 87–89.

56. Lance Hill, *The Deacons for Defense: Armed Resistance and the Civil Rights Movement* (Chapel Hill, N.C., 2004), 38–47.

57. Strain, 111–115.

58. Harrison interview, March 29, 2010.

59. Hebert, 2–3.

60. Ibid., 5–8.

61. "City Bus Strike Will Continue, Talks Planned," *Morning Advocate*, June 16, 1953, 6-A, col. 2.

62. "City Bus Strike Is Still On," *Morning Advocate*, June 17, 1953, 8-A, col. 4.

63. "Bus Strike Talks Continuing, Said More Favorable," *Morning Advocate*, June 18, 1953, 1-A.

64. "City Bus Strike to End at Dawn Today: Attorney General Says City Seating Law Is Invalid," *Morning Advocate*, June 19, 1953, 1-A.

65. "Negroes Here Continue Bus Boycott; Company May Curtail Service," *Morning Advocate*, June 20, 1953, 1-A.

66. Ibid., 2-A, col. 3.

67. "BR Negroes May Petition for Separate Bus System: Leaders Say Boycott Plan to Be Continued," *Morning Advocate*, June 21, 1953, 8-A, col. 5.

68. "New Ordinance on Bus Seating Is Kept Secret," *Morning Advocate*, June 23, 1953, 1-A.

69. BR Negroes May Petition for Separate Bus System: Leaders Say Boycott Plan to Be Continued," *Morning Advocate*, June 21, 1953, 8-A, col. 5.

70. "New Ordinance On Bus Seating Is Kept Secret," *Morning Advocate*, June 23, 1953, 6-A, col. 7.

71. "Bus Fight Settlement Is Possible," *Morning Advocate*, June 24, 1953, 1-A.

72. "City Council Passes New Bus Ordinance; Bond Election Called," *Morning Advocate*, June 25, 1953, 1-A.

73. Ibid., 6-A, col. 6.

74. "Negroes End Bus Boycott," *Morning Advocate*, June 26, 1953, 6-A, col. 4.

75. "Bus Business Is Off as Negroes Resume Riding," *Morning Advocate*, June 27, 1953, 1-A.

76. Aldon D. Morris, *The Origins of the Civil Rights Movement: Black Communities Organizing for Change* (New York, 1984), 25.

77. V. P. Franklin, "Patterns of Student Activism at Historically Black Universities in the United States and South Africa," *Journal of African American History* 88, no. 2, The History of Black Student Activism (spring 2003): 206.

78. Ibid., 205.

79. "Montgomery Boycott Leader Visits Baton Rouge Church," *Southern University Digest* 27, no. 4 (December 1, 1956), 1.

80. Harrison interview, March 29, 2010.

81. "NAACP Chapter Formed on Campus," *Southern University Digest* 27, no. 5 (December 2, 1955), 1.

CHAPTER 5

1. Donald Matthews and James Protho, "Negro Students and the Protest Movement," in *Black Power and Student Rebellion,* ed. James McEvoy and Abraham Miller, 383 (Belmont, Calif., 1969).

2. Seymour Martin Lipset, *Rebellion in the University: A History of Student Activism in America* (Boston, Mass., 1971), 10–11.

3. Parker, 196–197.

4. "Integration Action in N.C. Spreads," *Morning Advocate,* February 9, 1960, 1-A; "Chanting Negroes Parade in Alabama Against Segregation, *Morning Advocate,* March 2, 1960, A-1; "Negroes Continue Demonstrations for Integration," *Morning Advocate,* March 4, 1960, 1-A; "11 Negroes Arrested for Trespassing," *Morning Advocate,* March 8, 1960, 1-A.

5. "Demonstrations by Negroes Hit Two Big Cities," *Morning Advocate,* March 9, 1960, 1-A.

6. "400 Students Parade in Support of Civil Rights," *Campus Digest,* March 1, 1960, 1.

7. "State College Heads Warned on 'Incidents,'" *Morning Advocate,* March 16, 1960, 1-A.

8. Major Johns and Ronnie Moore, *It Happened in Baton Rouge, U.S.A.* (New York, 1962), 1.

9. "Negro Protests Spread," *Morning Advocate,* March 27, 1960, 1-A.

10. Johns and Moore, 1.

11. "Negro Students Arrested Here after Sit-Down," *Morning Advocate,* March 29, 1960, 1-A.

12. "Long Suggests That Dissatisfied Negroes Leave," *Morning Advocate,* March 29, 1960, 1-A.

13. "Third St. Boycott by Negroes Urged after New Sit-Down Case," *Morning Advocate,* March 30, 1960, 1-A.

14. D'Army Bailey, *The Education of a Black Radical: A Southern Civil Rights Activist's Journey* (Baton Rouge, La., 2009), 49.

15. Harrison interview, March 29, 2010.

16. Huel D. Perkins, former student and dean of Arts and Humanities, Southern University and A&M College, interview by author, tape recording, Baton Rouge, La., March 30, 2010.

17. Louis E. Lomax, *The Negro Revolt* (New York, 1963), 211.

18. Ibid., 212.

19. "Suspensions Follow BR Demonstrations," *Morning Advocate,* March 31, 1960, 1-A.

20. "Leader Asks Whole Southern U. Student Body to Quit School," *Morning Advocate,* April 1, 1960, 1-A.

21. Baily, 52–53.

22. "Negro Students Leaving Campus in Small Numbers," *Morning Advocate,* April 4, 1960, 1-A.

23. Adam Fairclough, *Race and Democracy: The Civil Rights Struggle in Louisiana, 1915–1972* (Athens, Ga., 1995), 270.

24. Ibid., 266.

25. Russel L. Honoré, former student and retired Army lieutenant general, Southern University and A&M College, interview by author, tape recording, Baton Rouge, La., March 30, 2010.

26. Joy Ann Williamson, *Radicalizing the Ebony Tower: Black Colleges and the Black Freedom Struggle in Mississippi.*(New York, 2008), 147.

27. "ROTC Activities Serve Wide Variety of Interests on Campus," *Southern University Digest* (October 15, 1960), 3.

28. "Otis D. Jones Heads Staff of S.U. Digest," *Southern University Digest* (October 15, 1960), 1; "Three Seniors Named for Regular Army Appointments," *Southern University Digest* (February 4, 1961), 1; D'Army Bailey, "Campus Expose,'" *Southern University Digest* (March 23, 1961), 3; Bailey, *The Education of a Black Radical*, 64.

29. "Voluntary and Compulsory ROTC," *Southern University Digest* (March 23, 1961), 6.

30. "Home Economics Major Enlists in Army Dietetics Program," *Southern University Digest* (May 25, 1961), 1.

31. "60 Per Cent of Tuskegee's Air Force ROTC Graduates Now on Active Duty," *Campus Digest*, January 20, 1961, 1.

32. "Graduates Are Navy Officers Now," *Campus Digest*, October 27, 1961, 5.

33. "Southern University Military Department," *Southern University Digest* (May 25, 1961), 8–9.

34. "Armed Forces Day Will Be Observed," *Campus Digest*, May 12, 1961, 5.

35. "Army Engineer Recruits TI Engineering Students," *Campus Digest*, November 17, 1961, 6.

36. See Army advertisement, *Southern University Digest* (February 17, 1962), 5; see Air Force advertisement, *Southern University Digest* (April 4, 1962), 10; Army advertisement, *Southern University Digest* (November 20, 1962), 5; Air Force advertisement, *Southern University Digest* (October 17, 1963), 6.

37. "Why Academic Electives in ROTC," *Southern University Digest* (May 3, 1963), 2.

38. Neiberg, 184.

39. Michael Harrington, *The Other America: Poverty in the United States* (New York, 1962).

40. George C. Herring, *America's Longest War: The United States and Vietnam, 1950–1975* (Philadelphia, Pa., 1986), 14.

41. David Kaiser, *American Tragedy: Kennedy, Johnson, and the Origins of the Vietnam War* (Cambridge, Mass., 2000), 484.

42. President's Task Force on Manpower Conservation, *One Third of a Nation: A Report on Young Men Found Unqualified for Military Service* (Washington, D.C.: Government Printing Office, 1964).

43. Ibid., 2.

44. Christian Appy, *Working-Class War: American Combat Soldiers and Vietnam* (Chapel Hill, N.C., 1993), 31.

45. "Your Public Image," *Southern University Digest* (October 16, 1964), 4.

46. "Southern ROTC Honor Graduate Killed in Action in South Viet Nam," *Southern University Digest* (April 21, 1964), 8.

47. "A Hero's Arrival and Departure," *Southern University Digest* (April 21, 1964), 8.

48. Adam Garfinkle, *Telltale Hearts: The Origins and Impact of the Vietnam Antiwar Movement* (New York, 1997), 71.

49. "A Message from the Professor of Military Science at Southern," *Southern University Digest* (October 16, 1964), 4.

50. Herring, 108.

51. Cherry Burroughs, "Students, Faculty Discuss Viet Nam," *Campus Digest*, May 24, 1965, 10.

52. Leon S. White, "Viet Nam Poll," *Campus Digest*, October 23, 1965, 2.

53. "Our Stake in Vietnam—Freedom from Peril," *Southern University Digest* (February 6, 1965), 4.

54. "We Will Go to Jail by the Thousands King Pledges in Alabama Black Belt," *Southern University Digest* (February 6, 1965), 1.

55. Jacob Bouie Jr., "Politically Speaking," *Southern University Digest* (March 9, 1965): 2.

56. Wade Hudson, "Freedom?" *Southern University Digest* (April 7, 1965), 2.

57. Eddie Sanderford, "Malcolm X—The Man Without the Mask," *Southern University Digest* (April 7, 1965), 4.

58. "Bouie Awarded for Services in South Vietnam," *Southern University Digest* (November 25, 1966), 6.

59. "Distinguished ROTC Students Named by Military Science Dept.," *Southern University Digest* (October 21, 1966), 1.

60. "Leggett Invited to Student Government Conference in N.O.," *Southern University Digest* (October 21, 1966), 1.

61. Memorandum, Robert McNamara, Secretary of Defense, to Lyndon B. Johnson, President of the United States, 3/2/66, Ex ND 12/2/65-11/21/66, WHCF, Box 148, LBJ Presidential Library, Austin, Texas.

62. Homer Bigart, "Military Plans to 'Salvage' 40,000 Rejected in Draft," *New York Times*, August 24, 1966, 18.

63. Ibid.

64. Peter Barnes, *The Plight of the Citizen-Soldier* (New York, 1972), 44.

65. Ibid., 45.

66. Howard Schuman, "Two Sources of Antiwar Sentiment in America," *American Journal of Sociology* 78, no. 3 (November 1972): 514.

67. Robert W. Mullen, *Blacks in America's Wars: The Shift in Attitudes from the Revolutionary War to Vietnam* (New York, 1973), 64.

68. Randall Fisher, *Rhetoric and American Democracy: Black Protest through Vietnam Dissent* (New York, 1985), 96–97.

69. Shapiro, 121–122.

70. Karin L. Stanford, *If We Must Die: African American Voices on War and Peace* (Lanham, Md., 2008), 226.

71. Ibid., 136.

72. "Dept. of Political Science Holds 'Black Power' Seminar," *Southern University Digest* (November 4, 1966), 7.

73. "The War Must Be Won," *Southern University Digest* (December 16, 1966), 2; "The Roving Report," *Southern University Digest* (December 16, 1966), 2.

74. "What Good Can Military Training Do You? The Values of a ROTC Program Discussed," *Southern University Digest* (December 16, 1966), 4.

75. Mullen, 70.

76. Judy Tzu-Chun Wu, "An African-Vietnamese American: Robert S. Browne, the Antiwar Movement, and the Personal/Political Dimensions of Black Internationalism," *Journal of African American History* 92, no. 4, New Black Power Studies: National, International, and Transnational Perspectives (autumn 2007): 501.

77. Kwame Ture and Charles V. Hamilton, *Black Power: The Politics of Liberation* (New York, 1992), xix.

78. Eldridge Cleaver, *Soul on Ice* (New York, 1992), 149–153.

79. H. Rap Brown, *Die Nigger Die!* (Chicago, Ill., 2002), 38.

80. Wu, 505.

81. Marian Judkins, "Should the U.S. Remain in Vietnam?" *Campus Digest*, May 8, 1965, 2.

82. Alton Hornsby Jr. "A U.S. Commitment," *Campus Digest*, May 8, 1965, 8.

83. George Geddis, Chuck Griner, and Eddie Cotton, "Week-Long Protests Continue," *Campus Digest*, January 15, 1966, 1.

84. "Why They Protest," *Campus Digest*, March 5, 1966, 2.

85. "Essayist: Lives Are Sacrificed," *Campus Digest*, May 28, 1966, 2.

86. Ibid.

87. "War vs. War," *Campus Digest*, October 1, 1966, 4.

88. Ernest Stephens, "Carmichael to Speak," *Campus Digest*, October 8, 1966, 1.

89. Johnson, 182.

90. Ibid., 184.

91. Ibid., 186.

92. Ibid., 188.

93. "ROTC Necessary," *Campus Digest*, December 3, 1966, 2.

94. "Open Season on Negroes," *Campus Digest*, December 19, 1966, 1.

95. Ibid.

96. "The United States Is the Greatest Purveyor of Violence in the World Today," *Campus Digest*, April 15, 1967, 3.

97. Ibid.

98. "Letters to the Editor," *Campus Digest*, April 15, 1967, 5.

99. "Letters to the Editor," *Campus Digest*, November 11, 1967, 4.

100. "The Great Society—In Uniform," *Newsweek*, August 22, 1966, 47.

101. Ibid.

102. Ibid., 48.

103. Ibid., 47.

104. Ibid., 47–48.

105. Simeon Booker, "Negroes in Vietnam: 'We, Too, Are Americans,'" *Ebony*, November 1965, 89.

106. Ibid., 91.

107. Ibid., 96.

108. "Negro Deaths Exceed Whites' in Viet Nam," *Pittsburgh Courier*, May 28, 1966, 8.

109. Ibid.

110. Ibid.

111. "Amendments to Policies and Procedures Relating to Student Life at the University," *Southern University Digest* (November 16, 1967), 1.

112. "Four Senior Cadets Designated Distinguished Military Students," *Southern University Digest* (October 20, 1967), 3.

113. "Administrators Concede to Senate's Letter of Demands," *Southern University Digest* (November 16, 1967), 1.

114. "Grambling Students Boycott for Academic Excellence," *Southern University Digest* (November 16, 1967), 2.

115. "Student-Administration Meetings Benefit Both," *Southern University Digest* (November 16, 1967), 1.

116. "Let's Give a Hand to the Senate," *Southern University Digest* (November 16, 1967), 2.

117. "Governor McKeithen Visits SU to Survey Campus Needs," *Southern University Digest* (March 22, 1968), 1.

118. "Black Power Conference Advocated by Senators," *Southern University Digest* (December 18, 1967), 1.

119. Ibid.

120. "Letters to the Editor," *Southern University Digest* (January 19, 1968), 2.

121. Timothy E. Pratt, "The Invaders," *Southern University Digest* (January 19, 1968), 5.

122. Parker, 107.

123. Colin Powell, *My American Journey* (New York, 1995), 25–26.

124. Harvard Sitkoff, *The Struggle for Black Equality, 1954–1980* (New York, 1981), 217.

CHAPTER 6

1. Maurice Isserman and Michael Kazin, *America Divided: The Civil War of the 1960s* (New York, 2000), 180–186.

2. Johnson, 179–190.

3. Russel Honoré interview, March 30, 2010.

4. Mullen, 66–67.

5. Wallace Terry, *Bloods: An Oral History of the Vietnam War by Black Veterans* (New York, 1984), xiv.

6. Mullen, 66.

7. Paul Boyer, *Promises to Keep: The United States since World War II* (Lexington, Mass., 1995), 335.

8. Shapiro, 135.

9. "Students March on the Capital to Protest White Racist Killing," *Southern University Digest* (May 17, 1968), 7.

10. Ibid.

11. Ibid.

12. "Compulsory ROTC—Give Us a Choice," *Southern University Digest* (May 17, 1968), 2.

13. Vincent, 207.

14. Letter, Vice Admiral D. H. Guinn, Chief of Naval Personnel, to G. Leon Netterville, President, Southern University and A&M College, October 17, 1970, File: Naval ROTC, Box Marked: General Information, 1971–1972, Southern University Archives, Southern University and A&M College, Baton Rouge, La.

15. "Highlights of Student Leadership Conference," *Southern University Digest* (October 14, 1968), 3.

16. "Comment . . . ," *Southern University Digest* (November 1, 1968), 2.

17. Frank Williams, "R.O.T.C. Vs The Man," *Southern University Digest* (December 18, 1968), 10.

18. Neiberg, 173.

19. Ibid., 171

20. Michael Useem, *Conscription, Protest, and Social Conflict: The Life and Death of a Draft Resistance Movement* (New York, 1973), 267.

21. Memorandum, Martin L. Harvey, Dean of Student Affairs, to G. Leon Netterville, President, Southern University and A&M College, November 18, 1968, File: ROTC—1969, Cabinet 16, Southern University Archives, Southern University and A&M College, Baton Rouge, La.

22. Ibid.

23. "Against the Black Digest," *Southern University Digest* (March 27, 1969), 2.

24. Ronald Walters and Robert Smith, "The Black Education Strategy in the 1970s," *Journal of Negro Education* 48, no. 2 (spring 1979): 156.

25. Ibid.

26. Harlette Smith, "SUNO REVOLTS," *Southern University Digest* (May 23, 1969), 2.

27. Appy, *Working-Class War*, 37.

28. "Netterville Meets with SUNO Leaders," *Morning Advocate*, April 19, 1969, 16-A.

29. Art Adams, "Protestors from SUNO Gather Here," *Morning Advocate*, May 3, 1969, 1-A.

30. Bill Crider, "Students Leave SU in Orleans; McKeithen Holds Back Guard," *Morning Advocate*, May 6, 1969, 8-A.

31. Ken Dixon, "SU Unrest Blamed on Untrue Reports," *Morning Advocate*, May 13, 1969, 1-A.

32. Ken Dixon, "Calm Prevails at SU after Governor Meet," *Morning Advocate*, May 15, 1969, 1-A.

33. "ROTC Is Doing OK," *Morning Advocate*, May 19, 1969, 2-A.

34. Harrison interview, September 9, 1998.

35. Ransburg interview, February 12, 1998.

36. Gibbs Adams, "Gov. McKeithen Tours Southern University Campus," *Morning Advocate*, May 20, 1969, 10-A.

37. "21 TU Students Are Disciplined," *Times-Picayune*, May 22, 1969, 1-A.

38. "Committee Set on ROTC in Lake Charles," *Morning Advocate*, April 20, 1969, 4-B.

39. "ROTC Made Voluntary by LSU Board," *Morning Advocate*, May 27, 1969, 1-A.

40. "Northeast ROTC Goes Elective," *Morning Advocate*, August 2, 1969, 5-B.

41. "Netterville States Policy on Disruptions," *Morning Advocate*, September 5, 1969, 5-B.

42. Frank S. Ransburg, former student, professor, and administrator, Southern University and A&M College, interview by author, tape recording, Baton Rouge, La., April 27, 2001.

43. Ibid.

44. Edward Augustus, "R.O.T.C. Goes Voluntary," *Southern University Digest* (September 26, 1969), 1.

45. Ibid., 9.

46. "Status of ROTC in Review at S.U.," *Southern University Digest* (October 17, 1969), 1.

47. "ROTC Flight Program at Southern University," *Southern University Digest* (October 24, 1969), 10.

48. Tim Spofford, *Lynch Street: The May 1970 Slayings at Jackson State College* (Kent, Ohio, 1988), 26.

49. Ibid., 30.

50. Ibid.

51. Ibid.

52. Ibid., 35.

53. Ibid.

54. Ibid., 38.

55. Ibid., 57.

56. "Jackson State Becalmed," *Newsweek*, March 1, 1971, 69.

57. "Dark Day in Jackson," *Newsweek*, May 25, 1970, 35.

58. "The South: Death in Two Cities," *Time*, May 25, 1970, 22.

59. "Dark Day in Jackson," 36.

60. "Jackson State Becalmed," 69.

61. Charles DeBenedetti, *An American Ordeal: The Antiwar Movement of the Vietnam Era* (Syracuse, N.Y., 1990), 279–280; Spofford, 38–41.

62. Johnson, 195.

63. The application was originally submitted on October 24, 1967, by President Felton G. Clark. Clark invited Navy officials to inspect Southern's facilities, which were deemed adequate for a unit.

64. Letter, Vice Admiral D. H. Guinn, Chief of Naval Personnel, to G. Leon Netterville, President, Southern University and A&M College, October 17, 1970, File: Naval ROTC, Box Marked: General Information, 1971–1972, Southern University Archives, Southern University and A&M College, Baton Rouge, La.

65. Wilbur Robinson, "RACE AND ROTC: Army Intelligence Was Devised Amid City Riots Five Years Ago," *Southern University Digest* (March 11, 1971), 2.

66. Ibid., 4.

67. Larry St. Amant, "NROTC Commission Date Set; Black Admiral to Do Honors," *Southern University Digest* (September 25, 1971), 6.

68. Ibid.

69. Bobby Gilliard, "Admiral Relates Navy Efforts to Improve Lot of Minority," *Southern University Digest* (October 16, 1971), 1.

70. "Campus Militants Won Skirmishes but Lost the War," *Southern University Digest* (December 3, 1971), 5.

71. Ibid.

72. "On Induction: New SS Policy Effective July 1," *Southern University Digest* (June 29, 1972), 1.

73. Ibid.

74. Hebert, 348–349.

75. Letter, M. W. King to E. C. Harrison, University Vice President, Southern University and A&M College, November 14, 1972, File: Student Unrest (Letters of Disruption), F. G. Clark Papers, Box Marked: S-W 1970–1974, Southern University Archives, Southern University and A&M College, Baton Rouge, La.

76. Hebert, 350; "A Deadly History . . . Chronology of Events That Led to Death of Students," *Southern University Digest* (January 19, 1973), 5; William J. Guste Jr., Attorney General, State of Louisiana, "Report of the Attorney General's Special Commission of Inquiry on the Southern University Tragedy of November 16, 1972" (Baton Rouge, La.: State of Louisiana Department of Justice, July 1973), 7, Southern University Archives, Southern University and A&M College, Baton Rouge, La.

77. Guste, 12.

78. Ibid.

79. Ibid., 15–18; Hebert, 350–351.

80. Stanley Morris, "Southern's Trouble Considered," *Morning Advocate,* November 16, 1972.

81. Charles Layton, "Netterville Is Firing Some Profs," *Morning Advocate,* November 19, 1972, 1.

82. "SU President Calls for Return to Reason for Jan. 3 Reopening," *Baton Rouge News Leader,* December 17, 1972, 6-A.

83. Progress Report of Special Projects Related to Student Grievances, December 21, 1972, File: Student Unrest (Reports of Various Committees), F. G. Clark Papers, Box Marked: S-W 1970–1974, Southern University Archives, Southern University and A&M College, Baton Rouge, La.

84. Symposium Resolutions, File: Student Unrest (Reports of Various Committees), F. G. Clark Papers, Box Marked: S-W 1970–1974, Southern University Archives, Southern University and A&M College, Baton Rouge, La.

85. Weusi Tshinde, "Students Say Deaths at SU Planned by Deputies," *Baton Rouge News Leader,* December 3, 1972, 3-B

86. Letter, Edith M. Johnson, English instructor, to Major William Pass, Campus Security, January 18, 1973, File: Student Unrest (Letters of Disruption), F. G. Clark Papers, Box Marked: S-W 1970–1974, Southern University Archives, Southern University and A&M College, Baton Rouge, La.

87. Vincent, 222.

88. "Murder at SU," File: 11-17-72 (Day of Infamy), F. G. Clark Papers, Box Marked: S-W 1972–1973, Southern University Archives, Southern University and A&M College, Baton Rouge, La.

89. Michael Lanning, *The African-American Soldier: From Crispus Attucks to Colin Powell* (Secaucus, N.J., 1997), 276.

90. Charles C. Moskos and Frank R. Wood, eds., *The Military: More Than Just a Job?* (Washington, D.C., 1988), 3–6.

91. Berwin McClinton, "Southern NROTC among First to Admit Women," *Southern University Digest* (March 25, 1972), 5.

92. "Women May Train as ROTC Officers," *Southern University Digest* (September 14, 1973), 1.

93. Johnson, 209.

94. Appy, *Working-Class War*, 6.

95. Moskos and Butler, 83–84.

CHAPTER 7: CONCLUSION

1. L. F. Koons, former student, Tuskegee University, interview by author, transcript, Tuskegee, Ala., April 30, 2000.

2. Neiberg, 167.

3. Ibid.

4. Moskos and Butler, 37.

5. Russel Honoré interview, March 30, 2010.

6. Nalty, 336.

7. Moskos and Wood, 3.

8. Ibid., 16.

9. Neiberg, 169.

10. Henry L. Essex, former professor, Southern University and A&M College, interview by author, transcript, Baton Rouge, La., n.d.

11. J. Alfred Phelps, *Chappie: America's First Black Four Star General—The Life and Times of Daniel James, Jr* (Novato, Calif., 1991), 273–275; Charles Honore, former student and retired Army major general, Southern University and A&M College, interview by author, transcript, Fair Oaks Ranch, Tex., n.d.

12. "Black Colleges Are the Primary Source of African American Army Officers," *Journal of Blacks in Higher Education*, no. 16 (summer 1997): 52.

13. Powell, 35.

14. Elaine Edwards, "African American Student Retention in the Reserve Officer Training Corps (ROTC) Leadership Program" (Ph.D. diss., Walden University, 2012), 3–4.

15. Ibid., 27.

16. Vincent, 159.

17. Walter L. Hawkins, *African American Generals and Flag Officers: Biographies of over 120 Blacks in the United States Military* (Jefferson, N.C., 1993).

18. Perkins interview, 1999.

19. John Sibley Butler, "Race Relations in the Military," in *The Military: More Than Just a Job?*, ed. Charles C. Moskos and Frank R. Wood, 121 (Washington, D.C., 1988).

20. James Lund, former student, Tuskegee University, interview by author, transcript, Superior, Wisc., n.d.

21. William O. Jones, former student, Tuskegee University, interview by author, transcript, Tuskegee, Ala., n.d.

22. Charles Honore interview, n.d.

23. Koons interview, April 30, 2000.

24. Perkins interview, 1999.

25. Moskos and Butler, 83.

26. Ibid., 83–84.

BIBLIOGRAPHY

MANUSCRIPT COLLECTIONS

Felton G. Clark Papers, Southern University Archives, Baton Rouge, Louisiana.
  Army Specialized Training Program, 1942 file.
  Civilian Defense (General Matters), 1941–1942 file.
  Civilian Defense Council, 1941 file.
  Civilian Defense Council, 1941–1942 file
  Civilian Defense Council (Campus), 1941–1942 file.
  Civilian Defense School, 1941–1942 file
  Community War Chest Fund, 1943 file.
  Defense Savings Bonds, 1941–1942 file.
  Department of State file.
  National Defense file.
  National Defense Program file.
  Naval ROTC file.
  Personal Letters—Confidential file.
  Reserve Officers' Training Corps, 1948–1952 file.
  ROTC, 1969 file.
  ROTC General Information file.
  ROTC Matters file.
  ROTC Unit Request, 1941–1946 file.
  ROTC Unit Request, 1946–1948 file.
  Selective Service, 1950–1952 file.
  Student Unrest file.
  United States Office of Education, 1943 file.
  War Department, 1941–1942 file.
  War Department, 1942–1943 file.

War Efforts (Faculty), 1942 file.
11-17-72 file.

Lyndon Baines Johnson Presidential Library, Austin, Texas.
Records of Robert McNamara, Secretary of Defense. Box 148.

National Archives II, College Park, Maryland.
Records of Homefront Campaigns, 1943–1945. Record Group 208.
Records of Louisiana College to Commanding General. Record Group 319
Records of Major General Charles L. Bolte. Record Group 407.
Records of Military Policy Implications. Record Group 107.
Records of Reserve Officer Training Corps Units. Record Group 107.
Records of Secretary of War Office. Record Group 107.
Records of Special Consultant to the Deputy Director of Public Relations. Record Group 107.
Records of the Adjutant General, U.S. Department of the Army. Record Group 319
Records of the Army Specialized Training Program. Record Group 107.
Records of the Office of Assistant Secretary of Defense. Record Group 319.
Records of the Office of Education. Record Group 12.

Frederick Douglass Patterson, Tuskegee University Archives, Tuskegee, Alabama.
National Defense file.
Hampton Institute file.
War file.
Land Grant Colleges file.
Tuskegee Army Air Field file.
Reserve Officer Corps Training Monthly Reports file.

PUBLIC DOCUMENTS

Guste, William J., Jr., Attorney General, State of Louisiana. *Report of the Attorney General's Special Commission of Inquiry on the Southern University Tragedy of November 16, 1972.* Baton Rouge: State of Louisiana Department of Justice, July 1973.

Pilot Training School: Tuskegee Institute. United States Army Air Force Training Edition. Washington, D.C.: Government Printing Office, 1944.

President's Task Force on Manpower Conservation. *One-Third of a Nation: A Report on Young Men Found Unqualified for Military Service.* Washington, D.C.: Government Printing Office, 1964.

U.S. Department of Labor, Office of Policy Planning and Research. *The Negro Family: The Case for National Action.* Washington, D.C.: Government Printing Office, 1965.

INTERVIEWS

Anonymous. Former student. Transcript, Tuskegee University. Baton Rouge, La., April 15, 2000.
Essex, Henry L. Former professor. Transcript, Southern University and A&M College. Baton Rouge, La., n. d.
Harrison, E. C. Former student and vice president of academic affairs, Southern University and A&M College. Baton Rouge, La., September 9, 1998.
———. Former student and vice president of academic affairs, Southern University and A&M College. Baton Rouge, La., March 29, 2010.
Honore, Charles. Former student and retired Army major general. Transcript, Southern University and A&M College. Fair Oaks Ranch, Tex., n. d.
Honoré, Russel L. Former student and retired Army lieutenant general, Southern University and A&M College. Baton Rouge, La., March 30, 2010.
Jones, William O. Former student. Transcript, Tuskegee University. Tuskegee, Ala., n. d.
Koons, L. F. Former student. Transcript, Tuskegee University. Tuskegee, Ala., April 30, 2000.
Lund, James. Former student. Transcript, Tuskegee University. Superior, Wisc., n.d.
Perkins, Huel D. Former student and dean of Arts and Humanities, Southern University and A&M College. Baton Rouge, La., October 21, 1999.
———. Former student and dean of Arts and Humanities, Southern University and A&M College. Baton Rouge, La., March 30, 2010.
Ransburg, Frank R. Former student, professor, and administrator, Southern University and A&M College. Baton Rouge, La., February 12, 1998.
———. Former student, professor, and administrator, Southern University and A&M College. Baton Rouge, La., April 27, 2001.

NEWSPAPERS

Afro-American, 1946–1951
Baton Rouge News Leader, 1955–1972.
Campus Digest (Tuskegee University), 1937–1972.
Chicago Defender, 1950–1954.
Morning Advocate (Baton Rouge, La.), 1948–1972.
New York Times, 1948.

Pittsburgh Courier (the *Courier*), 1950–1968.
Southern University Digest, 1941–1973.
Times Picayune (New Orleans, La.), 1942, 1969.

SECONDARY SOURCES

Ambrose, Stephen. *Citizen Soldiers: The U.S. Army from the Normandy Beaches to the Bulge to the Surrender of Germany*. New York: Simon and Schuster, 1997.

Ampey, Marguerite Smith. "Freedom's People Radio Programs." *Louisiana Colored Teachers Journal* 15, no. 4 (June 1942): 14–15.

Anderson, James. *The Education of Blacks in the South, 1860–1935*. Chapel Hill: Univ. of North Carolina Press, 1988.

Andrew, Rod, Jr. *Long Gray Lines: The Southern Military School Tradition, 1839–1915*. Chapel Hill: Univ. of North Carolina Press, 2001.

Appy, Christian G. *Cold War Constructions: The Political Culture of United States Imperialism, 1945–1966*. Amherst: Univ. of Massachusetts Press, 2000.

———. *Working-Class War: American Combat Soldiers and Vietnam*. Chapel Hill: Univ. of North Carolina Press, 1993.

Astor, Gerald. *The Right to Fight: A History of African Americans in the Military*. Novato, Calif.: Presido Press, 1998.

Axt, Richard G. *The Federal Government and Financing Higher Education*. New York: Columbia Univ. Press, 1952.

Bailey, D'Army. *The Education of a Black Radical: A Southern Civil Rights Activist's Journey*. Baton Rouge: Louisiana State Univ. Press, 2009.

Barbalet, J. M. *Citizenship: Rights, Struggle, and Class Inequality*. Minneapolis: Univ. of Minnesota Press, 1988.

Barnes, Peter. *The Plight of the Citizen-Soldier*. New York: Knopf, 1972.

Berman, William C. *The Politics of Civil Rights in the Truman Administration*. Columbus: Ohio State Univ. Press, 1970.

Berry, Mary Frances. *Military Necessity and Civil Rights Policy: Black Citizenship and the Constitution, 1861–1868*. Port Washington, N.Y.: Kennikat Press, 1977.

"Black Colleges Are the Primary Source of African American Army Officers." *Journal of Blacks in Higher Education*, no. 16 (summer 1997): 52.

Blassingame, John W. "The Union Army as an Educational Institution for Negroes, 1862–1865." *Journal of Negro Education* 34, no. 2 (spring 1965): 152–159.

Blight, David W. *Frederick Douglass' Civil War: Keeping Faith in Jubilee*. Baton Rouge: Louisiana State Univ. Press, 1989.

Blum, John Morton. *V Was for Victory: Politics and the American Culture during World War II*. New York: Harcourt Brace Jovanovich, 1976.

Booker, Simeon. "Negroes in Vietnam: 'We Too, Are Americans.'" *Ebony*, November 1965, 89–99.

Boyer, Paul. *Promises to Keep: The United States since World War II*. Lexington, Mass.: Heath, 1995.

Branson, Herman. "The Training of Negroes for War Industries in World War II." *Journal of Negro Education* 12, no. 3 (summer 1943): 376–385.

Brawley, Benjamin. *History of Morehouse College*. Manchester, N.H.: Cosimo Classics, 2009.

Brooks, Jennifer E. *Defining the Peace: World War II Veterans, Race, and the Remaking of Southern Political Tradition*. Chapel Hill: Univ. of North Carolina Press, 2004.

Brown, Christopher Leslie, and Philip D. Morgan. *Arming Slaves: From Classical Times to the Modern Age*. New Haven, Conn.: Yale Univ. Press, 2006.

Brown, Flora Bryant. "NAACP Sponsored Sit-Ins by Howard University Students in Washington, D.C., 1943–1944." *Journal of Negro History* 85, no. 4 (2000): 274–286.

Brown, H. Rap. *Die Nigger Die!* Chicago: Lawrence Hill Books, 2002.

Buckley, Gail. *American Patriots: The Story of Blacks in the Military from the Revolution to Desert Storm*. New York: Random House, 2001.

Budiansky, Stephen. *The Bloody Shirt: Terror after Appomattox*. New York: Viking Penguin, 2008.

Butler, John Sibley. "Race Relations in the Military." In *The Military: More Than Just a Job?*, edited by Charles C. Moskos and Frank R. Wood, 115–127. Washington, D.C.: Pergamon-Brassey's International Defense Publishers, 1988.

Cardozier, V. R. *Colleges and Universities in World War II*. Westport, Conn.: Praeger, 1993.

Cashman, Sean Dennis. *African-Americans and the Quest for Civil Rights, 1900–1990*. New York: New York Univ. Press, 1991.

Chamberlain, Charles. *Victory at Home: Manpower and Race in the American South during World War II*. Athens: Univ. of Georgia Press, 2003.

Clark, Felton G. "Administrative Control of Public Negro Colleges." *Journal of Negro Education* 3, no. 2 (April 1934): 245–256.

———. "The Control of State Supported Teachers Training Programs for Negroes." *Teachers College Record* (1934): 324–325.

———. "Negro Higher Education and Some Fundamental Issues Raised by World War II." *Journal of Negro Education* 11, no. 3 (July 1942): 279–291.

Cleaver, Eldridge. *Soul on Ice*. New York: Delta Trade Paperbacks, 1992.

Cohen, Rodney T. *Fisk University*. Mt. Pleasant, S.C.: Arcadia Publishing, 2001.

Cornish, Dudley Taylor. "The Union Army as a School for Negroes." *Journal of Negro History* 37, no. 4 (October 1952): 368–382.

"Crisis in the Making: U.S. Negroes Tussle with Issue . . ." *Newsweek,* June 7, 1948, 28–29.
Dabbs, Henry E. *Black Brass: Black Generals and Admirals in the Armed Forces of the United States.* Charlottesville, Va.: Howell Press, 1997.
Dalfiume, Richard M. *Desegregation of the U.S. Armed Forces: Fighting on Two Fronts, 1939–1953.* Columbia: Univ. of Missouri, 1969.
Daniel, Walter G., and Marion T. Wright. "The Role of Educational Agencies in Maintaining Morale among Negroes." *Journal of Negro Education* 12, no. 3 (summer 1943): 491–493.
"Dark Day in Jackson." *Newsweek,* May 25, 1970, 35.
Davis, John W. "Current Changes in Negro Higher Education to Meet the Immediate War Emergency." *Journal of Negro Education* 11, no. 3 (July 1942): 292–294.
———. "The Participation of Negro Land-Grant Colleges in Permanent Federal Education." *Journal of Negro Education* 7, no. 3 (July 1938): 282–291.
Davis, Leroy. *A Clashing of the Soul: John Hope and the Dilemma of African American Leadership and Black Higher Education in the Early Twentieth Century.* Athens: Univ. of Georgia Press, 1998.
Dawson, Martha E. *Hampton University: A National Treasure.* Silver Springs, Md.: Beckham Publications Group, 1996.
DeBenedetti, Charles. *An American Ordeal: The Antiwar Movement of the Vietnam Era.* Syracuse, N.Y.: Syracuse Univ. Press, 1990.
de Jong, Greta. *A Different Day: African American Struggles for Justice in Rural Louisiana.* Chapel Hill: Univ. of North Carolina Press, 2002.
Dower, John W. *War Without Mercy: Race and Power in the Pacific War.* New York: Pantheon Books, 1986.
Drewry, Henry N., and Humphrey Doermann. *Stand and Prosper: Private Black Colleges and Their Students.* Princeton, N.J.: Princeton Univ. Press, 2001.
Dudziak, Mary L. *Cold War Civil Rights, Race and the Image of American Democracy.* Princeton, N.J.: Princeton Univ. Press, 2000.
Edwards, Elaine. "African American Student Retention in the Reserve Officer Training Corps (ROTC) Leadership Program." Ph.D. diss., Walden University, 2012.
Enloe, Cynthia. *Does Khaki Become You?* London: South End Press, 1993.
———. *Maneuvers: The International Politics of Militarizing Women's Lives.* Berkeley, Calif.: Univ. of California Press, 2000.
Estes, Steve. *I Am a Man!: Race, Manhood, and the Civil Rights Movement.* Chapel Hill: Univ. of North Carolina Press, 2005.
Evans, James C.. "The Contribution of Negro Higher Education to the War Effort." *Journal of Negro Education* 11, no. 3 (July 1942): 304–313.

Evans, James C., and Albert Parker. "ROTC Programs and Negro Youth." *Journal of Negro Education* (spring 1956): 130–131.

Fairclough, Adam. *Race and Democracy: The Civil Rights Struggle in Louisiana, 1915–1972*. Athens: Univ. of Georgia Press, 1995.

Farber, David. *The Age of Great Dreams: America in the 1960s*. New York: Hill and Wang, 1994.

Finkle, Lee. *Forum for Protest: The Black Press during World War II*. Cranbury, N.J.: Associated Univ. Presses, 1975.

Fisher, Randall. *Rhetoric and American Democracy: Black Protest through Vietnam Dissent*. New York: Univ. Press of America, 1985.

Flynn, George O. *The Draft, 1940–1973*. Lawrence: Univ. Press of Kansas, 1993.

Franklin, John Hope, and Alfred A. Moss Jr., *From Slavery to Freedom: A History of African Americans*. New York: McGraw Hill, 1994.

Franklin, V. P. "Patterns of Student Activism at Historically Black Universities in the United States and South Africa." *Journal of African American History* 88, no. 2, The History of Black Student Activism (spring 2003): 204–217.

Frazier, E. Franklin. "Ethnic and Minority Groups in Wartime, with Special Reference to the Negro." *American Journal of Sociology* 48 (1942): 369–377.

Garfinkle, Adam. *Telltale Hearts: The Origins and Impact of the Vietnam Antiwar Movement*. New York: St. Martin's Griffin Edition, 1997.

Gasman, Marybeth, and Christopher L. Tudico, eds. *Historically Black Colleges and Universities: Triumphs, Troubles, and Taboos*. New York: Palgrave Macmillian, 2008.

Gerhardt, James M. *The Draft and Public Policy: Issues in Military Manpower Procurement, 1945–1970*. Columbus: Ohio State Univ. Press, 1971.

Gibson, Truman K., Jr. *Knocking Down Barriers: My Fight for Black America*. Evanston, Ill.: Northwestern Univ. Press, 2005.

Gooding, James Henry, and Virginia M. Adams. *On the Altar of Freedom: A Black Soldier's Civil War Letters from the Front*. Amherst, Mass.: Univ. of Massachusetts Press, 1999.

"The Great Society—In Uniform." *Newsweek*, August 22, 1966, 47.

Harrington, Michael. *The Other America: Poverty in the United States*. New York: Collier Books, 1962.

Harris, J. John, III, Cleopatra Figgures, and David G. Carter. "A Historical Perspective of the Emergence of Higher Education in Black Colleges." *Journal of Black Studies* 6, no. 1 (September 1975): 55–68.

Hawkins, Walter L. *African American Generals and Flag Officers: Biographies of over 120 Blacks in the United States Military*. Jefferson, N.C.: McFarland, 1993.

Hebert, Mary Jacqueline. "Beyond Black and White: The Civil Rights Movement in Baton Rouge, Louisiana, 1945–1972." Ph.D. diss., Louisiana State University, 1999.

Heineman, Kenneth J. *Campus Wars: The Peace Movement at American State Universities in the Vietnam Era.* New York: New York Univ. Press, 1993.

Herring, George C. *America's Longest War: The United States and Vietnam, 1950–1975.* Philadelphia, Pa.: Temple Univ. Press, 1986.

Hill, Lance. *The Deacons for Defense: Armed Resistance and the Civil Rights Movement.* Chapel Hill: Univ. of North Carolina Press, 2004.

Holland, Antonio F. *Nathan B. Young and the Struggle over Black Higher Education.* Columbia: Univ. of Missouri Press, 2006.

Honey, Maureen, ed. *Bitter Fruit: African American Women in World War II.* Columbia: Univ. of Missouri Press, 1999.

Horne, Gerald. *Communist Front: The Civil Rights Congress, 1946–1956.* Rutherford, N.J.: Associated Univ. Presses, 1988.

Humphreys, Margaret. *Intensely Human: The Health of the Black Soldier in the American Civil War.* Baltimore, Md.: Johns Hopkins Univ. Press, 2008.

Isserman, Maurice, and Michael Kazin. *America Divided: The Civil War of the 1960s.* New York: Oxford Univ. Press, 2000.

"Jackson State Becalmed." *Newsweek,* March 1, 1971, 69.

Jakeman, Robert. *The Divided Skies: Establishing Segregated Flight Training at Tuskegee Alabama, 1934–1942.* Tuscaloosa: Univ. of Alabama Press, 1992.

Jencks, Christopher, and David Riesman. *The Academic Revolution.* New York: Transaction Publisher, 1968.

Jefferson, Robert F. *Fighting for Hope: African American Troops of the 93rd Infantry Division in World War II and Postwar America.* Baltimore, Md.: Johns Hopkins Univ. Press, 2008.

Johns, Major, and Ronnie Moore, *It Happened in Baton Rouge, U.S.A.* New York: Congress of Racial Equality, 1962.

Johnson, Charles, Jr. *African Americans and ROTC: Military, Naval and Aeroscience Programs at Historically Black Colleges, 1916–1973.* Jefferson, N.C.: McFarland, 2002.

Jordan, William G. *Black Newspapers and America's War for Democracy, 1914–1920.* Chapel Hill: Univ. of North Carolina Press, 2001.

Kaiser, David. *American Tragedy: Kennedy, Johnson, and the Origins of the Vietnam War.* Cambridge, Mass.: Belknap Press of Harvard Univ. Press, 2000.

Keniston, Kenneth. *Youth and Dissent: The Rise of a New Opposition.* New York: Harcourt Brace Jovanoich, 1971.

Kennedy, David M. *Freedom from Fear: The American People in Depression and War, 1929–1945.* New York: Oxford Univ. Press, 1999.

Knight, Felice F. "Portrait of a Community Activist: William 'Bill' Saunders and the Black Freedom Struggle in Charleston, SC, 1951–2004." Master's thesis, College of Charleston, 2006.

Krebs, Ronald R. *Fighting for Rights: Military Service and the Politics of Citizenship.* Ithaca, N.Y.: Cornell Univ. Press, 2006.

Kryder, David. *Divided Arsenal: Race and the American State during World War II.* Cambridge, U.K.: Cambridge Univ. Press, 2000.

Lane, Ulysses Simpson. "The History of Southern University, 1879–1960." Ph.D. diss., Utah State University, 1969.

Lanning, Michael. *The African-American Soldier: From Crispus Attucks to Colin Powell.* Secaucus, N.J.: Carol Publishing Group, 1997.

Laver, Harry S. "Refuge of Manhood: Masculinity and the Militia Experience in Kentucky." In *Southern Manhood: Perspectives on Masculinity in the Old South,* edited by Craig Thompson Friend and Lorri Glover, 1–21. Athens: Univ. of Georgia Press, 2004.

Levine, Bruce. *Confederate Emancipation: Southern Plans to Free and Arm Slaves during the Civil War.* New York: Oxford Univ. Press, 2006.

Lewis, David Levering. *W.E.B. Du Bois: The Fight for Equality and the American Century, 1919–1963.* New York: Holt, 2000.

Lewis, Lionel S. *The Cold War and Academic Governance: The Lattimore Case at John Hopkins.* New York: State Univ. of New York Press, 1993.

———. *Cold War on Campus: A Study of the Politics of Organizational Control.* New Brunswick, N.J.: Transaction Books, 1988.

Lipset, Seymour Martin. *Rebellion in the University: A History of Student Activism in America.* Boston: Little, Brown, 1971.

Lloyd, R. Grann. "Loyalty Oaths and Communistic Influences in Negro Colleges and Universities." *School and Society* 75 (January–June 1952): 8.

Logan, Rayford W. *What the Negro Wants.* Chapel Hill: Univ. of North Carolina Press, 1944.

———. *Howard University: The First Hundred Years, 1867–1967.* New York: New York Univ. Press, 2004.

Lomax, Louis E. *The Negro Revolt.* New York: American Library, 1963.

Longacre, Edward G. *A Regiment of Slaves: The 4th United States Colored Infantry, 1863–1866.* Mechanicsburg, Pa.: Stackpole, 2003.

Lowry, Thomas P. *Sexual Misbehavior in the Civil War: A Compendium.* Bloomington, Ind.: Xlibris, 2006.

———. *The Story the Soldiers Wouldn't Tell: Sex in the Civil War.* Mechanicsburg, Pa.: Stackpole, 1994.

"The Loyalty of the Negro." *Ebony,* November 1950, 94–95.

MacGregor, Morris J., Jr. *Integration of the Armed Forces, 1940–1965.* Washington, D.C.: Center of Military History, U.S. Army, 1981.

McCoy, Donald, and Richard Ruetten. *Quest and Response: Minority Rights and the Truman Administration.* Lawrence: Univ. Press of Kansas, 1973.

Marten, James. "The Ambiguous Legacy of Blacks in Wartime America." *USA Today,* January 9, 1991, 80–84.

Martinez, J. Michael. *Carpetbaggers, Cavalry, and the Ku Klux Klan: Exposing the Invisible Empire during Reconstruction.* Lanham, Md.: Rowman and Littlefield, 2007.

Matthews, Donald, and James Protho. "Negro Students and the Protest Movement." In *Black Power and Student Rebellion,* edited by James McEvoy and Abraham Miller, 379–418. Belmont, Calif.: Wadsworth, 1969.

May, Elaine Tyler. *Homeward Bound: American Families in the Cold War Era.* New York: Basic Books, 1988.

Mershon, Sherie, and Steven Schlossman. *Foxholes and Color Lines: Desegregating the U.S. Armed Forces.* Baltimore, Md.: Johns Hopkins Univ. Press, 1998.

Meyer, Leisa D. *Creating GI Jane: Sexuality and Power in the Women's Army Corps during World War II.* New York: Columbia Univ. Press, 1996.

Modell, John, and Timothy Haggerty. "The Social Impact of War." *Annual Review of Sociology* 17 (1991): 205–224.

Moore, Brenda. *To Serve My Country, To Serve My Race.* New York: New York Univ. Press, 1996.

Morehouse, Maggie M. *Fighting in the Jim Crow Army: Black Men and Women Remember World War II.* Lanham, Md.: Rowman and Littlefield, 2000.

Morris, Aldon D. *The Origins of the Civil Rights Movement: Black Communities Organizing for Change.* New York: Free Press, 1984.

Moskos, Charles C., and John Sibley Butler, *All That We Can Be: Black Leadership and Racial Integration the Army Way.* New York: Basic Books, 1996.

Moskos, Charles C., and Frank R. Wood, eds., *The Military: More Than Just a Job?* Washington, D.C.: Pergamon-Brassey's International Defense Publishers, 1988.

Moynihan, Daniel. "One-Third of a Nation." *New Republic,* November 5, 1982, 20.

Mullen, Robert W. *Blacks in America's Wars: The Shift in Attitudes from the Revolutionary War to Vietnam.* New York: Monad Press, 1973.

Murray, Paul T. " Blacks and the Draft: A History of Institutional Racism." *Journal of Black Studies* (September 1971): 64–67.

Nalty, Bernard. *Strength for the Fight: A History of Black Americans in the Military.* New York: Free Press, 1996.

Neiberg, Michael S. *Making Citizen Soldiers: ROTC and the Ideology of American Military Service.* Cambridge, Mass.: Harvard Univ. Press, 2000.

Nelson, Scott, and Carol Sheriff. *A People at War: Civilians and Soldiers in America's Civil War.* New York: Oxford Univ. Press, 2007.

Nichols, Lee. *Breakthrough on the Color Front.* New York: Random House, 1954.

O'Neill, William L. *A Democracy at War: America's Fight at Home and Abroad in World War II.* New York: Free Press, 1993.

Parker, Christopher S. *Fighting for Democracy: Black Veterans and the Struggle Against White Supremacy in the Postwar South.* Princeton, N.J.: Princeton Univ. Press, 2009.

Perkins, Iris Johnson. "Felton Grandison Clark, Louisiana Educator." Ph.D. diss., Louisiana State University, 1976.

Pfeffer, Paula F. *A. Philip Randolph, Pioneer of the Civil Rights Movement.* Baton Rouge: Louisiana State Univ. Press, 1990.

Phelps, J. Alfred. *Chappie: America's First Black Four Star General—The Life and Times of Daniel James, Jr.* Novato, Calif.: Presido Press, 1991.

Ploski, Harry A., and Ernest Kaiser, eds. *The Negro Almanac.* New York: Bellwether, 1971.

Plummer, Brenda Gayle. *Rising Wind: Black Americans and Foreign Affairs, 1935–1960.* Chapel Hill: Univ. of North Carolina Press, 1996.

———. *Window on Freedom: Race, Civil Rights, and Foreign Affairs, 1945–1988.* Chapel Hill: Univ. of North Carolina Press, 2003.

Powell, Colin. *My American Journey.* New York: Ballantine Books, 1995.

"Races: The Unbunching." *Time,* February 22, 1954, 30.

Rhodes, Lelia Gaston, *Jackson State University: The First Hundred Years, 1877–1977.* Jackson: Univ. Press of Mississippi, 1979.

Roach, Ronald. "From Combat to Campus: GI Bill Gave a Generation of African Americans an Opportunity to Pursue the American Dream." *Black Issues in Higher Education* 14, no. 13 (August 21, 1997).

Roebuck, Julian B., and Komanduri S. Murty. *Historically Black Colleges and Universities: Their Place in American Higher Education.* Westport, Conn.: Praeger, 1993.

Rozwenc, Edwin, and Kenneth Lindfors. *Containment and the Origins of the Cold War.* Boston: Heath, 1967.

Samito, Christian G. *Becoming American Under Fire: Irish Americans, African Americans, and the Politics of Citizenship during the Civil War Era.* Ithaca, N.Y.: Cornell Univ. Press, 2009.

Sanson, Jerry Purvis. *Louisiana during World War II: Politics and Society, 1939–1945.* Baton Rouge: Louisiana State Univ. Press, 1999.

Savage, Barbara Dianne. *Broadcasting Freedom: Radio, War, and the Politics of Race.* Chapel Hill: Univ. of North Carolina Press, 1999.

Scipio, Albert L., II. *Pre-War Days at Tuskegee*. Silver Springs, Md.: Roman Publications, 1987.
Shakoor, Jordana Y. *Civil Rights Childhood*. Jackson: Univ. of Mississippi Press, 1999.
Sherry, Michael. *In the Shadow of War: The United States since the 1930s*. New Haven, Conn.: Yale Univ. Press, 1995.
Schiffman, Joseph. "The Education of Negro Soldiers in World War II." *Journal of Negro Education* 18 (1949): 22–28.
Schuman, Howard. "Two Sources of Antiwar Sentiment in America." *American Journal of Sociology* 78, no. 3 (November 1972): 513–536.
Shapiro, Herbert. "The Vietnam War and the American Civil Rights Movement." *Journal of Ethnic Studies* 16, no. 4 (winter 1989): 118–135.
Sims, Serbrenia J. *Diversifying Historically Black Colleges and Universities: A New Higher Education Paradigm*. Westport, Conn.: Greenwood Press, 1994.
Singletary, Otis A. "The Negro Militia during Radical Reconstruction." *Military Affairs* 19, no. 4 (winter 1955): 177–179.
Sitkoff, Harvard. "Racial Militancy and Interracial Violence in the Second World War." *Journal of American History* 3 (1971): 668–681.
———. *The Struggle for Black Equality, 1954–1980*. New York: Hill and Wang, 1981.
"The South: Death in Two Cities." *Time*, May 25, 1970, 22.
Southern, David W. *Gunnar Myrdal and Black-White Relations: The Use and Abuse of an American Dilemma, 1944–1969*. Baton Rouge: Louisiana State Univ. Press, 1987.
Spofford, Tim. *Lynch Street: The May 1970 Slayings at Jackson State College*. Kent, Ohio: Kent State Univ. Press, 1988.
Stanford, Karin L. *If We Must Die: African American Voices on War and Peace*. Lanham, Md.: Rowman and Littlefield, 2008.
Stillman, Richard J., II. *Integration of the Negro in the U.S. Armed Forces*. New York: Praeger, 1968.
Strain, Christopher B. *Pure Fire: Self-Defense as Activism in the Civil Rights Era*. Athens: Univ. of Georgia Press, 2005.
Terry, Wallace. *Bloods: An Oral History of the Vietnam War by Black Veterans*. New York: Ballantine Books, 1984.
Townsend, Kenneth William. *World War II and the American Indian*. Albuquerque: Univ. of New Mexico Press, 2000.
Ture, Kwame, and Charles V. Hamilton. *Black Power: The Politics of Liberation*. New York: Vintage Books, 1992.
Tyson, Timothy B. *Radio Free Dixie: Robert F. Williams and the Roots of Black Power*. Chapel Hill: Univ. North Carolina Press, 1999.
Useem, Michael. *Conscription, Protest, and Social Conflict: The Life and Death of a Draft Resistance Movement*. New York: A Wiley-Interscience Publication, 1973.

Vincent, Charles. *A Centennial History of Southern University and A&M College, 1880–1980*. Baton Rouge, La.: Moran Industries, 1981.

Washington, George L. *The History of Military and Civilian Pilot Training of Negroes at Tuskegee, Alabama, 1939–1945*. Washington, D.C.: George L. Washington, 1946.

Walker, Martin. *The Cold War: A History*. New York: Holt, 1993.

Walters, Ronald, and Robert Smith. "The Black Education Strategy in the 1970s." *Journal of Negro Education* 48, no. 2 (spring 1979): 156–170.

Watkins, William H. *The White Architects of Black Education: Ideology and Power in America, 1865–1954*. New York: Teachers College, 2001.

Westheider, James E. *Fighting on Two Fronts: African Americans and the Vietnam War*. New York: New York Univ. Press, 1997.

White, John. *Black Leadership in America, 1895–1968*. London: Longman Group, 1985.

Williams, Heather Andrea. "Commenced to Think Like a Man: Literacy and Manhood in African American Civil War Regiments." In *Southern Manhood: Perspectives on Masculinity in the Old South*, edited by Craig Thompson Friend and Lorri Glover, 196–219. Athens: Univ. of Georgia Press, 2004.

———. *Self-Taught: African American Education in Slavery and Freedom*. Chapel Hill: Univ. of North Carolina Press, 2005.

Williamson, Joy Ann. *Radicalizing the Ebony Tower: Black Colleges and the Black Freedom Struggle in Mississippi*. New York: Teachers College Press, 2008.

Wu, Judy Tzu-Chun. "An African-Vietnamese American: Robert S. Browne, the Antiwar Movement, and the Personal/Political Dimensions of Black Internationalism." *Journal of African American History* 92, no. 4, New Black Power Studies: National, International, and Transnational Perspectives (autumn 2007): 491–515.

Wynn, Neil A. *The Afro-American and the Second World War*. New York: Holmes and Meier Publications, 1975.

Young, Marilyn. *The Vietnam Wars, 1945–1990*. New York: HarperCollins, 1991.

INDEX

Note: *t* denotes a table

Acheson, Dean, 63
African American ROTC Army commissions, 1964–1967, 132*t*5.1
African Americans: achievements in the 1950s, 88–89; antiwar leaders, 85–87; attitudes towards military service and training, 2–3, 5–7, 101–102, 168–170, 175; citizenship during Civil War, 11; civil rights and, 55–56; education at black colleges, 19–24; education during Civil War, 14–16; female gender roles, effects of, 82–83; higher education, progress through, 44–46; illiteracy during wartime, 43–44; integration of the military, 75–76, 80–81, 89, 99, 133; Korean War heroes, 79–80; land-grant schools and, 26; military tradition of, 10–14, 16–18, 19–24; militia in Reconstruction south, 18–19; post-World War II era and, 5–7; ROTC, activism against, 156–158; ROTC, support for, 155–156; social equality, quest for, 7, 10, 24, 74–75, 101; voting rights, 12, 19, 20, 56, 96, 104, 140; war morale in the 1940s, 35–36, 40–43; wartime contributions of, 30–32

African Americans and ROTC: Military, Naval and Aerospace Programs at Historically Black Colleges, 1916–1963 (Johnson, C.), 2–3
Afro-American (newspaper), 53, 58–59, 75–76, 79, 80
AGCT (Army General Classification Test), 43–44
Alabama A&M College, 23, 65, 65*t*3.1, 155–156, 159, 169
Alabama State University, 63, 104, 144
Albany State College, GA, 63, 152
Alcorn A&M College, MS, 63, 65*t*3.1, 155–156, 169
Allen University SC, 104
all-volunteer force, 151, 169–170, 170–171
American Council on Education, 47, 62
American Legion Post 502 (Baton Rouge, LA), 68
American Missionary Association, 15
American Revolution, 3
Amiss, Al, 161, 164, 165
Anderson, Eddie, 88
Andrew, Rod, 26
anti-lynching laws, 56
antiwar leaders, 85–87
antiwar movement. *See* Vietnam War
Appy, Christian, 146

INDEX

Arkansas A&M College, 65t3.1
Arkansas Constitutional Convention, 20
Armstrong, Samuel Chapman, 20–21
Army Air Corps, 38
Army Engineers Training School, 46
Army Enlisted Reserve Corps, 32
Army General Classification Test (AGCT), 43–44
Army of Tennessee, 13
Army Specialized Training Program (ASTP), 46
Associated Negro Press, 33, 88
Association of Land-Grant Colleges and Universities, 63
Association of the United States Army, 73, 110, 129
ASTP (Army Specialized Training Program), 46
Atlanta University, 22, 23, 62, 63, 65t3.1, 66t3.1
"Attitudes of the Negro Soldier," 41

Bailey, D'Army, 110
Baker, George W., 162
Ballard, Joe N., 174
Banks, Nathaniel, 15
Barkley, Alben, 63
Barksdale bill (1865), 13
Barnett, Claude, 33, 88
Bashful, Emmitt, 147
Bates, Pervis M., 117
Baton Rouge bus boycott (1953), 92–98
Baton Rouge Bus Company (BRBC), 93–98
Baton Rouge News Leader (newspaper), 112
Bauer, E. A., 71
Benedict College (SC), 104, 144, 169
Bennett College (NC), 104
Benson, George C. S., 158
Bergin, William E., 64
Bethune, Mary McLeod, 39
Beukema, Herman, 46
Bibbens, Jodie, 141–142

Bishop College (TX), 23, 169
Black Draft Counseling Center, 146
Black Panther Party, 125
Black Power movement, 2, 6–7, 123–124, 125–126, 136–137, 145, 160, 168
black press, 75–77, 132–133. *See also specific titles*
black student newspapers, 77–78. *See also specific titles*
Board of Education (LA). *See* Louisiana
Board of Foreign Scholarships, 62
Bolden, Frank E., 41–42
Booker, Simeon, 133
Boston University (MA), 105
Bouie, Jacob, Jr., 119, 120
Branch Normal School (AR), 22, 24
Brandeis University (MA), 105
Brannan, Charles, 63
Bres, Edward S., 57
Brown, H. Rap, 7, 125, 126
Brown, Leonard Douglas, 164
Browne, Robert S., 125, 126
Brown v. Board of Education (1954), 8, 98
Bunche, Ralph, 86
bus boycotts. *See* Baton Rouge bus boycott; Montgomery bus boycott
Butler, John Sibley, 175, 177

Cade, John B., 38, 66–67
Cadence Call, 73
Cadoria, Sherian, 174
Caliver, Ambrose, 39, 46
Capitol High School (LA), 95, 96
Carmichael, Stokely, 7, 123, 124, 125–126, 128, 138
Central State (OH), 132t5.1
Chicago Defender (newspaper), 74, 75–76, 79, 80, 84, 88
citizenship rights, 1, 7, 10, 74–75, 90, 170
Civilian Defense Exposition (1942), 37
civilian defense programs at Southern University, 36–39

Civil Rights Congress (CRC), 86
civil rights movement: Baton Rouge bus boycott, 92–98; Jackson State demonstration, 152–155; Kent State demonstration, 151–155; lunch counter demonstrations, 98, 104, 105, 118; military link to, 103–104; military service as activism, 89–92; Montgomery bus boycott, 98; ROTC and, 55–56; Selma to Montgomery march (1965), 91, 103; student protests, 103–104, 104–106. *See also* Jemison, T. J.; King, Martin Luther; racial discrimination
Civil War, 3, 11, 12–16, 17, 19, 24, 114
Claflin College (SC), 21
Clark, F. G. (Felton Grandison): Board of Education battle, 106–109; Board of Foreign Scholarships appointment, 62; the early years, 27–29; education as social progress, 44–46; racial discrimination and, 47–48; retirement from Southern University, 142–143; ROTC at Southern University, and, 52–53, 54, 60; tarnished legacy of, 109–110; war chest poem of, 49; "Win the War Campaign," 48–49; World War II, support for, 32–35, 39–40, 43–44, 50–51
Clark, J. S. (Joseph Samuel), 4, 27
Cleaver, Eldridge, 125, 126
Cleburne, Patrick R., 13
Clement, Rufus E., 45
Cocreham, Roland, 36
Cold War, 8, 60–62, 62–64, 75, 83, 88
Cole, Nat King, 88
Cole, William, 121
Collins, Walter, 146
Colored Land-Grant College Presidents' Association, 58–59
Columbia University (NY), 141
Commission on Universal Military Training, 57
Committee Against Jim Crow in Military Service and Training, 6, 57, 59

Committee on Civilian Components of the Armed Forces, 55
Committee on Equality of Treatment and Opportunity in the Armed Services, 77, 79
Committee on Participation of Negroes in the National Defense Program, 33
Communism, 63–64, 113–114, 116–117, 118, 127
compulsory ROTC. *See* ROTC
Confederate States of America (CSA), 13
Conference of Presidents of Land-Grant Colleges of Negroes, 55–56, 59
Consolidated Chemicals, 93
Conti, Paul, 122
Continental Convention of the State of Louisiana (1879), 24–25
The Control of State Supported Teachers Training Programs for Negroes (Clark), 28
corner boys, 153, 154
Council for Democracy, 33
Crenshaw, Craig C., 174
CSA (Confederate States of America), 13

Davis, Jefferson, 13
Davis, John W., 38
Davis, Joseph A., 104
Davis, Russell, 153
Deacons for Defense and Justice, 92
defense planning, 36–39, 52–53
Defense Savings Bond and Stamp Program, 32, 34–35
Delandro, Donald, 99, 174
Delany, Martin, 12, 16
Delaware State College (DE), 65t3.1
Demas, Henry, 25
Department of Defense (DoD), 65, 113, 144, 158, 177
Department of War, 33–34, 38, 46
Dillard University (LA), 24, 26, 104
discrimination. *See* racial discrimination
DISSENT (civil rights group), 128
Dixiecrat Party, 59

INDEX

Dixon, Wilbur, 85
Dodd, F. T., 67
Dodd, William J., 147
Doermann, Humphrey, 3
Douglass, Frederick, 12, 17
Dow Chemical Company, 141
Drewry, Henry, 3
Du Bois, W.E.B., 86

Ebony (magazine), 75, 86, 132–133
education: American Council on Education, 47, 62; at black colleges, 19–24; Civil War, during, 14–16; Cold War and, 60–62; as key to progress, 44–46; military service and, 14–16, 43–44; as social opportunity, 10–11, 14–16, 43. *See also* Negro Land-Grant Colleges; *specific institution*
Edwards, Edwin, 160, 164, 165
Eisenhower, Dwight D., 59, 62, 89
Elders, Glen H., 90
Engineering, Science, and Management War Training (ESMWT), 32
Enlisted Reserve Corps (ERC), 32, 38
Enloe, Cynthia, 83
ERC (Enlisted Reserve Corps), 32, 38
ESMWT (Engineering, Science, and Management War Training), 32
Essex, Henry L., 172
Ethyl Corporation, 93
Evans, James, 54
Evans, James C., 60, 68, 69
Ewell, Richard S., 14
Executive Order 8802, 33
Executive Order 9981, 59–60
expansion of military programs during the Cold War, 64–65

1st South Carolina Colored Volunteers, 14
54th Massachusetts Infantry Regiment, 15
59th U.S. Colored Infantry, 17
503rd Field Artillery Battalion, 80

Fair Employment Practices Committee (FEPC), 32
Fayetteville State (NC), 144, 169
female gender roles in the military, 82–84
FEPC (Fair Employment Practices Committee), 32
Fisher, Randall, 123
Fisk University (TN), 23, 51, 63, 104
Florida Agricultural and Mechanical College, 21, 22, 63, 132t5.1, 168
Flowers, Myrtle L., 111
Flynn, George, 6
Forman, James, 103
Fort Bliss (TX), 144
Fort Bragg (NC), 144
Fort Eustis (VA), 66, 69
Fort Hood (TX), 87
Fort Jackson (SC), 144
Fort Lee (VA), 82
Fort McIntosh, 15
Fort Sam Houston (TX), 53
Fortune, Dorothy, 166
Fort Valley State College (GA), 65t3.1, 169
Foster, L. H., 104
Fourth Army, 53, 67, 70, 71, 144
Franklin and Marshall College (PA), 144
Freedom's People Radio Program, 39

Gaiter, Leonce, 66
Gates Commission, 170
Gay, Hobart R., 70
gender roles, 4, 60, 81–82, 82–84, 124, 166
General Order Number 79, 22–23
Georgia State Industrial College, 21, 22, 23
Gibbs, Phillip Lafayette, 154
Gooding, James Henry, 17
Grambling College (LA), 63, 65t3.1, 134–135, 155–156, 168
Gravely, Samuel, 157–158
Gray Board, 58
"Great Society," 122, 123, 131, 167
Green, Earl, 154

Greene, Walter, 91
Griffin, D. A., 157
Grinnell College (IA), 144
Gross, Walter, 129–130
Gulf of Tonkin, 116

Haggerty, Timothy, 81
Hampton Normal and Agricultural Institute. *See* Hampton University
Hampton University (VA), 19–24, 63, 104–105, 128–129, 132t5.1, 139
Harrington, Michael, 113
Harrison, Elton C., 54, 67, 106, 148, 160
Harvard University (MA), 105, 144
Harvey, Martin L., 88, 99, 144–145
Hastie, William O., 33, 86
HBCUs: anti-Vietnam War movements at, 102–103, 117–119; military training programs at, 19–24, 65–66; ROTC compulsory requirements at, 19–24, 128–131; ROTC expansion, 55–56, 168–169; student protests at, 104–106; wartime, support for, 49–50. *See also specific institution*
Hebron Baptist Church, 94
Hedberg, L. Eugene, 59
Herman, Ruby E., 82
Herring, George, 114, 117
Hickey, Patrick, 18
Higginson, Thomas Wentworth, 14
higher education. *See* education
Hill, Lance, 92
Historically Black Colleges and Universities. *See* HBCUs
Hoffman, Hugh, 67
Holliday, Terrell C., 53
Holmes, Lieutenant, 131
Homeward Bound (May), 83
Honey, Maureen, 82–83
Honor, Edward, 174
Honore, Charles E., 172, 174, 176
Honoré, Russel L., 109, 140, 169, 174
Hope, John, 50

Horne, Gerald, 86
Horne, Lena, 88
Hornsby, Alton, Jr., 127
Howard University (Washington, D.C.): ASTP and, 48; Martin Luther King address, 123; ROTC and, 23–24, 129, 132t5.1; SATC and, 23; Selective Service Act and, 22; Vietnam War and, 42, 139; war protests at, 42; wartime, support at, 49–50
Howell, G. L., 112
Hudson, Wade, 119
Human Rights Commission, 56
Hunt, James L., 161

illiteracy during wartime, 15, 27, 43–44
Irish Americans in the Civil War, 11

Jackson, Shelby, 106
Jackson State College. *See* Jackson State University (MS)
Jackson State University (MS), 63, 65t3.1, 152–155, 169
James, C. L. R., 42, 86
James, Daniel Chappie, 172
Jefferson, William, 149
Jemison, D. V., 96, 97
Jemison, T. J., 94–98, 98–99
Jenkins, Seman, 131
Jenkins, Silas, 85
"Jim Crow" laws, 25, 29, 30, 40, 42, 93, 104–106, 171
Johns, Major, 104, 108
Johnson, B.W., 66
Johnson, Charles, Jr., 2
Johnson, Charles S., 39
Johnson, Eugene, 130
Johnson, Joseph, 162
Johnson, Lyndon B., 113, 116, 121, 123, 130
Johnson, Mordecai W., 36
Johnson, Richard Francis, 69
Joint Committee for the Selection of Non-Federal Educational Institutions, 47

Jones, Otis D., 110
Jones, Prentiss C., 85
Jones, R. W. E., 64
Jones, Sam H., 36, 50
Jones, William O., 176
Jordan, Clevester, 43
Journal of Negro Education, 45
Journal of Negro History, 39

Kaiser, David, 114
Keesler Air Base (MS), 77
Kelly, Fred J., 47
Kennedy, John F., 113–114, 138
Kent State University (OH), 151–155
Kentucky State College (KY), 63, 65t3.1
Kenworthy, E. W., 77
King, Cornelius, 39
King, Martin Luther, 99, 118, 123, 141–142
Kitt, Eartha, 88
Koons, L. F., 168, 176–177
Korean War, 68–69, 75–76, 79–80, 86, 88, 90–91
Kress drugstore lunch counter demonstration, 105. *See also* lunch counter demonstrations
Ku Klux Klan, 18, 91–92

Lagare, Jimmie "Scrooge," 146
land-grant schools. *See* Negro Land-Grant Colleges
Langston, John Mercer, 12
Lanham Act, 50
Lanning, Michael, 165
Lautier, Louis R., 33, 80
Laver, Harry S., 16
League for Nonviolent Civil Disobedience Against Military Segregation, 59
Lee, Robert E., 13
Leggett, Isiah, 120
Legislative Committee on Public Education (LA), 24–25
Leland University (LA), 25–26

Levine, Bruce, 14
Lewis, Cleophus C., 87
Lewis, Esau, 66
Lincoln University (MO), 15, 23, 132t5.1
Lincoln University (PA), 65t3.1, 152, 160
Lloyd, R. Grann, 63
Lofton, Harry F., 74
Logan, Rayford W., 33
Lomax, Louis E., 107
Long, Earl K., 105
Long Gray Lines: The Southern Military School Tradition, 1839–1915 (Andrew), 3
Louis, Joe, 88
Louisiana: Baton Rouge, 92–98; Board of Education, 46–47, 104–106, 106–109, 137, 142, 147–148, 159, 161; Capitol High School, 95, 96; Congressional delegation, 53; Continental Convention of 1879, 24–25; Legislative Committee on Public Education, 24–25; McKinley High School, 95; "Win the War Campaign," 38. *See also* Southern University and A&M College (LA)
Louisiana A&M College (LA), 23
Louisiana College (LA), 64
Louisiana Colored Teachers Association, 38
Louisiana Colored Teachers Journal, 38–39
Louisiana Congressional delegation, 53
Louisiana State University, 25, 65, 87
Louisiana Weekly (newspaper), 109
loyalty oaths, 63
Loyola University (LA), 65, 87
lunch counter demonstrations, 98, 104, 105, 118
Lund, James, 175

Making Citizen Soldiers: ROTC and the Ideology of American Military Services (Neiberg), 3
Malcolm X, 7, 119, 124
manhood and military service, 16–18, 74–75, 90

Marchbanks, Vance H., 112
Marching Cavalettes, 72, 87
Marching Cavaliers, 72
Marrs, Elijah, 17
Marshall, George C., 76
Marshall, Thurgood, 84–85, 108–109
Massachusetts Institute of Technology, 105
Matthews, Donald, 102
Matthews, Ralph, 79
May, Elaine Tyler, 83
McKeithen, John, 136, 148
McKinley High School (LA), 95
McNamara, Robert, 120–121
McNeese State College (LA), 64, 149
Meager, Robert C., 166
Medical Specialist Corps Reserve, 111
Meharry Medical College (TN), 23
Meredith, James, 103
"Meredith March Against Fear," 92
Merrill, Lewis, 18
Metoyer, Bryford G., 116
MFDP. *See* Mississippi Freedom Democratic Party
Michigan State University, 152
Miles College (AL), 152
military service and training: African American attitudes towards, 2–3, 84–85, 101–102, 110–112, 131–134; black press, support by, 75–77; civil rights movement and, 1, 89–92, 103–104; discrimination and segregation, 59–60; education and, 14–16; expansion of programs in U.S., 64–65, 168–169; female gender roles and, 82–84; growing popularity at Southern University, 66–68; at HBCUs, 19–24; integration of, 75–76, 80–81, 88–89, 99, 133; manhood, effects on, 16–18, 74–75, 90; as opportunity for advancement, 3–4, 76, 99–100, 112–113, 172–173; racial integration in, 8, 70, 75–77, 79, 80–81, 88–89, 99, 133; rejection rates in, 114–115; ROTC compulsory requirements and, 66–68; at Southern University, 46–48, 52–62; surviving turmoil in, 110–112
Mims, Samuel, 134–136
Miners Teachers College (Washington, D.C.), 63
minorities. *See* African Americans; racial discrimination
Mississippi Freedom Democratic Party, 6, 103, 111, 123, 131
Mississippi Valley State, 169
Modell, John, 81
Montgomery bus boycott (1955), 98
Moore, Amize, 91
moral conduct and the Cold War, 60–62
Morehouse College (GA), 23, 50, 63
Morgan State College. *See* Morgan State University
Morgan State University (MD), 2, 63, 128–129, 130, 132, 132t5.1, 155
Morning Advocate (newspaper), 96, 162
Morrill Land-Grant Act of 1890, 26
Morris, Aldon, 97
Morris, Stanley, 162
Moskos, Charles, 170, 177
Moss, Donald, 108
Mount Zion Baptist Church (Baton Rouge), 99
Moynihan, Daniel Patrick, 115
Mullens, Robert, 122
Muller, General, 66
Murphy, Carl, 53, 58–59

NAACP. *See* National Association for the Advancement of Colored People
Nalty, Bernard, 170
National Association for the Advancement of Colored People, 33, 56, 84–85, 96–97, 99
National Baptist Convention, 96
National Defense Advisory Commission, 31
National Guard, 7, 58, 135, 139, 152–154, 159, 166
National Urban League, 33, 66

National Youth Administration, 39
Naval Reserve Officers Training Corps, 55, 59, 143, 156–157
Negro Agricultural and Technical College (NC), 22
Negro Division for Louisiana Civilian Defense, 37
Negro Employment and Training Branch, 31, 33
Negro Land-Grant Colleges, 11, 26, 31, 47, 56–57, 144
Negro Manpower Service, 31
Negro Newspaper Publishers Association, 33
Neiberg, Michael S., 3, 169, 171
Nell, William Cooper, 12
Netterville, G. Leon: campus unrest, 159–161, 162; as president of Southern University, 144, 146–148, 156; resignation of, 164–165; as VP of Southern University, 135, 142
New Orleans University. *See* Dillard University (LA)
Newsweek (magazine), 131–132, 141, 155
Newton, Alexander, 17
Nicholls, Francis T., 25
Nixon, Richard M., 165
Norfolk State University (VA), 169
North Carolina A&T College (NC), 23, 48, 132t5.1
Northeast Louisiana State College (LA), 64, 150
North Korean People's Army, 68, 79
NROTC. *See* Naval Reserve Officers Training Corps

Office of War Information, 33, 42–43, 49
One Third of a Nation: A Report on Young Men Found Unqualified for Military Service (task force report), 114–115
The Other America (Harrington), 113
"Our Stake in Vietnam—Freedom From Peril" (Army pamphlet), 118

Paine College (GA), 152
Parker, Albert, 54
Parker, Christopher, 103
Parks, Dorothy R., 82
Patin, Jude W. P., 174
Patterson, F. D., 36, 39, 61
Patterson, William, 86
Pearl Harbor attack, 36
Peoples, John, 154
Perkins, Huel D., 40–41, 54, 67, 106, 175, 177
Perry, Nelson, 43
Pershing Rifles National Honor Military Society, 72–73, 87, 110
Pertee, A. P., 40, 42
Petersen, Howard C., 56, 57
Pinchback, P.B.S., 24–25
Pittsburgh Courier (newspaper), 29, 41–42, 75–76, 82, 133
Plessy v. Ferguson (1896), 98
Plummer, Brenda, 88
Powell, Adam Clayton, 89
Powell, Colin, 137–138, 172–173
Powell, David D., 87
Prairie View State Normal and Industrial College (TX): Army Specialized Training Program and, 48; as land-grant institution, 31; loyalty oath pledge, and, 63; ROTC program at, 19, 24, 132t5.1, 155, 168; SATC program, and, 23; Vietnam War and, 139; vocational training, establishment of, 22
Prairie View State Normal and Industrial College (TX): wartime support for, 49–50
Pratt, Timothy E., 137
President's Committee on Youth Employment, 114
Princeton University, NJ, 152
Project 100,000, 120–122, 125
Prothro, James, 102

race problems. *See* racial discrimination
racial discrimination: criticism of in black community, 84–85; defense industries,

in, 56; military, in, 42–43, 46–48; military segregation and, 59–60, 84–85; ROTC and, 55; ROTC summer camp, at, 69–70. *See also* civil rights movement
racial integration in the military, 8, 70, 75–77, 79, 80–81, 88–89, 99, 133
Ramsey, Julius B., 22
Randolph, A. Philip, 6, 57–58, 59, 63
Ransburg, Frank S., 67, 148, 150
Ready Reserves. *See* National Guard
Reaves, John R., 87
Reconstruction south, 18–19
recruitment during Cold War, 62–64
Redeemers of the Democratic Party, 19
Reed, Adolph, Sr., 109
rejection rates in the military, 114–115
Reserve Officer Training Corps. *See* ROTC
Reynolds, Grant, 57–58
Rhodes, Warren B., 143, 151
Rixson, Benjamin, 128
Roberts, T. N., 37–38
Robeson, Paul, 39, 86
Robinson, Jackie, 88
Robinson, Marvin, 108
Robinson, Sugar Ray, 88
Robinson, Wilbur, 156–157
Roosevelt, Eleanor, 50
Roosevelt, Franklin D., 31, 33
ROTC: African American Army commissions, 1964–1967, 132t5.1; African Americans activism against, 156–158; African Americans attitudes towards, 2–3, 101–102, 168–170, 175; all-volunteer force, 151, 169–170, 170–171; Antiaircraft Artillery unit request, 67–68; colleges with Senior ROTC, 65t3.1; compulsory requirements, 128–131, 140–141, 142, 143, 148–149, 149–150; expansion at HBCUs, 55–56, 155–156, 158–159; Infantry unit request, 67–68; Jackson State demonstration, 151–155; Kent State demonstration, 151–155; Marching Cavalettes, 72, 87;
Marching Cavaliers, 72; new programs established, 144–145, 168–169; Pershing Rifles National Honor Military Society, 72–73, 87, 110; Prairie View State Normal and, 24, 54, 132t5.1, 155; Southern University and, 70–71, 166, 173–174; Special Regulations 44 and, 23–24; student incentives for, 112–113; summer camp, 69–70, 87–88, 171; units deactivated, 144–145; Vietnam War and, 116–119, 120; women and, 72, 87, 166
Round-the-World study project, 63
Rountree, Gregory, 174

2nd Louisiana Native Guards, 15
62nd U.S. Colored Troops, 15
65th U.S. Colored Troops, 15
Samito, Christian G., 11
Sampson, Edith, 86
Sanderford, Eddie, 119
Sanders, Jared Y., Sr., 26–27
SATC. *See* Student Army Training Corps
Saunders, William, 91
Savannah State University (GA), 168
Scabbard and Blade, 73, 110
Schneider, J. Thomas, 62
Scotlandville, LA, 38, 54, 93, 105, 107, 157
Scott, Raymond, 94, 96
Scott, Raymond P., 68
Selective Service Act of 1917, 22
Selective Service Extension Act of 1950, 68
Selective Service System: attitudes towards post-World War II, 5–7; inequalities of, 120, 146, 165; policy changes and, 158. *See also* Project 100,000
Selma to Montgomery march (1965), 91, 103
Sengstacke, John H., 88
sex discrimination. *See* gender roles
Shapiro, Herbert, 123
Shreveport Alumni Association, 70–71
Small Rural Industries Program, 38
Smith, Denver Allen, 164

Smith, Isaac D., 174
Smith, T. Roosevelt, 96
social equality, quest for, 7, 10, 24, 74–75, 101
Socialist Workers' Party, 85
Solvay Process Company, 93
South Carolina A&M College, 22, 23, 24
South Carolina State, 132t5.1
South Carolina State Agricultural and Mechanical College, 21, 22
South Caroline State College, 57
Southeastern Louisiana College, 64–65
Southern University and A&M College (LA): African American ROTC Army Commissions, 1964–1976, 132t5.1; "Agriculture, the First Line of Defense" celebration, 37–38; Antiaircraft Artillery unit request, 67–68; antiwar movement, 139–141; Army Air Corps and, 38; army specialized training at, 46–48; Association of the U.S. Army, 73; Black Draft Counseling Center, 146; Black Power movement, 123–124, 136–137, 145; Board of Education battle, 106–109; Cadence Call, 73; campus unrest, 134–137, 159–161, 161–163, 162; civilian defense programs at, 36–39; Clark, Felton Grandison, 27–29, 106–109, 142–143; Clark, Joseph Samuel, 27; Cold War, during, 52–53; Discipline Committee at, 61–62; education as key to progress, 44–46; Enlisted Reserve Corps (ERC), 38; establishment of, 24–27; expulsion of students at, 106–109; Infantry unit request, 67–68; Korean War effects, 68–69; loyalty oath requirement, 63; Marching Cavalettes of, 72, 87; Marching Cavaliers of, 72; Martin Luther King's death, effect on, 141–142; McKeithen visit, 149; military training, 46–48, 52–53, 53–54, 66–68, 72–73; Netterville, G. Leon and, 135, 142, 144, 146–148, 156, 164–165; NROTC program approved, 156–157; Pershing Rifles at, 87; poor war morale and, 40–43; "Power for Peace," 111–112; regional defense training center, as, 31, 34–35; ROTC, activism against, 142, 159–162; ROTC air unit request, 53, 151; ROTC and women, 72; ROTC compulsory requirements, 66–68, 128–131, 132; ROTC flag officers, 174; ROTC program, 70–71, 166, 173–174; Scabbard and Blade, 73; *Southern University Digest*, 77–78, 87–88, 110, 112, 137, 145; student activism during Vietnam War, 134–138, 146–148; Student Afro-American Society, 147; Students United, 159, 162–163, 165; survey and research results, 174–178; Transportation Corps at, 60, 70, 73; Vietnam War and, 139; Vocational Education for War Production Workers program, 40; wartime support, for, 39–40, 43–44, 49–50; "Win the War Campaign" at, 48–49; World War II and, 32–35, 50–51
Southern University Digest, 77–78, 84, 87–88, 110, 112, 124, 137, 145
Special Regulations 44 (1919), 23–24
St. Amant, Larry, 157
Stamps, T. B., 25
Stand and Prosper: Private Black Colleges and Their Students (Drewry and Doermann), 3
Standard Oil Company, 93, 127
Stanford, John, 129
Stanford University (CA), 144
State University of New York, 151
St. Augustine's College (NC), 169
Storer College (WV), 63
Straight College. *See* Dillard University (LA)
Straight University. *See* Dillard University (LA)
Studebaker, J. W., 31, 47
student activism. *See* civil rights movement; Vietnam War
Student Afro-American Society, 147
Student Army Dieticians' Program, 111
Student Army Training Corps, 22–23

Student Nonviolent Coordinating Committee, 7, 103, 124–125, 145, 146
student protests. *See* civil rights movement; Vietnam War
Student Protests 1969 (Urban Research Corporation), 146
Students for a Democratic Society (SDS), 147
Sturrup, Randolph, 131
Sumner High School (MO), 22
Sweney, John, 16, 17

3rd New York Infantry Regiment, 18
24th Infantry Regiment, 79
33rd U.S. Colored Troops, 14
Talladega College (AL), 21, 23
Tarver, Robert F., 71
Task Force on Manpower Conservation, 114
Taylor, Ordie P., 79
Taylor, Thomas B., 68, 69
Temple University (PA), 151
Tennessee A&I University, 23–24, 104, 129
Tennessee A&M College, 23
Tennessee State, 169
Terry, Wallace, 140
Texas Southern University, 23, 28, 63, 65t3.1, 104
Texas State University for Negroes. *See* Texas Southern University
"The Freedom Movement and the War in Vietnam" (Browne), 125
Thigpen, Pascal, 122
Thomas, Earnest "Chilly Willy," 91–92
Thomas, Jessie O., 34–35
Time (magazine), 89
Tomkinson, Kenneth D., 131
"To Secure These Rights," 1946 (civil rights committee), 56, 59–60
training, military. *See* military service and training
Transportation Corps, 60, 70, 73
Tri Quang, Thich, 125
Truman, Harry S., 6, 52, 56, 59–60, 68

Tulane University (LA), 65, 149
Turner, Harold J., 72, 87
Turner, Henry McNeal, 17
Tuskegee Airmen, 5
Tuskegee Normal and Industrial Institute. *See* Tuskegee University (AL)
Tuskegee University (AL): African American ROTC Army commissions, 1964–1967, 132t5.1; Air Force ROTC and, 111–112; background of, 5, 10–11; gender roles in military, 81–82; pro-communist label and, 63; ROTC and, 19, 21–22, 23–24, 31, 112, 129, 155–156; SATC and, 23; student activism, 104, 129–130, 139; Tuskegee Airmen, 5; Vietnam War and, 117–118, 127–128, 139; wartime, support for, 49–50

Union Normal School. *See* Dillard University (LA)
United Defense League, 94–98
United Service Organization (USO), 38
University of Arizona, 151
University of Illinois, 144
University of Maryland, College Park, 152
University of Michigan, 144
U.S. 7th Calvary, 18
U.S. Colored Troops, 14, 15, 79
U.S. News and World Report (magazine), 158
U.S. Office of Education, 31, 39, 114

Vann, Robert, 29
Victory Book Campaign, 38
"Vietnam and the American Conscience" (public forum), 128–129
Vietnam War: African American views on, 6, 140–141; American involvement begins, 116–117; antiwar movements, 117–119, 139–141, 148, 151–155; civil rights movement and, 101–102, 127–128; criticism of, 102–103, 122–123, 126–127; Project 100,000, 120–122; ROTC programs and,

Vietnam War (*continued*)
  116–119; student activism at Southern University, 134–138; U.S. withdrawal from, 165; War on Poverty, effects on, 113–115
Villanova University (PA), 151
Virginia Normal and Industrial College. *See* Virginia State University
Virginia State College. *See* Virginia State University
Virginia State University, 24, 104, 132t5.1
Virginia Union University, 23, 63
Vocational Education for War Production Workers program, 40
voting rights, 12, 19, 20, 56, 96, 104, 140

WAC (Women's Army Corps), 72, 82, 111
WAF (Women in the Air Force), 81
Wallace, George, 129–130
War Manpower Commission, 32, 47–48
war morale in the black community, 35–36, 40–43
War of 1812, 3
War on Poverty, 113–115, 128, 130
Washington, Booker T., 5, 21
Weakley, Vernon, 153
Weaver, Robert C., 33
W.E.B. Du Bois Clubs, 145
Weckerling, John, 71
Weidmann, Hugo, 37
Wells, Franklin D., 124
Wendell Phillips High School (IL), 22
Western University (KS), 22
Westover, Wendell, 58, 59
West Virginia Collegiate Institute, 21, 23–24
West Virginia State College, 38, 132t5.1
Whittaker, M. F., 57
Wilberforce University (OH), 10, 21, 23–24
Wilborne, Mary W., 82

Wiley University. *See* Texas Southern University
Williams, Frank, 143
Williams, Heather Andrea, 15
Williams, Hosea, 90, 103
Williams, Robert F., 91
Williams, Stacy T., Jr., 78
Williamson, Joy Ann, 110
Wilson, Eleanor B., 82
Wilson, Joseph T., 15, 17
Wilson, L. Alex, 74, 80
Wilson, Louis, 66
"Win the War Campaign," 38, 48–49, 53
Wirtz, Willard, 114
women. *See* gender roles
Women in the Air Force (WAF), 81
Women's Army Corps (WAC), 72, 82, 111
Wood, Frank, 170
Woodson, Carter G., 39
Woolworth's lunch counter demonstrations, 104. *See also* lunch counter demonstrations
World War I, 28, 40
World War II: African American attitudes postwar, 5–7, 89–90, 168; citizenship-civil rights links, 55–56, 75, 92; educational opportunities, rise of, 45–48; HBCUs' support of, 49–50; illiteracy rates during, 43–44; participation in, 30–35; social change, struggle for, 103–104; Southern University and, 32–35, 50–51; "Win the War Campaign," 48–49, 53

Xavier University (LA), 65t3.1

Yale University (CT), 144
Young, Clarence J., 116
Younge, Samuel L., 127, 129

www.ingramcontent.com/pod-product-compliance
Lightning Source LLC
Chambersburg PA
CBHW022004220426
43663CB00007B/958